Shakespeare's Comic Commonwealths

Shakespeare's Comic Commonwealths

Camille Wells Slights

UNIVERSITY OF TORONTO PRESS
Toronto Buffalo London

© University of Toronto Press 2012
Toronto Buffalo London
www.utppublishing.com
Printed in Canada

ISBN 978-0-8020-2924-9 (cloth)
ISBN 978-1-4426-1504-5 (paper)

Canadian Cataloguing in Publication Data

Slights, Camille Wells
Shakespeare's comic commonwealths

Includes bibliographical references and index.
ISBN 978-0-8020-2924-9 (bound). ISBN 978-1-4426-1504-5 (pbk.)

1. Shakespeare, William, 1564–1616 – Comedies.
I. Title.

PR2981.S55 1993   822.3'3   C93-09376-X

This book has been published with the help of a grant from the Canadian Federation for the Humanities, using funds provided by the Social Sciences and Humanities Research Council of Canada.

Contents

ACKNOWLEDGMENTS

1 INTRODUCTION 3

Part I Belonging

2 Egeon's Friends and Relations: *The Comedy of Errors* 13
3 The Raw and the Cooked in *The Taming of the Shrew* 32

Part II Cultural Values and the Values of Culture

4 Common Courtesy in *The Two Gentlemen of Verona* 57
5 Learning and Language in *Love's Labor's Lost* 74

Part III Change and Continuity

6 The Changes and Chances of Mortal Life in
   A Midsummer Night's Dream 103
7 Deserving and Diversity in *The Merchant of Venice* 125

Part IV Court and Country

8 Pastoral and Parody in *The Merry Wives of Windsor* 151
9 The Unauthorized Language of *Much Ado About Nothing* 171

Part V Renewal and Reciprocity

10 Changing Places in Arden: *As You Like It* 193
11 The Principle of Recompense in *Twelfth Night* 216

12 Conclusion 236

NOTES 245

BIBLIOGRAPHY 273

INDEX 285

Acknowledgments

'I hate ingratitude more,' says Viola, 'Than lying, vainness, babbling, drunkenness, / Or any taint of vice whose strong corruption / Inhabits our frail blood.' Viola's judgment must be daunting to anyone writing about Shakespeare's plays. When I first started thinking about this book, I determined that I wouldn't presume to add to the body of Shakespeare criticism without fully taking into account the work others had done. The sheer volume and accelerating pace of published discussions of Shakespeare's plays have defeated that naïve intention. Still, I have learned much from scholars and critics who have preceded me, and I am grateful to them. While my notes acknowledge specific debts, I have a larger, more diffuse debt to the teachers, colleagues, and students who over many years have shaped my ideas and guided my responses to literary texts. I regret that I undoubtedly have missed relevant critical and scholarly work that could have saved me from some of the mistakes and misunderstandings recorded in the following chapters.

I am deeply grateful to the Social Sciences and Humanities Research Council of Canada for research grants that enabled me to write this book. I am grateful also to the staff of the British Library and especially the staff of the Huntington Library for their kind and efficient help. I want to thank too the friends and colleagues at the Huntington who provided me with an intellectual and scholarly community in which to work when I most needed one. I am indebted to friends who generously read parts of the manuscript. Anthony Dawson, Elizabeth Donno, Anthony Harding, Lynne Magnusson, Michael Shapiro, and Paul Stevens gave encouragement and criticism that saved me from embarrassing errors. I owe thanks to Roma Kail and to Susan McDonald for verifying quotations and to Jessica Slights, who typed and verified quotations, and whose delight in these plays sustained my enthusiasm for this project. My largest debt is to William Slights, who patiently read and re-read the various stages of composition and whose advice permeates the whole, even the parts he disagrees with. Finally, earlier versions of several chapters have appeared elsewhere, and I am grateful for permission to use material from 'The Raw and the Cooked in *The Taming of the Shrew*,' *Journal of English and Germanic Philology*, 88 (1989); 'Pastoral and Parody in *The Merry Wives of Windsor*,' *English Studies in Canada*, 11 (1985); '*The Two Gentlemen of Verona* and the Courtesy Book Tradition,' *Shakespeare Studies*, 16 (1983); 'The Principle of Recompense in *Twelfth Night*,' *Modern Language Review*, 77 (1982); 'In Defense of Jessica: The Problem of the Run-away Daughter in *The Merchant of Venice*,' *Shakespeare Quarterly*, 31 (1980), and 'The Unauthorized Language of *Much Ado About Nothing*,' *Elizabethan Theatre*, 12 (1992).

Shakespeare's Comic Commonwealths

CHAPTER ONE

Introduction

After Titania's declaration of love, Bottom muses, 'reason and love keep little company together now-a-days. The more the pity that some honest neighbors will not make them friends' (*MND*, III.i.143–6).[1] What interests me most about these remarks is not the commonplace observation of love's irrationality but the assumption that reconciliation is a job for 'honest neighbors.' When Bottom's attention is on dramatic performance, he assumes a play-world populated by lovers and tyrants, but in considering a situation in his own life, he thinks in terms of people performing roles in a closely knit human community. Like Bottom, critics of Shakespeare's comedies usually describe conflicts between lovers and tyrants, and although they have good reason for tracing such traditional comic structures, this approach has limited usefulness in explaining the dramatic energy of the plays. For example, it cannot account for Costard's apology for Sir Nathaniel's stage fright during the Pageant of the Worthies: 'There an't shall please you, a foolish mild man, an honest man, look you, and soon dash'd. He is a marvellous good neighbor, faith, and a very good bowler; but for Alisander – alas, you see how 'tis – a little o'erparted' (*LLL*, V.ii.580–4). Similarly, when the Host of the Garter Inn undertakes to resolve the quarrel between Parson Evans and Doctor Caius, he exemplifies Bottom's idea of an honest neighbor far more effectively than he contributes to the plot concerning Anne Page's romantic problems. In fact, neither *Love's Labor's Lost* nor *The Merry Wives of Windsor* conforms satisfactorily to the standard model of confrontation between youthful passion and oppressive age. Just as Bottom thinks of himself as an actor, a weaver, and the Duke's loyal subject rather than as a lover, most of the characters and events in the so-called romantic comedies are defined less by their relation to love than by their place within a human society. My defense for presuming to add to the number of books about Shakespeare, then, is the relative neglect of the social dimensions of the comedies. My object is to explore how the ten comedies from *The Comedy of Errors* through *Twelfth Night* represent the problems and satisfactions of people living together in an ordered commonwealth.

Although most theories of genre recognize that comedy emphasizes the group rather than the individual, criticism of Shakespeare's comedies usually has given only perfunctory attention to their social bases and concerns in order to concentrate either on questions of dramatic technique and tradition or on the topic of romantic love.[2] One popular trend is to insist that Shakespeare's art is involved exclusively in its own artifice and to dismiss as naïvely presumptuous attempts to discover meanings that reflect or illuminate the ordinary reality either of Shakespeare's world or of ours. Warnings against the asininity of expounding Bottom's dream are almost as frequent as efforts to do so. Interpretive studies that assume vital connections between the plays and the life external to their fictional worlds have by and large focused on the portrayal of love as an individual psychological and spiritual experience.[3]

The most influential theories of Shakespearean comedy have been C.L. Barber's, tracing comic form to medieval holiday customs of temporary license, and Northrop Frye's, presenting Shakespeare's comic structure as a variation on the Roman New Comedy formula, in which youth and love triumph over age and social bondage.[4] Any study of the social dimensions of the plays will be indebted to their work, but neither Barber's model of 'festive' comedy nor Frye's of 'green world' comedy is applicable to all the plays. Moreover, both Barber's formulation of a pattern of action that moves through release to clarification and Frye's of a movement to a 'green world,' where comic resolution is achieved unhampered by social restraint, derive from psychological models.

The emphasis on the individual psyche in criticism since the nineteenth century is unsurprising given the predominance in Western thought of the notion of the autonomous individual existing apart from any social role or function. From this perspective, the Renaissance was a crucial period in the transition from a medieval, static view of people as defined by their social roles to a

Introduction

new view of people able to fulfill themselves, unhampered by historical limitations. But we should not impose on the Renaissance a modern idea of individual autonomy that assumes a personal identity apart from and prior to all social roles. Undoubtedly the Renaissance saw a growth in self-consciousness and an increased awareness of personal choice, of possibilities for self-fulfillment through individual will and effort. Indeed, Thomas Greene has suggested that Erasmus' formulation of the individual's power to shape his own identity – '*Homines non nascuntur, sed finguntur* – men are fashioned rather than born' – could serve as a motto of the humanist revolution in thought.[5] The humanists, however, conceived of these possibilities in terms of the individual's place in society. Their visions of human possibility characteristically took the form of portraits of an ideal society (More's *Utopia*, Bacon's *New Atlantis*) or of an ideal social role (Castiglione's *The Courtier*, Elyot's *The boke named the governour*, Ascham's *The Scholemaster*). In Elizabethan England, as Robert Hellenga says, people conceived of individual identity 'not in opposition to but by participation in social roles.'[6]

In recent years we have become increasingly aware of our tendency to identify the institutions and values of our own culture as immutable truths. Despite the erudition and insight, sometimes brilliance, of the considerable body of critical commentary on Shakespeare's comedies, it is not innocent of imposing ideas and values derived from post-Enlightenment liberal democratic traditions on texts embedded in the culture of late sixteenth- and early seventeenth-century England. In particular, the emphasis in our time and place on the unique individual self has led to a critical neglect of the social assumptions and political implications of the plays. Such scholars as Stephen Greenblatt and Louis Montrose have demonstrated powerfully the dangers of a parochially universalizing criticism and the need to integrate Renaissance literature, including Shakespearean drama, into the culture that produced it.[7] But while recent scholarship has convincingly contested formalist assumptions about the non-referentiality of literary texts, its primary concern with manifestations of political power has directed attention for the most part to Shakespeare's histories and tragedies, rather than to the early comedies. In addition, neglect of artistic form and skepticism of poetry's power to shape and modify attitudes and beliefs as well as to disseminate received wisdom have led to an undervaluing of the imaginative insights of literary works. In this study I combine formalist with historical analysis of the representation of society in Shakespeare's comedies.

These post-structuralist times provide us with no consensus about the purpose of the critical endeavor or the nature of the literary text except, perhaps, that there are no stable, unmediated texts and no disinterested, non-ideological criticism. The questions I have asked of Shakespeare's comedies have been generated from the material and educational security of my privileged position as a white, middle-class, North American academic and the insecurity and vulnerability of my experiences as an immigrant, often unemployed woman. The process of asking and answering has convinced me that, while these plays embody no universal, eternal verities, their representations of forms of isolation and community can illuminate our own ambiguous negotiations with the various societies that include and exclude us. I draw ideas and insights from formalists, new and old historicists, feminists, sociologists, historians, and cultural anthropologists, for I believe that erecting barriers between post-structuralist theory and humanist scholarship is counter-productive. Analysis of literary form need not be ahistorical, and the historical rootedness of texts does not preclude individual agency. The plays that are the focus of this book are not autonomous repositories of transcendental truths, but cultural events inextricably involved in and limited by the historical conditions of their production. They are also consequences of human agency, verbal constructs which transform the reality they represent; in Wallace Stevens' terms, they 'press back against the pressure of reality.'[8]

'Society' and 'social,' the terms that identify the direction of my inquiry, are ambiguous. As Anthony Giddens observes, 'society' has two primary meanings:

> One is the generalized connotation of 'social association' or interaction; the other is the sense in which 'a society' is a unity, having boundaries which mark it off from other surrounding societies. The ambiguity of the term ... is less unfortunate than it looks. For societal totalities by no means always have clearly demarcated boundaries, although they are typically associated with definite forms of locale ... All societies both are social systems and at the same time are constituted by the intersection of multiple social systems.[9]

Introduction

I rely on what Giddens calls this 'useful double meaning' (xxvi) and consider in the category of Shakespeare's representations of society such diverse collectivities as late sixteenth-century England in which the plays were produced, the middle-class milieu depicted in *The Merry Wives of Windsor*, and the court of Navarre in *Love's Labor's Lost*. While the concept of the social is multivalent, usefully registering the intersection of social groups and institutions, it also sets limits, albeit flexible and permeable ones. Members of a society may hold differing values and beliefs, but they have 'some sort of common identity ... [some awareness] of belonging to a definite collectivity' (Giddens, 165). Societies are situated geographically, as Giddens suggests in the long quotation above and as Shakespeare's plays represent them. They also have a temporal dimension, some continuous duration. Thus the Elizabethan social theorist Thomas Smith explicitly excepts groups constituted for particular short-term purposes when he defines 'a commonwealth' as 'a societie of common doing of a multitude of free men, collected together, and united by common accord & covenants among themselves, for the conservation of themselves as wel in peace as in warre.'[10]

A frequently debated question relevant to my concerns is the relation between a particular text and the general culture – the degree to which texts are necessarily complicit in the prevailing ideology and, more particularly, whether Shakespeare's plays support or subvert the hierarchical structures of early modern England. The plays were written and performed first in an undemocratic, racist, sexist culture. While making no claims to verisimilar representation of actual social relations, they repeatedly portray characters achieving happiness within undemocratic, racist, sexist societies. Although this acquiescence to sixteenth-century social hierarchies can seem dismaying in the late twentieth century, the plays themselves foreground and problematize the political, economic, and gender inequities that trouble us. They are historically conditioned and speak in the terms available within a particular culture, but no culture is univocal or wholly stable, early modern England less so than many. It was a time of significant social, political, and economic change and a place where local traditions and practices varied widely in different regions. While there was virtually universal agreement among sixteenth-century political theorists that monarchy was the best form of government for England, there was interest among humanists in the ideals of republican government and considerable debate about the source and extent of monarchical power. Male social and political supremacy was not seriously contested, but questions about the nature and social place of women were of intense concern. English men and women at the end of the sixteenth century agreed on the hierarchical nature of society but often argued about the criteria for status. They shared ideals of deference and obedience to superiors but also insisted on traditional rights and liberties. If the *Homily on Obedience* was central to the culture, so too was the proverbial question, 'When Adam delved and Eve span / Who was then the gentleman?'

A simple dichotomy of subversion and endorsement is too crude to explain the relations between artistic productions and social norms. Shakespeare's plays explore contemporary social realities, and the cultural discourse of the time provided language and conceptual positions from which to examine, for instance, the sexism of *The Taming of the Shrew*, the racism of *The Merchant of Venice*, and the imperialism of *Much Ado About Nothing*. The comedies are culturally specific: it takes a leap of historical imagination for us to accept the Dromio twins' social status or to rejoice in Kate's marriage. They continue to speak to us today because there are also continuities between Shakespeare's age and our time, because the plays are part of the history that has made us what we are, and because they are exemplary models of art questioning the cherished orthodoxies of its own culture, exposing, for example, the coercion required to keep the Dromios and Kate in their places. Although characters in the comedies take a variety of stances towards particular social institutions and practices, with few exceptions they pride themselves on their civic virtue and condemn their enemies for uncivil behavior. But if the characters assume a binary opposition between the rude or savage and the civilized, the plays as wholes undermine this simple dichotomy, repeatedly showing savagery as a function of the civilized. Yet even while acknowledging that society may be rude, they never offer solitude as a permanent alternative. Their consistent assumption is that people must work out their lives within a given social order.

In the following chapters, then, I try to demonstrate that Shakespeare's comedies can be studied most fruitfully not as endorsements of the prevailing ideology of sixteenth-century English society nor as subversions of that culture, but as imaginative forms that present cultural practices, institutions, and beliefs as human constructions susceptible to critical scrutiny. I investigate the complicated relations between conflict and conciliation, savagery and civilization, autonomy and dependence, isolation and community in order to argue that the plays satirize the absurdities and celebrate the virtues of the civilized community. They dramatize individual action in the context of the web of relationships that constitute society. The characters are defined for themselves and the audience in terms of their relations with others. The settings may be fantastic – the forest of Arden or an Athens ruled by a legendary Theseus – but they are never merely atmospheric backdrops. Rather, they are clearly realized social structures that give meaning to the characters' actions. The eruption of social discord is characteristically the basis for the pathos and suspense that the dramatic action generates and for the absurd situations that produce comic incongruity. Much of the special charm of the plays stems from characters' success in coping with social disorder, and the resolution of social dissension provides the satisfying completion of the comic form. Love and courtship function in the plots not primarily as crucial experiences in individual characters' emotional development, but as problems of marriage – an institution combining radical individual change with social tradition and stability and providing a dramatic juncture of the intimate and personal with the public. The knock-about comedy of *The Comedy of Errors*, the verbal games of *Love's Labor's Lost*, and the ironic wit of *As You Like It* all depend less on individual eccentricities than on misunderstandings of characters' places in society. Of course, no formula serves as a blueprint for all the plays. Each is a fresh experiment in comic form, yet the diverse forms – from rollicking farce to witty comedy of manners – express varying perspectives on the forces that make and mar human communities.

Part One

Belonging

CHAPTER TWO

Egeon's Friends and Relations: *The Comedy of Errors*

'We being strangers here, how dar'st thou trust ...' (I.ii.60)

Preaching on Ephesians 5, a text that seems to lie behind the setting of *The Comedy of Errors*,[1] John Donne offers an analysis of the essential nature of all human societies since the birth of Eve's first son: 'from that beginning to the end of the world, these three relations, of *Master* and *Servant, Man* and *Wife, Father* and *Children,* have been, and ever shall be the materialls, and the elements of all society, of families, and of Cities, and of Kingdomes.'[2] Whether or not all societies of all times consist of these three relationships, as Donne alleges, *The Comedy of Errors* does. The reunion of Egeon with his wife and sons provides the *telos* of the plot, and the scenes of mistaken identity that constitute the action ring changes on confused relations between master and servant and husband and wife. The comedy is also consistent with Donne's analysis in its representation of these relations as forms of power. According to Donne, '(because the principall foundation, and preservation of all States that are to continue, is *power*) the first relation was between *Prince* and *Subject*, when God said to Man, *Subjicite* & *dominamini*, subdue and govern all Creatures; The second relation was between *husband* and *wife* ...; And the third relation was between *parents* and *children*' (113–14). In the play, a ruler demonstrates his power by sentencing a man to death in the first scene and by rescinding the sentence in the last. In the intervening scenes, confusions of identity are manifested by masters beating the wrong servants and by a husband and wife's struggle for power.

A third significant parallel between the play's representation of society and Donne's account is the connection between the human and non-human worlds. In Donne's exposition, the relationship between prince and subject was established 'when God said to Man, *Subjicite & dominamini*, subdue and govern all Creatures.' In the comedy, Luciana explains that 'Man' is

> Lord of the wide world and wild wat'ry seas,
> Indu'd with intellectual sense and souls,
> Of more pre-eminence than fish and fowls. (II.i.21–3)

As the immediate context of these lines specifies, the man who dominates physical nature in Luciana's account is not inclusively human but, rather, exclusively male:

> There's nothing situate under heaven's eye
> But hath his bound in earth, in sea, in sky.
> The beasts, the fishes, and the winged fowls
> Are their males' subjects and at their controls:
> Man, more divine, the master of all these,
> Lord of the wide world and wild wat'ry seas,
> Indu'd with intellectual sense and souls,
> Of more pre-eminence than fish and fowls,
> Are masters to their females, and their lords. (II.i.16–24)

In both accounts, then, the relations of dominance and subjection in human affairs are natural and necessary and posited on human control of physical nature.

Donne's version suggests that these arrangements serve human convenience – the 'preservation of all States' – but the emphasis is on the divine institution of this distribution of power: 'God said to Man, *Subjicite & dominamini*.' In fact, Donne derives the structure of human society from the nature of the Godhead: 'God was always *alone* in heaven, there were no *other Gods* ... but he was never *singular*, there was never any time, when there were not *three persons* in heaven ... As then God seemes to have been eternally delighted, with this eternall generation, (with persons that had ever a relation to one another, *Father*, and *Sonne*) so when he came to the Creation of this lower world, he came presently to those three relations, of which the whole frame of this world consists' (5:113). Luciana, intent on reconciling her angry sister to her wayward husband, describes men as 'more divine' than the rest of creation and refers to 'heaven's eye,' thus suggesting divine approval of the distribution of human power. But the play as a whole treats human society not as divinely ordained but as practically necessary. The misadventures of Shakespeare's hapless twins occur in a world where human society is a necessary protection against the harsh conditions of physical existence. In the opening scene, Egeon's account of the shipwreck that started his troubles evokes the dangerous world beyond the boundaries of the city. The violence of wind and water and 'mighty rock' (I.i.101) dispersed his family. Subjected to an unjust Fortune (I.i.105) and unpitied by the 'merciless' gods (I.i.98–9), Egeon hopes only that people will know that his misfortune 'Was wrought by nature, not by vile offense' (I.i.34).

Although Egeon protests that the world of physical nature is unjust and merciless, he does not perceive it as random or chaotic. He registers no surprise or awe at the ocean storm that began his misfortune, recalling matter-of-factly:

> A league from Epidamium had we sail'd
> Before the always-wind-obeying deep
> Gave any tragic instance of our harm. (I.i.62–4)

As the waves obeyed the wind, so the people in their makeshift boat were 'obedient to the stream' (I.i.86) until the more powerful sun dispersed the storm and calmed the seas. Egeon assumes that the physical world follows its own laws by which the inferior is obedient to the superior. Egeon and his family, without their ship and abandoned by its crew, are helpless against the superior power of violent nature. After the shipwreck, Egeon and his wife managed to save their lives and those of the two pairs of infant boys in their care by fastening themselves to the small masts which 'sea-faring men provide for storms' (I.i.80) until they were rescued by ships from Corinth and Epidaurus. Evidently, then, men can become lords 'of the wide world and wild wat'ry seas' (II.i.21) only in concert with others of their kind. In an orderly society people can protect themselves and establish control over nature. Thus when Egeon's search for his family brings him to Ephesus, he defers without protest to Ephesian authority. Solinus, the Duke of Ephesus who sentences Egeon to death as an enemy alien, justifies his action not as an expression of his divinely granted personal right to rule but as the application of a law he is powerless to change. He justifies the law not as an embodiment of natural law or of transcendental justice but as an exercise of the power and responsibility of the state to protect its citizens against an external enemy. He explains that both the Syracusians and the Ephesians have decreed

> To admit no traffic to our adverse towns:
> Nay more, if any born at Ephesus be seen
> At any Syracusian marts and fairs;
> Again, if any Syracusian born
> Come to the bay of Ephesus, he dies,
> His goods confiscate to the Duke's dispose,
> Unless a thousand marks be levied
> To quit the penalty and to ransom him. (I.i.15–22)

Personally, Solinus pities Egeon as an innocent victim of 'dire mishap' (I.i.141), but officially, he sentences him to death according to Ephesian law. The power of the state exists to protect its own citizens; Egeon, deprived of relationships with his ruler and his family, is outside society and so 'Hopeless and helpless' (I.i.157).

Throughout *The Comedy of Errors* the importance attached to belonging to society is suggested both by the amount of dialogue directly concerned with social machinery like making appointments and paying bills and by the play's imagery, which typically is drawn from the details of social activity. For example, when Antipholus of Syracuse woos Luciana, after one fairly perfunctory reference to her as a 'fair sun', he avoids the roses, stars, and pearls of traditional love talk and praises her instead as 'My food, my fortune, and my sweet hope's aim' (III.ii.56, 63). Nature imagery in this play usually suggests danger and destruction rather than beauty or fertility. Thus Egeon thinks how old age brings changes that hide his identity in 'sap-consuming winter's drizzled snow' (V.i.313). And Antipholus of Syracuse expresses his loneliness far from home by likening himself to 'a drop of water' in the vast, formless ocean (I.ii.35). Even Antipholus' vision of Luciana as a mermaid contains as much fear as admiration:

> Sing, siren, for thyself, and I will dote;
> Spread o'er the silver waves thy golden hairs,
> And as a bed I'll take them, and there lie,
> And in that glorious supposition think
> He gains by death that hath such means to die. (III.ii.47–51)

Although Antipholus feels willing to submit to the destructive sexual element at this point, he soon decides to flee from the 'mermaid's song' that has 'almost made me traitor to myself' (III.ii.164, 162).

The characters in *The Comedy of Errors* are social beings who habitually contrast the familiarity and safety of human society with the dangers outside its boundaries. They see the world of nature as threatening but ordered according to a hierarchical pattern in which people participate. They defer to the Duke and look to him to settle their disputes. The subjection of servants to masters is similarly unquestioned. The relationship of the two Dromios to their masters is neither servile nor solemnly formal. Antipholus of Syracuse, for example, is obviously fond of the 'trusty villain' who, 'When I am dull with care and melancholy, / Lightens my humor with his merry jests' (I.ii.19–21), but there is no question but that the servant must submit to his master's power. As Dromio ruefully acknowledges, he must obey orders 'although against my will, / For servants must their masters' minds fulfill' (IV.i.112–13).

Some critics have seen a conflict between two incompatible views of marriage in Adriana's bitter complaints about her husband and Luciana's advocacy of wifely submission. To Peter Phialas, for example, Luciana represents romantic love, whereas Adriana is the shrewish wife, 'who thinks of love in terms of possession, ownership, and mastery' and 'rejects the notion that the man should be master in the home.'[3] But Luciana makes an odd advocate for romantic love. Her primary motive is to quell open dissension. She reprimands Adriana for being insufficiently submissive, and she urges Antipholus to conceal his infidelities from his wife: 'if you like elsewhere, do it by stealth'; 'Be secret-false: what need she be acquainted?' (III.ii.7, 15). Adriana's complaints serve not to contrast with her sister's romanticism but to elicit a defense of the gender hierarchy within marriage. When Adriana asks, 'Why should their [men's] liberty than ours be more?' (II.i.10), Luciana tells her at length in the passage quoted earlier. And in spite of protesting against Antipholus' infidelities, Adriana never questions her duty to love, honor, and obey her husband. She describes Antipholus to the Duke as 'my husband, / Who I made lord of me and all I had' (V.i.136–7). Nor is this public orthodoxy belied by private rebellion. Her self-abasement to the man she takes to be her strangely standoffish husband should satisfy the most demanding proponent of male domination:

> Thou art an elm, my husband, I a vine,
> Whose weakness, married to thy stronger state,

> Makes me with thy strength to communicate:
> If aught possess thee from me, it is dross,
> Usurping ivy, brier, or idle moss,
> Who, all for want of pruning, with intrusion
> Infect thy sap, and live on thy confusion. (II.ii.174–80)[4]

Thus, although Luciana's counsels of avoidance and appeasement contrast with Adriana's bitterness, their basic understandings of marital obligations do not differ. In spite of twentieth-century interpretations of Adriana as a portrait of a sixteenth-century shrew, her insistence on her husband's marital responsibilities is remarkably similar to John Donne's interpretation of St. Paul on marriage. According to Donne, 'The generall duty, that goes through all these three relations, is ... *Submit your selves to one another, in the feare of God*; for God hath given no Master such imperiousnesse, no husband such a superiority, no father such a soveraity, but that there lies a burden upon them too ... The wife is to submit herselfe; and so is the husband too' (5:114). The nature of that submission, he says, 'is *love: Husbands love your wives*' (115). Although the Ephesians in *The Comedy of Errors* give no evidence of knowing St. Paul much less the Dean of St. Paul's, they assume a similar view of social hierarchy. Even in her defense of male supremacy, Luciana stipulates that 'There's nothing situate under heaven's eye / But hath his bound' (II.i.16–17), and she and Balthasar, as well as Adriana, try to recall Antipholus to his 'husband's office' (III.ii.2. cf. III.i.85–106).

The corollary of the duty of mutual submission and assistance, Donne observes, is the interdependence of master and servant, husband and wife, father and son: 'They depend upon one another, and therefore he that hath not care of his fellow, destroys himselfe' (114). Similarly, Balthasar assumes the mutual dependency of husband and wife when he argues that Antipholus' violent assault on the locked door of his house would dishonor both him and his wife, and Adriana invokes this concept when she berates Antipholus for rejecting her. She begs Antipholus not to 'look strange and frown' (II.ii.110) because 'thou art then estranged from thyself':

> Thyself I call it, being strange to me,
> That, undividable incorporate,
> Am better than thy dear self's better part.
> Ah, do not tear away thyself from me. (II.ii.120–4)[5]

For either wife or husband to violate their marriage vows is to damage both:

> For if we two be one, and thou play false,
> I do digest the poison of thy flesh,
> Being strumpeted by thy contagion.
> Keep then fair league and truce with thy true bed,
> I live dis-stain'd, thou undishonored. (II.ii.142–6)

This plea for love and fidelity is not the tirade of a comic virago bent on mastery.

Parental authority does not cause the frustration and suffering that the power of masters and husband does for the Dromios and Adriana. No one neglects his or her obligations as parent or child, and no character is moved to instruct another in the duties of care and love. But the obligations of parents and children are nevertheless a source of dramatic tension. Egeon's narrative of the shipwreck assumes that parents are responsible for protecting their children and emphasizes his helpless inability to save his babies from disaster. Even more poignantly, in the last scene Egeon mistakes Antipholus of Ephesus, who has not seen his father since infancy, for his twin brother. Egeon's initial certainty that his son will save his life withers before Antipholus' blank incomprehension, and Egeon concludes that his son is ashamed to acknowledge a miserable old man as his father.

Since for these characters, as for Donne, the constitutive elements of society are personal relationships, a man without political or family ties remains pretty much at sea. Antipholus of Syracuse is not threatened with death as his father is, but he is nonetheless aware of his vulnerability as an outsider. Arriving in a strange city without any established relationships, he feels that he is losing his individual identity:

> I to the world am like a drop of water,
> That in the ocean seeks another drop,
> Who, falling there to find his fellow forth
> (Unseen, inquisitive), confounds himself.
> So I, to find a mother and a brother,
> In quest of them (unhappy), ah, lose myself. (I.ii.35–40)

Loss of personal relationships brings physical danger as well as psychological disorientation. 'We being strangers here' must be constantly on guard (I.ii.60), Antipholus warns his servant Dromio.

If the literal loss of home and family is fraught with danger, so too is the disruption of basic relationships. Adriana warns her husband that he cannot neglect their relationship without injuring her identity and his own:

> For know, my love, as easy mayst thou fall
> A drop of water in the breaking gulf,
> And take unmingled thence that drop again,
> Without addition or diminishing,
> As take from me thyself and not me too. (II.ii.125–9)

While Antipholus of Syracuse uses the water-drop analogy to express fear that his personal identity is dissolving in a sea of undifferentiated humanity, Adriana uses the same image to argue the complementary point that a separable, autonomous self cannot exist independent of human relationships. Anyone who deliberately damages his basic social relationships is dangerously self-destructive and anti-social. In *The Comedy of Errors* conflict arises not from competing values or goals but from mistaken identities in the context of universal dependence on social roles.

Despite my misleadingly solemn account of attitudes towards society in *The Comedy of Errors*, dependence on social relations is central to the play's comic tone. Its humor is posited on the decorum demanded by social roles. The scenes of mistaken identity are not of the kind where a dignified, solemn man is taken for and treated as a notorious libertine. Individual temperament has little – and the responsibilities of social role much – to do with the comedy. For example, Adriana's eloquent plea against marital estrangement creates humor rather than pathos because it is addressed to the wrong man and elicits the comically deflating response – but I *am* a stranger:

> Plead you to me, fair dame? I know you not:
> In Ephesus I am but two hours old,
> As strange unto your town as to your talk. (II.ii.147–9)

The assumption that the husband is master of the house creates comic incongruity when Antipholus of Ephesus brings friends home for dinner. As the scene begins, Antipholus is feeling some misgivings at being late and arranges for a friend to provide an excuse for his tardiness, but his apology that 'My wife is shrewish when I keep not hours' (III.i.2) is clearly jovial in tone. He confidently expects his wife to welcome his guest. To Balthasar's courteous demur, 'Small cheer and great welcome makes a merry feast'

(III.i.26), Antipholus responds with the polite diffidence of a man who takes pride in the hospitality he offers:

> Ay, to a niggardly host and more sparing guest:
> But though my cates be mean, take them in good part;
> Better cheer you may have, but not with better heart.
>
> (III.i.27-9)

This elaborate exchange of compliments anticipates the civilities with which King Duncan is made welcome to Dunsinane and serves a similar purpose, indicating through a minor social ritual the intricate network of pride, humility, deference, and hospitality that binds a community together. The shattering of the promised welcome is much less sinister in the comedy than in the tragedy, but no less complete. Antipholus finds the door locked against him and himself defied and ridiculed by his servants and repudiated by his wife. At these blows to his belief that the household is his to command, Antipholus passes quickly and ludicrously through bewilderment, embarrassment, shock, and rage.

A similar comedy of crossed purposes takes place when Luciana hears declarations of love from a man she believes to be her sister's husband or when one of the Dromios delivers a message to his master's uncomprehending twin. For example, when Dromio of Ephesus proudly delivers the rope he has been sent to find while his master impatiently expects the bail money that can release him from arrest, they sound like Abbott and Costello discussing 'Who's on first':

> **E.Ant.** How now, sir? have you that I sent you for?
> **E.Dro.** Here's that, I warrant you, will pay them all.
> **E.Ant.** But where's the money?
> **E.Dro.** Why, sir, I gave the money for the rope.
> **E.Ant.** Five hundred ducats, villain, for a rope?
> **E.Dro.** I'll serve you, sir, five hundred at the rate.
> **E.Ant.** To what end did I bid thee hie thee home?
> **E.Dro.** To a rope's end, sir, and to that end am I return'd.
> **E.Ant.** And to that end, sir, I will welcome you.
> *[Beats Dromio.]*
>
> (IV.iv.9-17)

The comic point is that in spite of their mutual acceptance of the terms of their relationship both the master's power and the servant's obedience are totally futile.

Thus the usual judgment that *The Comedy of Errors* relies on farce and physical comedy is only partly accurate. The play certainly contains a good deal of slapstick and lacks scenes of such multiple ironies as that where Rosalind disguised as Ganymede plays the part of Rosalind and warns Orlando that as a wife she will be 'more jealous of thee than a Barbary cock-pigeon over his hen' (*AYL*, IV.i.150–1). But the earlier comedy is not simple. When Adriana turns her sarcasm and eloquence on her husband's genuinely mystified twin brother or when she unleashes Doctor Pinch on her true husband because she is trying to do her duty by the 'poor distressed soul' (IV.iv.59), Shakespeare has given several twists to the stock portrayal of shrewish wives and tormented husbands. The central irony is that the bitterest quarrels grow out of fundamental agreement. In the last scene when Antipholus appeals to the Duke for justice against Adriana, he charges that his wife has 'shut the doors upon me' (V.i.204). Antipholus' complaint interrupts Adriana's appeal for justice against the Abbess, who 'shuts the gates' (V.i.156) and so frustrates her determination to take her husband home where she can care for him:

> I will attend my husband, be his nurse,
> Diet his sickness, for it is my office,
> And will have no attorney but myself. (V.i.98–100)

Antipholus' outrage and Adriana's insistence on the duties of her 'office' (V.i.99) emphasize their mutual adherence to the norms of conduct defined by social role. Similarly, Antipholus of Syracuse, who delivers short lectures on the art of domestic service – 'If you will jest with me, know my aspect, / And fashion your demeanor to my looks' (II.ii.32–3) – is understandably exasperated when his servant appears to flout him deliberately and repeatedly. And, of course, both Dromios are no less frustrated that their faithful diligence consistently provokes scoldings and beatings.

A complex picture of the strength and fragility of the human relationships that constitute society emerges from these confusions. The complications of plot pit the individual characters' sense of themselves as unique and irreplaceable against their dependence on other people for their sense of who they are and against the fact that to other people they are indistinguishable from each other. In III,i, when an unknown and unseen porter calling himself Dromio refuses entrance to the master of the house, the response by Dromio of Ephesus epitomizes the baffling predicament experienced by all the major characters:

O villain, thou hast stol'n both mine office and my name:
The one ne'er got me credit, the other mickle blame.
If thou hadst been Dromio to-day in my place,
Thou wouldst have chang'd thy face for a name, or thy name
   for an ass. (III.i.44–7)

On the one hand, Dromio is denied the social role that defines his identity. On the other, the faithful performance of that role has unpredictable, incomprehensible, often unpleasant results. Dromio himself is aware of that much about his own experience. Only the audience appreciates the further irony that the man addressed has, in fact, 'been Dromio to-day in [his] place' and beaten as an ass.

The Comedy of Errors presents the tension between the characters' sense of uniqueness and their dependence on precarious social identities as both terrifying and absurd. After the introductory dialogue between Egeon and Duke Solinus demonstrates the life-and-death stakes of belonging, the play transforms nightmare into absurdity, projecting the deep fear of being excluded or rejected from society in a series of hilarious misadventures. All the major characters undergo the Kafkaesque experience of suddenly finding themselves in a nightmare world of strange transformations and inexplicable events. But, of course, in Shakespeare's play the audience knows the simple facts that can explain the inexplicable and replace bewildering rejection with recognition and acceptance. Our awareness that all will end happily when the pairs of twins eventually meet (as we are sure they will) dissipates the potential terror and enables us to laugh freely at the increasing confusion.

The mistakes that make up the plot take the form of violations of social conventions. Since such artificial systems as those governing time, money, and law provide the coherence and stability necessary for society, even minor infractions of these conventions disturb social harmony.[6] In Shakespeare's Ephesus, persistent violations almost destroy all social order. In one sense, of course, time is a natural reality over which people have no control. Egeon, for example, attributes his son's failure to recognize him to the unavoidable changes brought by 'time's extremity' (V.i.308). Even Luciana's exposition of man's dominion over nature acknowledges that 'Time is their master' (II.i.8). But of more importance in this play than the ineluctable passing of time is the human ordering of time. Significantly, Luciana continues: 'Time is their master, and when they see time, / They'll go or come' (II.i.8–9). The confusions pivot on how people see and measure time. Because Antipholus of Ephesus does not come home at the conventional dinner hour, his wife goes out to find him and brings his twin home in his place. Because Angelo the jeweler fails to deliver the chain Antipholus of Ephesus has ordered at the time and place arranged, he gives it instead to the wrong Antipholus. Thus, failures in punctuality lead to Antipholus' humiliating exclusion from his house and to his arrest for debt when he refuses to pay for a chain he never received. These actual mistimings are hopelessly entangled with apparent ones. In the first scene of mistaken identity, Antipholus of Syracuse and Dromio of Ephesus accuse each other of being guilty of mistiming. Dromio, sent by his impatient mistress to bring her delinquent husband home to dinner, accuses Antipholus of being late, while Antipholus, who has ordered his servant to wait for him at the inn, accuses the wrong Dromio of returning too soon and interprets his talk of a waiting wife and dinner as jokes that are 'out of season' (I.ii.68). Similarly, when Antipholus next meets the true Dromio of Syracuse, he beats his servant for denying the earlier conversation 'a second time,' and Dromio protests at being 'thus beaten out of season' (II.ii.46, 47).

Just as Antipholus' and Dromio's real and apparent mistimings are interpreted as breaches of their duties as husband and servant, so too the confusions over money are perceived as violations of the obligations imposed by social role. Money is valued primarily not for any intrinsic worth nor as a means for securing goods and services but as a symbol of the trust necessary for the social exchanges that form human relationships. The chain Antipholus has promised his wife is the source of most of the confusion. When Antipholus decides to give the chain to the courtesan in revenge for Adriana's locking him out, he is symbolically rejecting his role as husband, although he wants to see his action as an expensive prank rather than a serious repudiation of his marriage.[7] When he denies receiving the chain and refuses to pay for it, the jeweler is most outraged by the impeachment of his 'credit' and 'reputation' (IV.i.68, 71). Conversely, when Antipholus of Syracuse receives the chain and the money intended for his brother's bail, they have little value to him because they have no part in comprehensible human relationships. In spite of the mysterious generosity of the Ephesians, he plans to flee as quickly as possible from a place where 'every one knows us, and we know none' (III.ii.152).

While most of the incidents in the plot revolve around discrepancies in how people see time and money, the law is the primary concern at the beginning and end of the play. As we have seen, in Act I the violation of a law directed against natives of Syracuse puts Egeon's life at risk. By Act V all the confusions over time and money have become questions of law, as the Ephesians appeal for justice to the Duke as the guardian of social order. But both the Duke's conscientious execution of his office and the respect for his authority by both Ephesians and strangers are ineffectual. Until the two pairs of twins finally meet at the end of the play, respect for law and order merely exacerbates confusion. The comedy of errors reaches its climax in Act V as Adriana and Antipholus of Ephesus, supported by a bewildering cloud of contradictory witnesses, demand justice and testify to totally incompatible versions of what has happened, and the poor Duke concludes that they are all mad. With the Duke's inability to dispense justice and establish order, the relations between parents and children, master and servant, husband and wife, and creditor and debtor have broken down, and all social structure seems ready to collapse in chaos.

When social structures cease to function in this world where individuals are helpless against nature and fate, the only possible responses seem to be hopeless resignation, ineffectual anger, or patient suffering of what cannot be avoided. The first alternative is Egeon's habitual reaction. Far from begging for mercy from the Duke, he urges on his own execution:

> Proceed, Solinus, to procure my fall,
> And by the doom of death end woes and all. (I.i.1–2; cf. 26–7)

As he reluctantly tells the story of his misfortunes, he reveals that in the earlier catastrophe also he 'would gladly have embrac'd' (I.i.69) death but that the tears of his wife and babies forced him to 'seek delays' (I.i.74). To the Duke's offer of time in which to raise money for the fine and so to save his life, he responds despairingly:

> Hopeless and helpless doth Egeon wend,
> But to procrastinate his liveless end. (I.i.157–8)

The other characters react to their troubles with a good deal more excitement and energy. Anger is the usual response. Antipholus of Ephesus threatens to pluck out his wife's eyes. Adriana reviles her husband as deformed in mind and body and threatens to crack her servant's skull. Both Antipholi repeatedly curse, threaten, and beat whichever Dromio is within reach. Like Egeon's hopelessness, the Ephesians' violence is not new. In the first scene of mistaken identity, Dromio of Ephesus' answer to Antipholus of Syracuse's inquiry about his thousand pounds indicates the angry violence of ordinary life in Ephesus:

> I have some marks of yours about my pate;
> Some of my mistress' marks upon my shoulders;
> But not a thousand marks between you both.
> If I should pay your worship those again,
> Perchance you will not bear them patiently. (I.ii.82–6)

Patience, the third response, is often preached but seldom practiced. When Luciana counsels Adriana to bear her husband's transgressions patiently, Adriana interprets the advice as the ignorance of inexperience:

> So thou, that hast no unkind mate to grieve thee,
> With urging helpless patience would relieve me;
> But if thou live to see like right bereft,
> This fool-begg'd patience in thee will be left. (II.i.38–41)

Her husband, who is frequently advised to be patient, is even more decisive in his contempt for patience. When Antipholus and Dromio escape from Doctor Pinch's ungentle ministrations, the finishing touch to their revenge is a sarcastic exhortation to patience:

> My master and his man are both broke loose,
> Beaten the maids a-row, and bound the doctor,
> Whose beard they have sing'd off with brands of fire,
> And ever as it blaz'd, they threw on him
> Great piles of puddled mire to quench the hair;
> My master preaches patience to him, and the while
> His man with scissors nicks him like a fool. (V.i.169–75)

Appeals to patience are no more effective than appeals to marital love and loyalty in the face of outright denial of identity and relationship.

The aggressive impatience of the characters in this reworking of a Plautine comedy comments irreverently on the classical concept of patience. Although some Renaissance humanists found moral guidance in discussions by classical authors of the virtue of enduring adversity with equanimity, others contrasted the classical concept of patience as passive endurance based on control of passion by reason with Christian patience, an active virtue based on faith and hope. While classical patience was summed up in the proverb 'Bear and forbear,' a patient Christian, maintaining faith in a providential order in spite of adversity, avoids both wrath and despair and lives in obedience and charity.[8] The virtue recommended in Ephesus is essentially the self-protective discretion of classical patience. Thus, Luciana argues that a wife should 'forbear' (II.i.31) if her husband strays because jealousy is 'self-harming' (II.i.102), and Balthasar advises Antipholus to control his anger because creating a public scandal would damage his reputation. Christian patience is exemplified by the Abbess, who turns out to be Aemilia, the long-lost wife and mother. Her reputation as a 'virtuous and a reverend lady' (V.i.134), her religious vocation during the years of the family's dispersal, and the calm dignity with which she performs the 'charitable duty of [her] order' (V.i.107) contrast with the intemperate anger of Adriana and Antipholus of Ephesus and with the despairing hopelessness of Egeon. In spite of her life of 'long grief' (V.i.407), she neither wishes for death nor strikes out at others but sets herself against 'grim and comfortless despair' and the 'infectious troop / Of pale distemperatures and foes to life' (V.i.80, 81–2).

When all this has been said, however, it is still evident that *The Comedy of Errors* is not a cautionary tale demonstrating the evil consequences of impatience.[9] The patient Abbess doesn't appear until the last scene where her despairing husband and impetuous and angry sons fare as well as she. The characters' follies and vices do not cause the plot complications. In fact, their occasional lapses into patience cause as much confusion as their more usual impatience. When Antipholus of Ephesus threatens to break down the door of his house, Balthasar counsels patience: 'Have patience, sir, O, let it not be so!'; 'Be rul'd by me, depart in patience' (III.i.85, 94). Antipholus uncharacteristically agrees, 'You have prevail'd. I will depart in quiet' (III.i.107) – and so effectively postpones the discovery of his unknown twin.

The bizarre experiences suffered in Shakespeare's Ephesus do not demonstrate the need for patience or test individual character in adversity so much as they demonstrate that without shared social structures reality becomes unintelligible. In the last scene, Duke Solinus responds to the deluge of incompatible evidence by observing, 'I think you all have drunk of Circe's cup' (V.i.271), and then a few lines later concludes, 'I think you are all ... stark mad' (V.i.282).

The Duke is not alone in deciding that everyone in Ephesus is either mad or bewitched. Although conventions such as the time set for meals and the alacrity with which bills should be paid are artificial and arbitrary, they are so basic to social functioning that the persistent collision of discrepant views violently disrupts the relations between people. The loss of such social roles as husband, wife, and servant threatens the characters' sense of their own identities and destroys their sense of reality. To explain such utter confusion they have recourse to theories of madness or magic. Antipholus of Syracuse finds the experience of being assigned new identities by strangers so disorienting that he doubts his own sanity, wondering whether he is 'Sleeping or waking, mad or well-advis'd' (II.ii.213; cf. IV.iii.42). More often, he favors the theory that he is surrounded by the supernatural. In his first appearance he remembers that Ephesus has a reputation for magic and sorcery, and his subsequent experiences confirm his suspicion that 'There's none but witches do inhabit here' (III.ii.156). Meanwhile the intermittent appearances of the two Antipholi convince the Ephesians that the Antipholus they know and love has gone mad. At first Adriana does not take literally Dromio's charge that his master is 'stark mad' (II.i.59). But when she hears that Antipholus is not merely inconsiderate of members of his household but publicly abusing social relationships, she changes her mind. After the courtesan reports that Antipholus has taken a ring from her in exchange for a chain and then refused to give her the chain, Adriana decides that such anti-social behavior justifies the conclusion that Antipholus is mad. 'His incivility,' she reasons, 'confirms no less' (IV.iv.46).

The hypotheses of insanity and witchcraft are essential to the play's structural dynamics, in which a movement towards isolation pulls against a movement towards cohesion. While the audience anticipates a meeting of the two Antipholi where all problems will instantly evaporate, these expectations are repeatedly frustrated by the characters' efforts to isolate madmen and to escape from sorcerers. Initially Antipholus of Syracuse is as open to experience as any traveler, planning to wander around Ephesus to 'view the manners of the town, / Peruse the traders, gaze upon the buildings' (I.ii.12–13), and he first reacts to the experience of being greeted by name and claimed as husband by a woman he has never before seen in a spirit of adventure, deciding to withhold judgment and 'in this mist at all adventures go' (II.ii.216). But in his next appearance he begins to make arrangements to leave Ephesus. In spite of the attractions of the enchanting Luciana, he plans to board the first ship leaving Ephesus, and in every subsequent appearance he repeats his intention of fleeing from the land of magic and sorcery. Dromio's delivery to the wrong Antipholus of the message that a ship is ready, the wind favorable, and their baggage on board promises some delay, but when Antipholus of Syracuse next appears he is more than ever convinced that the gifts showered on him are only 'imaginary wiles' (IV.iii.10) and receives the news that all is ready for departure. He then runs from the courtesan as a 'devil' (IV.iii.50) or 'fiend' (IV.iii.65), rejects Dromio's plea to stay a while, and exits in full flight for the ship leaving Ephesus that night.

By his growing determination to leave, Antipholus of Syracuse introduces the possibility that he may miss encountering his brother. For Antipholus of Ephesus, meanwhile, the consequence of being supplanted in his social identity by his twin is progressive isolation: locked out of his house, arrested for debt, and finally left bound and gagged in a dark room by Doctor Pinch, whom Adriana hires to cure her husband's madness. The absurdity of the Doctor Pinch episode consists in the fact that Adriana's solicitude for her husband convinces him that she is engaged in a sinister conspiracy against him. The further irony is that the cases of both Antipholi are seen as individual problems and treated by withdrawal and isolation whereas actually they are part of a common mistake that can be corrected only by convergence.

The reunion of twins that corrects errors and restores order does not result from recognizing the disintegrative effects of isolating the strange and incomprehensible. If human agency contributes to the happy ending, it is not through individual perspicacity but through the conventions of time, money, and law. By trying to collect the money owed them, Angelo and the Second Merchant interrupt the departure of Antipholus and Dromio of Syracuse and drive them to take refuge in the priory. Similarly, the expectation of justice from the Duke leads all the aggrieved citizens of Ephesus to converge around him. Moreover, although the presence of Antipholus and Dromio of Syracuse in the priory is a happy accident, the gathering in front of the priory at 5 o'clock is not entirely coincidental. Egeon's execution is scheduled for 5 o'clock near the abbey, so Adriana and Luciana, the Second Merchant and Angelo, the Duke and Egeon, and then Antipholus and Dromio of Ephesus congregate there by appointment. Thus the conventions which have caused so much dissension also serve to bring people together so that reunion is possible.

Primarily, however, the plot is satisfactorily resolved, as the Duke says, 'accidentally' (v.i.362). Working against the conscious efforts to withdraw and isolate that would segregate the twins and thus prevent the comic anagnorisis is the on-stage action that involves growing numbers of characters and increasingly frenetic activity. As the pace quickens, originally separate groups break apart and re-form in new combinations until it seems that the twins must meet eventually. This whirlwind of activity, which seems destined to throw together every possible combination of characters, can be read as the work of a beneficent fate or providence. In the text nothing precludes and nothing necessitates such an interpretation. But the change in the last scene from chaos to clarity focuses on factual explanation of the relations among people, not on moral or spiritual enlightenment. R.A. Foakes has suggested that the discovery of Aemilia saves Egeon's life 'as if, through her intervention, the harsh justice embodied in the Duke is tempered by a Christian grace and mercy.'[10] This reading seems to me to exaggerate the play's Christian overtones. In *The Comedy of Errors*, as in Donne's formulation of the orthodox social theory quoted at the beginning of this chapter, power is constitutive rather than instrumental: society consists of a set of unequal relationships. Although both the sermon and the play stipulate limits to human power, neither contests the authority of master over servant, husband over wife, parent over child, or ruler over subject. But while Donne situates the source and purpose of power in the Godhead, the law administered by Duke Solinus has no transcendental significance. Because the banning of Syracusians is a practical measure produced by particular political and economic circumstances, it can be reinterpreted in the light of new information. In waving aside Antipholus' offer to pay his father's fine, the Duke is neither contradicting his claim that personal sympathy cannot justify abrogating the law nor transcending the law in the name of mercy. When he tells Antipholus, 'thy father hath his life' (v.i.391), he is responding to a new set of circumstances: Egeon is no longer an alien from a hostile city but the father and husband of respected citizens of Ephesus. The revelation of Egeon's family relationships means that he is no longer an outsider. He belongs, and so the law against outsiders does not apply.

The ending of *The Comedy of Errors* doesn't subvert or redeem society through the intervention of a higher spiritual force. The play recognizes that actuality falls far short of an ideally harmonious society in which inferiors defer loyally to superiors who honor obligations to protect dependents. The quarrels between masters and servants and between husband and wife display the injustice and violence inherent in the hierarchical social order, but the play invites the audience to see them not as individual sins nor as symptoms of social injustice but, as the title directs, as errors. Antipholus' infidelity, Adriana's insubordination, and the Dromios' beatings, like Egeon's undeserved suffering and the bewilderment of Antipholus and Dromio of Syracuse, are consequences of the temporary loss of recognized social roles. The play emphasizes the need to belong to society, not the need to reform it. The dramatic action begins with the helplessness of an isolated individual and ends when individual lives are secured through social relationships. In the Abbess' last speech her metaphor of prolonged birth pains implies that being truly human involves the social manifestation of biological relations:

> Thirty-three years have I but gone in travail
> Of you, my sons, and till this present hour
> My heavy burthen ne'er delivered. (v.i.401–3)

The baptismal 'gossips' feast' (v.i.406) to which the company exits at the end of the play celebrates the entry of the Antipholus twins into a community in which reason is equated with civility and personal identity with social role. It is a community where the relations of master and servant, man and wife, and parents and children are presented as crucially important, but are experienced as sometimes reassuring, sometimes brutal, often ludicrous, and as terrifyingly precarious.

CHAPTER THREE

The Raw and the Cooked in *The Taming of the Shrew*

'I must dance barefoot on her wedding-day.' (II.i.33)

Like *The Comedy of Errors*, *The Taming of the Shrew* creates humor by violating the decorum of social roles and resolves comic confusion with the recognition that the major characters have found places in the social order. Although these two early comedies share the assumption that people are social beings, they explore the contrast between wildness and civilization and between belonging and not belonging from significantly different perspectives. Egeon's narrative at the beginning of *The Comedy of Errors* fills in a background of harsh physical nature and capricious fate against which the drama of losing and recovering social identity will play itself out. The Induction to *The Taming of the Shrew* serves a similar purpose, but this time the contrast isn't between the human and non-human but between the cultivated and the brutish. Christopher Sly, the drunken tinker, is a portrait of human degradation – destructive, irascible, lawless, ignorant, and scurrilous. In obvious contrast, the Lord who plays an elaborate practical joke on Sly is a highly civilized man. He is introduced as a hunter, easily dominant over animal nature. His relations with his servants exhibit gracious familiarity on his part and respectful deference on theirs. His effortless authority is complemented by his attitude of protective care of his hounds; his desire to derive fun from the helpless drunk is controlled by concern that the joke not go to cruel extremes (Ind.i.66, 136–8), and his plans for deceiving Sly are interspersed with instructions to treat him gently (Ind.i.45, 66–8, 72, 94–9). While Christopher Sly bestializes himself, degrading his human form into a 'monstrous beast' lying in a drunken stupor 'like a swine' (Ind.i.34), the Lord lives in a world where men's physical needs are supplied with fine clothes and delicious foods and their senses gratified with delicate fabrics, sweet smells, music, and art. Although the Lord's practical joke is neither morally nor intellectually superior to Sly's form of self-indulgence, the contrast is undeniable. It is also evident that the aristocratic refinement and the vulgar coarseness are both forms of human culture. The success of the Lord's ruse – changing Sly's sense of social identity by changing his physical environment and by providing him with new relationships – stresses the artificiality of social identity and the power of social rank. The humor of the scene suggests the complexity of social manners and Sly's residual control of the situation. He is funnier after than before his transformation precisely because he insists on drinking small ale instead of sack and wants to know whether to call his wife 'Al'ce madam, or Joan madam' (Ind. ii.110). In *The Comedy of Errors*, social identity is a birthright and its misapprehension produces confusion, but in *The Taming of the Shrew* social roles are arbitrary and must be learned.

While *The Comedy of Errors* emphasizes human dependence on social structure, *The Taming of the Shrew* focuses on the dynamics of human power and purpose. In *The Comedy of Errors*, being in a strange city means dangerous isolation. In *The Taming of the Shrew*, visitors have no such fears. Tranio indignantly and successfully challenges the rich citizen Gremio: 'Are not the streets as free / For me as for you?' (I.ii.231–2). A xenophobic law against foreigners, which in *The Comedy of Errors* imperils Egeon's life, in *The Taming of the Shrew* is a joke, part of Lucentio's amorous intrigue. By convincing an old man whom he finds on the road from Mantua that a quarrel with the Duke of Mantua has caused the Duke of Padua to proclaim 'death for any one in Mantua / To come to Padua' (IV.ii.81–2), Tranio persuades the old Pedant to masquerade as Lucentio's father. Petruchio and Tranio, of course, are even more eager than the Pedant to undertake the challenges offered by a new place. In *The Comedy of Errors*, Egeon and Antipholus come to Ephesus to search for their lost son and brother. In *The Taming of the Shrew*, visitors arrive in Padua anticipating new opportunities. Lucentio opens the play announcing that he has come to 'fair Padua, nursery of arts' to pursue a 'course of learning and ingenious studies' (I.i.2, 9), then immediately accepts Tranio's advice to mix study with pleasure, and before the scene is over falls in love. In the next scene Petruchio announces that he has come to Padua 'to wive and thrive as best I may' (I.ii.56). In the world of this play it is natural for young men to travel 'To seek their fortunes farther than at home' (I.ii.51), and being in a strange city means exhilaration rather than fear or bewilderment.

The wooing scenes in these two early plays also illustrate the contrast in their representation of attitudes towards social institutions. In both plays, humor depends on the existence of courtship conventions. The scene in which Antipholus of Syracuse declares his love to Luciana is comic not because his manner of courting is funny in itself but because he directs his eloquence to a woman who believes him to be her sister's husband. When his tender plea, 'Give me thy hand,' elicits the deflating response, 'O soft, sir, hold you still; / I'll fetch my sister to get her good will' (*CE*, III.ii.69–70), the effect is ludicrous. In contrast, Petruchio's wooing of Kate is comic not because of any misperception of social roles but because both Katherina and Petruchio intentionally flout the conventions of courtship.

The opening scene of *The Taming of the Shrew*, then, sketches the shape of the main action not only by demonstrating the artificiality of social roles and the extremes of civilized and uncivilized behavior but also by emphasizing intentional perversity and impudence rather than inadvertent error. The ruse that the Lord practices on Christopher Sly is potentially frightening. In *The Comedy of Errors* when Antipholus of Syracuse has a comparable experience of being assigned a strange new identity and an unknown wife, he doubts his own sanity, sees the people who claim to know him as witches and sorcerers, and plans to flee in terror from a place where 'every one knows us, and we know none' (III.ii.152). Christopher Sly, on the other hand, enthusiastically accepts the new identity created for him by the Lord and his servants. For him, after some initial excitement, the experience is, as the Lord predicts, 'a flatt'ring dream' (Ind.i.44). When the play opens on Sly's altercation with the Hostess, he is as notable for his pretensions as for his ignorance, replying to the Hostess' threat of 'A pair of stocks, you rogue': 'Y' are a baggage, the Slys are no rogues. Look in the chronicles; we came in with Richard Conqueror. Therefore *paucas pallabris*, let the world slide' (Ind.i.2–6). The deception that transforms the poor tinker into a rich lord fulfills his fantasies of aristocratic rank as well as affording him the sensory gratification of fine clothes, food, and entertainment. Indeed, Sly is so delighted with the deception that his old life seems to him a dream he 'would be loath to fall into ... again' (Ind.ii.126–7). And as a new identity is a dream-come-true for Christopher Sly in the Induction, in the main action most of the major characters (including Lucentio, Tranio, Hortensio, and the Pedant) put on new clothes and claim new identities for their own purposes. Most notably, Petruchio and Katherina achieve new social roles that satisfy their personal wishes. Both *A Comedy of Errors* and *The Taming of the Shrew* trace the achievement of secure social position, but while the former converts the nightmare of individual vulnerability into rollicking comedy, the latter dramatizes the dream of adapting society to one's own desires.

After the social extremes of the beggar and the aristocrat in the Induction, the major characters of *The Taming of the Shrew* are what contemporaries called the middling sort. The play has no lovelorn duke or legendary hero, no enchanted woods or fairy-tale castle, and no subplot involving characters of inferior social status: the action all involves a closely knit, materialistic, and conventional society. As a famous university town, Padua is an appropriate destination for Lucentio and Petruchio, who are looking for adventure, but so many commercial and personal ties bind the travelers to the native inhabitants that in no sense do they seem strangers to the culture they find there. Petruchio says that he has 'come abroad to see the world' (I.ii.58), but he has come first to Padua to see friends, especially his 'best beloved and approved friend, / Hortensio' (I.ii.3–4). Although he hasn't met Katherina previously, his father was well known to her father, Baptista, who welcomes Petruchio for his father's sake (I.ii.101–2; II.i.68–70). Lucentio, who doesn't have old friends in Padua, can rely on his father's renown. When Tranio, disguised as Lucentio, asks permission to court Bianca 'upon knowledge of my parentage' (II.i.95), Baptista accepts him because Vincentio, Lucentio's father, is well known to him by reputation. Even the Pedant from Mantua is glad to accept protection from the son of a well-known merchant.

While this network of family and business connections enables the young men visiting Padua to combine adventure with security, it also seems almost suffocatingly restrictive. When Lucentio wants to adopt a disguise in order to be near Bianca and win her love, the main obstacle to his plan is that there must be someone to play the part of Lucentio. And his role is to

> be in Padua here Vincentio's son,
> Keep house and ply his book, welcome his friends,
> Visit his countrymen, and banquet them. (I.i.195-7)

Being his father's son and heir is undoubtedly useful, so that Lucentio finds it convenient to provide himself with a substitute father; still, he is severely embarrassed when his real father turns up unexpectedly. And if the emphasis on family connections is inconvenient for Lucentio, it is yet more troublesome for Katherina and Bianca, who are confined and frustrated by being thought of almost exclusively in terms of their familial roles. Katherina is publicly humiliated for being an unmarried and unsought-after elder daughter and understandably reacts with resentment towards her father and violent jealousy towards her sister. As younger daughter, Bianca is not free to marry until Katherina finds a husband. Even when Tranio/Lucentio urges that he be added to Bianca's list of suitors, he does so on the grounds that *her father* is 'a noble gentleman,' deserving multiple suitors for his daughter (I.ii.238). Unsurprisingly Bianca treats her apparently unmarriageable elder sister with veiled hostility. Subject to her father's authority in education and marriage – the only significant activities her society expects of her – Bianca subverts his will in both: secretly defying tutors he provides and making a clandestine marriage. The family unit, then, is not fragmented or threatened with dissolution as it is in such comedies as *The Comedy of Errors* or *As You Like It*,[1] but the very strength of the family generates hostility and hypocrisy.

While there is no real evil in *The Taming of the Shrew*, no malevolent villain or threat of death, there is considerable tension generated by the tightly knit, paternalistic social structures. The materialism of the play's world also contributes to an oppressive atmosphere. It is a world of objects: the luxurious objects evoked to convince Christopher Sly that he is a rich lord – 'a couch, / Softer and sweeter than the lustful bed / On purpose trimm'd up for Semiramis,' horses with 'Their harness studded all with gold and pearl' (Ind.ii.37-9, 42); the expensive objects Gremio pledges to win Bianca – a house 'richly furnished with plate and gold, / Basins and ewers ... Tyrian tapestry ... ivory coffers ... cypress chests ... Costly apparel, tents, and canopies, / Fine linen, Turkey cushions ... Pewter and brass ... a hundred milch-kine ... Six score fat oxen' (II.i.347-58); the homely, shabby things that constitute Petruchio's equipage on his wedding day – 'a new hat and an old jerkin; a pair of old breeches ... a pair of boots that have been candle-cases ... an old rusty sword ... his horse hipp'd' with an old mothy saddle and stirrups of no kindred' (III.ii.43–50). As a character in a novel by Umberto Eco exclaims, 'there is nothing more wonderful than a list, instrument of wondrous hypotyposis,'[2] and the lists in *The Taming of the Shrew* create this reassuring sense of reality, of warmth and security. But they also suggest a world almost too cluttered to move about in freely.

The language of the play not only fills the dramatic world with solid objects, it suggests that they are the determinants of human identity. While in *The Comedy of Errors* the confusions over the gold chain, the rope, and the bag of gold lead Antipholus of Syracuse to distrust his own perceptions, to Christopher Sly the testimony of his senses is irrefutable evidence of his new identity:

> I do not sleep: I see, I hear, I speak;
> I smell sweet savors, and I feel soft things.
> Upon my life, I am a lord indeed. (Ind.ii.70–2)

The multiple disguises in the body of the play – Tranio as Lucentio, Lucentio as Cambio, Hortensio as Litio, and the Pedant as Vincentio – focus attention on how much social identity depends on arbitrary conventions of costume. Of course, the power of disguise is a dramatic convention assumed in many of the comedies, but while Rosalind's female identity continues to function dramatically in spite of her doublet and hose, in *The Taming of the Shrew* we are directed to believe that there are no perceptible differences among men except those of costume. All that is necessary for Tranio to bear Lucentio's part in Padua is to put on his master's hat and cloak, for they cannot 'be distinguish'd by [their] faces / For man or master' (I.i.200–1). And, although the Pedant no more resembles Vincentio than 'an apple doth an oyster' (IV.ii.101–2), he is the right age and 'In gait and countenance surely like a father' (IV.ii.65), so that, as Tranio tells him, it is necessary only 'to clothe you as becomes you' (IV.ii.121) for him to play Vincentio.

Shakespeare's Padua is also materialistic in the sense that the characters are preoccupied with wealth and possessions. Almost invariably they identify themselves and describe others in terms of their economic status. Petruchio assures Hortensio that he has 'Crowns in [his] purse ... and goods at home' (I.ii.57) and more formally assures Baptista that he has inherited his father's entire fortune and increased that inheritance (II.i.117–18). Baptista welcomes

Lucentio not simply because he has heard of Vincentio but because he has heard of him as a 'mighty man of Pisa' (II.i.104); similarly the Pedant remembers him as a 'merchant of incomparable wealth' (IV.ii.98). Bianca's suitors are conscious that her father is 'very rich' (I.i.124), and the inducement Hortensio uses to interest Petruchio in Katherina is that she will be 'very rich' (I.ii.63). Petruchio notoriously announces that he has come 'to wive it wealthily in Padua' (I.ii.75), and Hortensio, when he becomes disillusioned with Bianca, his 'treasure' and his 'jewel' (I.ii.118–19), decides immediately to marry 'a wealthy widow' (IV.ii.37).

The metonymical identification of people with their possessions is a salient characteristic of the play's farcical hilarity. In the noisy quarrel where Katherina has bound Bianca's hands and then berates her about her suitors, Bianca offers to take off 'these other gawds ... Yea, all my raiment' (II.i.3, 5) in return for her release. Bianca clearly understands that her finery symbolizes to Katherina her value on the marriage market. Bianca is their father's 'treasure, she must have a husband,' while poor Kate fears that she 'must dance barefoot on [Bianca's] wedding-day' (II.i.32–3). When Baptista announces that he will give Bianca to the highest bidder, he explains even more explicitly that the human deeds he cares about are the deeds to land and property:

> 'Tis deeds must win the prize, and he of both
> That can assure my daughter greatest dower
> Shall have my Bianca's love. (II.i.342–4)

Characters so universally equate personal with economic worth and so unabashedly declare their economic motives that the effect is not individual characterization so much as the establishment of the values and mores of an acquisitive society.

Finally, perhaps the most striking feature of Shakespeare's Padua is the conventionality of its inhabitants. The characters are all thoroughly imbued with the ideology of a patriarchal society and assume that men have power over their wives, children, and servants. The dramatic action rests on the unquestioned assumption that marriage is right for everyone, and the plot develops from Baptista's determination that his daughters' marriages follow the usual pattern, his elder daughter marrying before her younger sister. The conflict arises from the universal abhorrence of Katherina's refusal to conform to conventional ideas of femininity.

The play does not, however, simply pit rebellious youth against aged conventionality. On the whole, the young lovers defer to the values and opinions of the group as automatically as do their elders. If Baptista's auctioning of his younger daughter satirizes the way the old sacrifice love to social and financial considerations, Hortensio's snobbish outrage when he believes he has discovered Bianca making love with her tutor also reveals the timid conventionality of a man who adheres unquestioningly to dominant social values. He announces himself as

> one that scorn[s] to live in this disguise
> For such a one as leaves a gentleman,
> And makes a god of such a cullion, (IV.ii.18-20)

and he renounces Bianca because she has lost value by favoring a social and economic inferior. Lucentio is less of a prig as a suitor, but he is just as obviously controlled by literary conventions as Hortensio is by social ones. When Lucentio first sees Bianca, he confesses his love in conventional Petrarchan language:

> Tranio, I burn, I pine, I perish, Tranio,
> If I achieve not this young modest girl. (I.i.155-6)

He expresses his rapture in the clichéd images Shakespeare satirizes also in Sonnet 130.

> Tranio, I saw her coral lips to move,
> And with her breath she did perfume the air. (I.i.174-5)

The young women too are directed by the norms of their society. Bianca's fulfillment of the conventional ideal of feminine docility and modesty and her later imperiousness together testify to the importance she attaches to the approval of others. She tries to evade the disadvantages of a subordinate position, but she never challenges the principle of subordination or disregards public opinion. Despite Katherina's rebellious refusal to adopt the role of feminine passivity, she too desires above all the approval of her society. Her outbreaks of temper, indeed, arise directly from resentment that she is not valued by others. She berates Baptista for neglecting his parental duties by exposing her to derision (I.i.57-8), by failing to provide her with a husband (II.i.31-4), and by matching her with an unconventional suitor (II.i.285-9). And when Petruchio is late for the wedding, Baptista's horror at 'What will be said? What mockery will it be ...!' (III.ii.4) is echoed by Katherina: 'No shame but mine ... Now must the world point at poor Katherine' (III.ii.8, 18). The reactions of the rich merchant and his rebellious daughter are the same: anger and fear at what people will say.

The 'happy gale' (I.ii.48) that blows Petruchio to Padua brings a gust of uncomfortably bracing air to this stultifyingly tightly knit, materialistic, and conventional community. In the early scenes his brashness is a major source of humor. Within a few lines of his first appearance he is beating his servant for failing to understand and comply immediately with his orders. In the next scene, Gremio twice rebukes him for being 'too blunt' and 'marvellous forward' (II.i.45, 73). But despite his temper and impatience with social proprieties Petruchio does not provoke serious hostility. Unlike Katherina, whose reactions to social constraints are anti-social and self-defeating, Petruchio tempers his assertiveness with engaging frankness and friendliness and acts effectively in personal and social relationships, demonstrating that society's rules are flexible enough to be shaped to fit individual needs.

The most important demonstration of Petruchio's combination of self-assertion and sociability is his marriage. At first he doesn't challenge conventional matrimonial practices but brushes aside the cant surrounding them. When he bursts on the scene in Padua, he is an energetic young man eager to participate fully in whatever life has to offer. No longer a student like Lucentio, he has some travel, business, and military experience behind him and is ready to take his place in society as a married man. Common sense tells him that financial considerations are the normal basis for matrimony in his society, and his habitual honesty prevents his draping his intentions in robes of sentiment. He unapologetically announces that he means to wed wealthily and 'If wealthily, then happily' (I.ii.76), and briskly sets about arranging financial terms with Baptista. His startling frankness makes him a natural target for Grumio's sarcasm: 'Nay, look you, sir, he tells you flatly what his mind is. Why, give him gold enough, and marry him to a puppet or an aglet-baby, or an old trot with ne'er a tooth in her head, though she have as many diseases as two and fifty horses. Why, nothing comes amiss, so money comes withal' (I.ii.77–82). But Petruchio is not trying to be what others expect or desire him to be. He insists on making his own decisions and is impervious to both ridicule and solicitous advice.

Petruchio's honesty about his economic motives is refreshing, but it is his response to Katherina herself that clearly shows his independent spirit. While his original intention to marry a rich woman reflects the materialism of his society, his assumption that the character of his wife will be totally irrelevant to his marital happiness shows that he is relatively inexperienced with women. While he may have 'heard lions roar' and 'heard the sea ... Rage like an angry boar' (I.ii.200, 201-2), there is something comically naïve in the breezy self-confidence with which he contemplates marriage with a shrew:

> Have I not in a pitched battle heard
> Loud 'larums, neighing steeds, and trumpets' clang?
> And do you tell me of a woman's tongue,
> That gives not half so great a blow to hear
> As will a chestnut in a farmer's fire?
> Tush, tush, fear boys with bugs. (I.ii.205-10)

Petruchio obviously has never been in love and, unlike Lucentio or the young lovers in *A Midsummer Night's Dream*, has not been attracted by the poets' accounts to want or expect the experience Lucentio calls 'love in idleness' (I.i.151). His brash assumption that his affections will not alter whether his wife is 'as foul as was Florentius' love, / As old as Sibyl, and as curst and shrowd / As Socrates' Xantippe' (I.ii.69-71) is not cynicism or misogyny so much as the comic hubris of inexperience. Katherina forces Petruchio to rethink his assumptions about women, and his transformation convinces the audience that he is indeed the man capable of taming her.

While the other eligible men desire Bianca because she fits the stereotypical ideal of femininity and despise Katherina because she so emphatically does not, Petruchio is excited by Katherina's spirit. After he hears about her forthright way of dealing with an unwanted music teacher, he is intrigued:

> Now by the world, it is a lusty wench!
> I love her ten times more than e'er I did.
> O, how I long to have some chat with her! (II.i.160-2)

At this point he gives some thought as to how to 'woo her with some spirit' (II.i.169) and decides to smother her shrewishness under the banalities of conventional courtship:

> Say that she rail, why then I'll tell her plain
> She sings as sweetly as a nightingale;
> Say that she frown, I'll say she looks as clear
> As morning roses newly wash'd with dew. (II.I.170-3)

When he actually meets Katherina, he modifies this plan considerably.

She seizes the initiative with her first words, haughtily rebuking his informality in addressing her familiarly as Kate: 'They call me Katherine that do talk of me' (II.i.184). Petruchio is thrown off balance and retorts, 'You lie, in faith, for you are call'd plain Kate' (II.i.185). Kate's combativeness and verbal dexterity force Petruchio to abandon his plan of ignoring what she actually says and provoke him into a verbal battle in which both participants intentionally flout courtship conventions. Kate responds to Petruchio's proposal of marriage by warning him that she is 'Too light [quick] ... to catch' (II.i.204) and dangerously 'waspish' (210), by rudely calling him a join'd-stool (198), an ass (199), a jade (201), a buzzard (206), a crab (229), and a fool (212, 257), and even by striking him. Clearly her sharp-tongued belligerence deliberately repudiates the gentle modesty expected in a young woman waiting to be wooed and won by an eligible suitor. Petruchio is equally far from the conventional lovesick swain, but while Katherina's language is consistently abusive, Petruchio's is notable for its variety. He not only joins in the wordplay Kate initiates ('**Kath.** What is your crest? a coxcomb? / **Pet.** A combless cock, so Kate will be my hen' [II.i.225–6]), but the song accompanying his wooing dance also includes sarcastic flattery ('thy mildness prais'd in every town' [191]), obscenity ('What, with my tongue in your tail?' [217]), praise ('sweet as spring-time flowers' [246]), and unembellished literal statement – to threaten ('I swear I'll cuff you, if you strike again' [220]), to inform ('your father hath consented / That you shall be my wife; your dowry 'greed on' [269–70]), and to invite ('Now, Kate, I am a husband for your turn' [272]).

Petruchio's verbal flexibility makes his victory in the battle of wits appear both credible and desirable. As audience, we can laugh at their mutual travesty of courtship rituals, delight in their sexual and intellectual energy, sympathize with this variation of the traditional comic material of young love, and yet see that Kate's knee-jerk shrewishness is no match for Petruchio's more varied responses. We see that, although Petruchio decided to marry Kate sight unseen because she was rich, when he meets her he in fact responds to the actual woman. Engaging in this combat of wits shows Petruchio that a shrewish wife cannot simply be ignored, determines him to tame Katherina, and convinces him that she is worth taming. The bawdy puns that are his chief weapon suggest that Petruchio, who boasted earlier that if his bride is rich enough she cannot be too foul for him, is sexually excited by the exchange with Kate. It may be worth remembering in this connection the Lord's 'wanton pictures' (Ind.i.47) offered to Christopher Sly: Adonis pursued by Venus, Io 'beguiled and surpris'd' by Jupiter, and Daphne fleeing from Apollo (Ind.ii.55). Petruchio's exuberant ribaldry is a far cry from the aristocratic Lord's decadent taste for sexual violence among the Olympians, but it does show that he finds the battle of the sexes erotically provocative.

In the course of the scene with Kate, Petruchio converts from an eagerness to marry any rich woman to a determination to marry and win the love of a particular woman. And he stops talking about her wealth. When he returns to the plan of meeting her shrewishness with the softness of love, his language – more personal and original than the intended clichés about roses and nightingales – expresses genuine admiration and tenderness:

> Kate like the hazel-twig
> Is straight and slender, and as brown in hue
> As hazel-nuts, and sweeter than the kernels. (II.i.253–5)

Using a strategy similar to that in Sonnet 130 ('My mistress' eyes are nothing like the sun'), Shakespeare here convinces us of Petruchio's sincerity by the contrast between what he intended to say and what he does say, between Lucentio's stale Petrarchisms and Petruchio's homely similes. When Petruchio brings their private interview to a close, he does so in terms of such a linguistic contrast:

> And therefore setting all this chat aside,
> Thus in plain terms: your father hath consented
> That you shall be my wife; your dowry 'greed on;
> And will you, nill you, I will marry you.
> Now, Kate, I am a husband for your turn,
> For by this light whereby I see thy beauty,
> Thy beauty that doth make me like thee well,
> Thou must be married to no man but me. (II.i.268–75)

Dismissing their contest of wits as chat, Petruchio speaks in plain terms that acknowledge economic and social reality and also speak his admiration and affection convincingly. This contrast between verbal games and plain honest statement suggests that Petruchio's idea of taming Kate is not to enforce a narrow, rigid conformity but to replace constricting formulas with mutual responsiveness.

Petruchio falls in love with Kate's vivacity and nimble wit, but he is dismayed that she thinks and acts in terms of unexamined social conventions. Her rebellion is not free and spontaneous but a performance as the stereotypical shrew. Insecure and resentful but always painfully aware of how others see her, she is afraid of Petruchio's heterodoxy. Ignoring Petruchio's offer of affection, she primly reproves her father for wishing to marry her to a 'madcap ruffian' (II.i.288). In the courtship scene, Petruchio responds to Kate's underlying conventionality by teasing her with patently false accounts of what people say about her, reporting that he heard her 'mildness prais'd in every town' (II.i.191) and indignantly wondering 'Why does the world report that Kate doth limp?' (II.i.252). Then he begins his program for taming her by flouting social decorum. First, he firmly wards off outside interference with his announcement of their wedding date: 'I choose her for myself. / If she and I be pleas'd, what's that to you?' (II.i.302–3). Next he carefully plans their wedding as a social event, explicitly making arrangements for food, clothing, and guests, and then deliberately turns the occasion into a fiasco – arriving late dressed in outlandish clothes, interrupting the ceremony with bizarre behavior, and finally carrying his bride off before the wedding feast in a hilarious parody of a knight-errant rescuing a damsel-in-distress. While Petruchio's earlier *faux pas* were by-products of energetic spontaneity ('O, pardon me,' he apologizes at Gremio's chiding, 'I would fain be doing' [II.i.74]), his 'mad marriage' (III.ii.182) is a deliberate repudiation of social decorum. Whether Petruchio is a boorish brute or a wise and benevolent teacher and whether he breaks Kate's spirit, rescues her from a repressive society, or teaches her civility by negative example are hotly contested critical questions, but unquestionably he forces Kate to think consciously about the norms of acceptable behavior in her community.

His program for taming 'wild Kate' (II.i.277) obviously does not include high culture. Hortensio and Lucentio in their roles as tutors discover to their dismay Kate's resistance to the fine arts. Indeed, her reaction to the lute is even less gratifying than Christopher Sly's to Shakespearean comedy. While he is bored and in most productions falls asleep, she breaks the lute over Hortensio's head. At first, Petruchio's method of modifying Kate's behavior seems like a replication of the Lord's practice on Christopher Sly, changing her identity by changing her external environment. He provides her with a new image of herself: instead of hearing her sister's suitors reject her as a whore and a devil (I.i.55, 66), she hears her husband insist that she is 'patient, sweet, and virtuous' (III.ii.195). By denying her food, clothing, and sleep, he forces her out of the role of selfish aggressor into that of suffering victim. Like Sly, Kate is disorientated by a radically changed environment that supplants familiar reality: she seems to Curtis 'as one new risen from a dream' (IV.i.186). And like Sly, Kate finds herself adopting unfamiliar modes of behavior: she 'who never knew how to entreat' (IV.iii.7) and who asserted the freedom to say and do whatever she wished, usually at others' expense, learns to ask for help, to express gratitude and compassion, to conciliate and accommodate.

But Kate's experience is fundamentally different from Sly's. While he does not have to discover the fragility of a personal identity based on external trappings, Kate learns that personal worth does not depend on deferential servants and fashionable clothes. When Baptista charges that marrying Katherina in disreputable clothes is shameful, Petruchio replies that clothes do not make the man: 'To me she's married, not unto my clothes' (III.ii.117). After tantalizing Kate with promises of 'silken coats and caps, and golden rings' (IV.iii.55) and then capriciously denying her the proposed finery, he expounds the moral even more explicitly:

> For 'tis the mind that makes the body rich;
> And as the sun breaks through the darkest clouds,
> So honor peereth in the meanest habit.
> What, is the jay more precious than the lark,
> Because his feathers are more beautiful?
> Or is the adder better than the eel,
> Because his painted skin contents the eye?
> O no, good Kate; neither art thou the worse
> For this poor furniture and mean array. (IV.iii.172–80)

Kate's transformation, then, must be internal, not external like Sly's.

What Petruchio teaches Kate is not simply a sense of proportion which subordinates surfaces to substance or the conventional piety that exalts immaterial virtue over material wealth (his objections to the cut of the gown are at least as arbitrary and as superficial as the vagaries of fashion for gentlewomen). The most important lesson

Kate learns is that it is 'the mind that makes the body rich' (IV.iii.172) – the human power of understanding and choice that values the song of the lark more highly than the plumage of the jay. Although Kate is spirited and rebellious, she reacts to conventions with thoughtless, puppetlike predictability. Her shrewishness fulfills a socially defined stereotype as much as Bianca's docility does. By usurping Kate's role of aggressive ill-temper and subjecting her to a bewildering mixture of harshness and tenderness, Petruchio forces her to abandon her customary modes of perception and behavior. She learns to exercise choice instead of conforming automatically to the expectations of the people she lives with and to select ways to act from among alternatives rather than to react with habitual shrewishness.

Petruchio challenges conventions governing time as well as costume. In *The Comedy of Errors*, as we saw earlier, time, both as natural phenomenon and as social convention, is men's master. In *The Taming of the Shrew*, Petruchio asserts his mastery over time. His lack of punctuality, like that of Antipholus of Syracuse, is cause for complaint, but while Antipholus' tardiness makes his wife shrewish, Petruchio's is part of the cure for shrewishness. In Act III he defies social convention by deliberately arriving late for his wedding. In Act IV when he makes the return to Baptista's house contingent on his version of time, he enunciates the principle clearly:

> I will not go to-day, and ere I do,
> It shall be what a' clock I say it is. (IV.iii.194–5)

Hortensio's response – 'Why, so this gallant will command the sun' (IV.iii.196) – is prophetic. On the journey, when Katherina objects to his calling the moon the sun, Petruchio claims the power not only to name the intervals of time as he chooses but to impose his own meaning on the natural phenomena by which people measure time: 'It shall be moon, or star, or what I list' (IV.v.7). By finally agreeing – 'be it moon, or sun, or what you please' (IV.v.13) – Katherina acknowledges the arbitrariness of the human order imposed on the natural world and Petruchio's independence of that conventional order. She also shows her understanding that she too can control the world she lives in. In the next episode, where she gaily addresses old Vincentio as a 'Young budding virgin' (IV.v.37), she exercises her power to interpret age and sex to suit her needs. The fun, of course, depends on the limits of that power – there would be no joke if Vincentio *were* young and female, but Kate's ability to parody

Petruchio is a measure of her mastery of his strategy. The old Katherina could only chafe against temporal conventions ('What, shall I be appointed hours, as though (belike) I knew not what to take and what to leave?' [I.i.103-4]) or feel humiliated at their breach by Petruchio ('Who woo'd in haste, and means to wed at leisure' [III.ii.11]). By the time she returns to her father's house with Petruchio, she can cheerfully assert a personal view of a timeless world where 'every thing I look on seemeth green' (IV.v.47), and can also acknowledge common reality and social propriety by apologizing for her 'mad mistaking' (IV.v.49).

In contrast to Kate's unorthodox marriage, Bianca's reveals the absurd contradiction between literary convention and social convention by literalizing both. Lucentio, following the romantic tradition in which a woman is a sought-after ideal, puts on a disguise to get access to Bianca and defeats a rival for her love, while his stand-in, Tranio, outbids another suitor in a parody of sixteenth-century matrimonial custom in which a woman is a man's property. Although the contrast between the unconventionality of the Petruchio-Katherina plot and the conventionality of the Lucentio-Bianca plot has received considerable critical attention,[3] the differences are variations within a parallel movement from confinement to freedom through marriage. Petruchio indirectly helps to liberate Bianca as well as Kate. At the beginning of the play Bianca's father has 'closely mew'd her up' (I.i.183), and Petruchio's courtship of the elder sister is initiated as a means to 'set the younger free' (I.ii.266).[4] More directly, Bianca, like her sister, gains her independence through a lover who overcomes the social conventions that confine her. Lucentio usurps the authority of both fathers, supplanting his own father with a substitute and defying Bianca's by marrying her 'without asking [his] good will' (V.i.134).[5] The two bridegrooms' language of defiance marks their similar stances toward society. Lucentio anticipates how, once he is married, 'let all the world say no, / I'll keep mine own, despite of all the world ' (III.ii.141-2); a few lines later Petruchio challenges the same social world: 'I will be master of what is mine own ... touch her whoever dare' (III.ii.229, 233). Moreover, just as Petruchio's wedding costume and his attack on the tailor symbolize his disruption of social decorum, improprieties in clothing compose a striking visual image of Lucentio's overturning of social order. For example, when Vincentio turns up unexpectedly and is denounced as an impostor by Biondello and Tranio, it is Tranio's clothing that Vincentio finds most upsetting:

> O immortal gods! O fine villain! A silken doublet, a velvet hose, a scarlet cloak, and a copatain hat! O, I am undone, I am undone! (v.i.66-8)

Bianca, like Kate, is a strong-willed young woman determined to have her own way in spite of social coercion: 'I'll not be tied to hours, nor 'pointed times' (III.i.19). By proceeding at her own rate, marrying first and securing parental approval afterwards, she achieves her goal. Like her sister, she accepts the role defined for her by society only in her own good time and her own fashion. While current audiences admire Katherina's rebellion more than Bianca's outward conformity and find Kate's overcoming of internalized barriers more interesting than Bianca's eluding of external ones, we shouldn't regard Bianca as Kate's villainous antithesis. Kate surpasses her sister, but Bianca is not much wide of the mark, as Petruchio's last speech reminds Lucentio: "Twas I won the wager, though you hit the white' (v.ii.186).

For all their neglect of social amenities and their assertion of personal rights against paternal authority, neither Lucentio nor Petruchio is a radical social critic. Lucentio defies the social convention of arranged marriages to court Bianca, but once he is safely married, far from hurling defiance at an outraged world, he kneels submissively begging his father's pardon and moves immediately to conciliate Bianca's father. Petruchio talks of freeing Bianca but of taming Kate; his aim is not to produce a rebel but 'a Kate / Conformable as other household Kates' (II.i.277-8). He sees himself as a member of the community, and he shares its basic values. His success in gaining a rich bride, in having his courtship expenses paid by others, and in winning a wager on his wife's obedience all testify to his ease and facility in an acquisitive, materialistic society. His preference for 'a lusty wench' as a bride is exceptional, but his desire for 'peace ... and love, and quiet life' (v.ii.108) in marriage is entirely usual. He is unconventional in a conventional society not because he minimizes the importance of social usages but because he asserts his power to control them. When he contends that Kate is marrying him and not his clothes, he is not demanding that she come to terms with unaccommodated man as 'a poor, bare, fork'd animal' but rather asserting his right to wear what clothes he chooses.

In contrast, Kate at the beginning of the play has neither the critical detachment nor the understanding of herself as a social being that could help her to control social customs. She has absorbed the assumptions that the admiration and deference of others guarantee social acceptance and that becoming a wife is the only desirable goal for a woman. Her resentment at being undervalued creates hostility and aggression that paradoxically threaten to produce the fate she most fears: a future as that social anomaly, an old maid. Shakespeare's Padua, of course, is not unusual in its abhorrence of a mature, unmarried woman. Sixteenth-century England displayed a similar attitude. Marriage was the normal condition for both sexes, and women derived their social and economic position from their husbands. The few women who remained unmarried suffered from an ambiguous social status and humiliating economic dependence.[6] Moreover, such customs as the English tradition requiring a bride's unmarried elder sister to dance barefoot on the wedding day or the French one requiring an unmarried elder brother or sister to eat raw vegetables suggest that the uneasiness about unmarried women was not caused solely by practical economic considerations.[7] In Claude Lévi-Strauss' interpretation, 'dancing barefoot' is equivalent to 'dancing raw,' and these and other related customs all depend on a contrast between 'the raw' (equivalent to nature) and 'the cooked' (equivalent to culture) and reflect the idea that the person who remains celibate too long is not fully socialized. Shakespeare's apparently unmarriageable shrew with her fear that she 'must dance barefoot on [her sister's] wedding day' (II.i.33) dramatizes not only a psychological but a social problem, the presence within society of the raw or uncivilized, someone not fully integrated into the community. When Petruchio denies Kate food, insisting that the meat is too burned to eat (IV.i.161), he implicitly tells her that she is not civilized enough to eat the food cooked for civilized people. Although Lévi-Strauss says that, in cultures where magical thought is vestigial, customs based on the equivalence of 'the cooked' with 'the socialized' are not intended to change but to describe a situation,[8] Petruchio clearly intends to change Katherina's behavior. When she tries to counter similar objections to the fashionable clothing she wants by arguing that 'gentlewomen wear such caps as these,' he makes the point explicitly: 'When you are gentle, you shall have one too' (IV.iii.70–1).

In the Induction, the Lord and Christopher Sly portray the civilized and the uncivilized in terms of social rank. In Kate we see similar extremes within a single person. Kate the shrew is aggressive, destructive, abusive, and self-defeating. By the end of the play she is a respected, socially secure wife. In *The Taming of the Shrew* belonging to a human community is not simply a birthright as it is in *A Comedy of Errors*; it depends instead on the acquisition of civilized values and manners. Kate's transformation from despised shrew to happily married woman suggests that civilization depends on people with a critical attitude towards it.[9] By suffering deprivation of the necessities of food and clothing that she can't provide for herself, Kate learns that she depends on other people. From Petruchio's iconoclastic attacks on conventional forms and rituals, she learns to see social institutions and practices not as threatening and intractable givens but as human constructions amenable to human control. By examining social customs critically, she learns not to reject society but to live comfortably within it.

As Petruchio confides to the audience, he also has 'Another way ... to man [his] haggard' (IV.i.193), a way that involves intimacy and affection as well as deprivation. G.R. Hibbard quotes Gervase Markham's *Country Contentments* (1615) to elucidate the falconry metaphor: 'All hawks generally are manned after one manner, that is to say, by watching and keeping them from sleep, by a continual carrying of them upon your fist, and by a most familiar stroking and playing with them ... and by often gazing and looking of them in the face, with a loving and gentle countenance, and so making them acquainted with the man.'[10] So too the necessary complement to Petruchio's program of harshness and deprivation is constant attention and affection: he does it all 'in reverend care of her' (IV.i.204). Subjected to unremitting offers of affection and demands for acquiescence, Kate discovers not only how much she owes but how much she can give to other people. When she tells Vincentio that she mistook him for a young girl because her eyes had been 'so bedazzled with the sun' (IV.v.46), she is ironically alluding to Petruchio's identification of himself as 'my mother's son' (IV.v.6) and to his insistence that she call the sun the moon. Her playfulness demonstrates that she understands Petruchio not as a man unable to tolerate a wife with a mind of her own but as a loving husband asking her to show that she wants to please him. Kate, who originally thought that the mark of maturity was knowing 'what to take and what to leave' (I.i.104), has learned that living harmoniously with other people is a matter of knowing when to take and when to give.

The understanding and cooperation between Kate and Petruchio in the last act has prompted several of the play's most perceptive critics to comment on their creation of a separate world, what Marianne Novy calls 'a private world, a joke that the rest of the characters miss' or what J. Dennis Huston calls 'a select society, which includes themselves, the playwright, and perhaps a few members of his audience.'[11] I believe that this emphasis on a exclusive community in collusion against the rest of the world assumes a twentieth-century opposition between public and private worlds that distorts the play's conceptual and structural dynamics.[12] Unlike Christopher Sly, who remains suspended in his dream of aristocratic splendor, Kate returns to her old environment.[13]

The action rises to a climax in Act III with the farcical violence of Petruchio rescuing his bride from her family and friends, but neither Kate nor Petruchio expresses any wish to remain isolated in Petruchio's country house. Acts IV and V dramatize Kate's gradual reintegration into society. Certainly the play works against Norbert Elias' thesis that the civilizing process depends on the coercive power of a strong central government:[14] the basis of Kate's transformation is the self-understanding she develops in her relationship with her husband. But her domestication is complete only when it is made public. Hortensio assures Petruchio that 'the field is won' (IV.v.23) as soon as Kate yields to him over what to call the sun, but Petruchio arranges a series of increasingly public demonstrations of Kate's new civility. The incident with Vincentio adds a stranger to the audience that already includes Hortensio and the servants. Next, Petruchio demands a kiss in the public street. Finally, Kate wins the wager on whose wife is most obedient before the assembled group of family and friends. Her education culminates, then, not in achieving intimacy with Petruchio but in winning recognition and approval from the social group. The pattern of interrupted feast, solitary fast, and celebratory feast marks the stages of her separation from and return to society. Significantly her final speech explaining the rationale of her obedience is not a private act of submission to Petruchio but a public demonstration of her full acceptance of her position as Petruchio's wife and a public reprimand of the Widow and Bianca for their failures 'to serve, love, and obey' (V.ii.164) their husbands.

Kate's demonstration of obedience is presented as a victory, not a humiliation. Her offer to place her hand under Petruchio's foot acknowledges her subordination in a hierarchical relationship, but the gesture also expresses gratitude at being cherished and pride at fulfilling her husband's desires. Petruchio certainly demands that Katherina submit to his will, but we know, as she does, that he won't step on her hand. Shakespeare, then, does not ironically subvert the patriarchal power structure portrayed in *The Taming of the Shrew*. As David Underdown has demonstrated, in the period between 1560 and 1640 a perceived threat to patriarchal order from unruly women produced a widespread fascination with literary shrews as well as a marked increase in legal proceedings against assertive women.[15] The representation of Kate's domestication as a paradigm of the civilizing process responds to that cultural anxiety by affirming women's subordination. Readings of Kate's endorsement of patriarchy as ironic are, I think, unconvincing.[16] Unlike Petruchio's claim that Kate is 'My horse, my ox, my ass, my any thing' (III.ii.232), which is qualified by the farcical context, Kate's exposition of wifely submission stands unqualified and unrefuted. Similarly, in *The Comedy of Errors* the Abbess' lecture to Adriana on how a nagging wife can drive a man mad (V.i.68–86) is consonant with the view of marriage in the play as a whole. Neither play is designed merely to teach uppity women their places. Both suggest that husbands and wives should be subject to each other in love, but both also endorse a hierarchical view of marriage in which wives owe obedience to husbands that husbands do not owe wives.

As tempting as it is to explain away Kate's final speech, such revisionism deflects needed attention from the patriarchal ideology the play enacts. As Lynda Boose convincingly argues, 'the impulse to rewrite the more oppressively patriarchal material in this play serves the very ideologies about gender that it makes less visible by making less offensive.'[17] Similarly, to ignore the play's consistent exclusion of physical brutality also obstructs the feminist project of writing the history of the construction of gender in Western society. While endorsing women's subordination within patriarchal marriage, *The Taming of the Shrew* mitigates the violence used to control unruly women in the real world and in the shrew-taming literary tradition. Although sparring verbally with Katherina excites Petruchio in their pre-marital battle of the sexes, his goal is 'peace ... love, and quiet life' (V.ii.108), and he puts a stop to the violence she initiates. His use of physical and economic force to deprive Katherina temporarily of food and sleep is relatively mild compared with the horrifying brutalities of actual social practice and with the sadism of earlier versions of the shrew story.[18] For example, in contrast to the hero of *A meery Jeste of a Shrewde and curste Wyfe lapped in Morrelles skin*, who subjects his bride to a brutal sexual initiation, Petruchio on their wedding night lectures Kate on continence. Not only do the methods employed in Petruchio's taming-school appear humane in the context of a society that tortured women judged to be scolds with cucking stools and scold's bridles, the play also demystifies the patriarchal authority it confirms. Discussions of unruly women in the years around 1600 usually represent female insubordination as a perversion of natural order and a symptom of an incipient breakdown of all social order. In contrast, Kate's shrewishness is a danger to no one but herself. Although Kate invokes the familiar analogy between familial and political order in her final speech, her subjection to Petruchio is presented not as an inevitable alignment with the natural relations between men and women but as the result of protracted negotiations between two people, anticipating Locke's theory of a contractual basis for marriage rather than reinscribing the family as the divinely instituted origin of political power.[19] Kate's exposition of a wife's duties is general and normative rather than personal, but she justifies wifely obedience on the basis not of the religious sanctity of the conventional sexual hierarchy but of its justice and convenience. The only inherent superiority she attributes to men is their greater physical strength, and she describes a wife's duties of 'love, fair looks, and true obedience' (V.ii.153) as just recompense to a husband who endures 'painful labor' to care for her (149).[20]

The Taming of the Shrew offers Kate and Bianca no alternative to the limited choice between spinsterhood and patriarchal marriage. In the context of contemporary discussions of domestic relations, it supports the ideal of marriage based on mutual love within the framework of masculine authority.[21] Petruchio's announced desire for a rich wife and Baptista's offer of his youngest daughter to the highest bidder allude unmistakably to the practice among the propertied classes of arranging marriages on an economic basis, and the play explicitly subordinates these financial motives to the emotional responses of the female characters. Petruchio's success consists not in winning a rich wife but in winning the love and obedience of a shrewish one and is proved not by Kate's humiliation but by her triumph. Her prompt response when Petruchio sends for her and her long final speech demonstrate to the community she lives in and to the audience that she is no longer wild but self-assured, self-controlled, and considerate – a civilized woman who understands human relationships as a balance of duties and privileges. By her public submission to her husband and her dominance over the Widow and Bianca, she simultaneously acknowledges her dependence and asserts her personal worth. Kate, in short, achieves what she has always wanted: a dominant place as a valued member of society.

The comedy's happy ending embodies the achievement of mutual love and understanding recommended by the proponents of companionate marriage who insist also on husbands' authority over their wives. *The Taming of the Shrew* is distinctive not in its unresolved tension between mutuality and inequality but in its uncompromising acknowledgment of the demand that women choose their own subordination. The play exposes the inequities and potential brutality of male power, the patriarchal attitudes and institutions only temporarily disguised by courtship rhetoric such as Lucentio's, and the voluntary subjection required of women by love within a framework of gender inequality. At the same time it shows men and women achieving happiness by actively asserting control over those structures. By the last scene all the major characters have been able to fulfill their personal desires through their relationships with each other. Petruchio has a rich and spirited wife as well as 'peace ... and love, and quiet life, / ... and right supremacy' (V.ii.108–9). Lucentio has Bianca, and Bianca has parental approval for the husband she has chosen for herself; moreover, she is still learning her lessons as she pleases. Baptista and Vincentio have seen their children married to their social equals with appropriate financial settlements. Even Gremio and Hortensio, who lose Bianca to Lucentio, have the satisfaction of watching their successful rival's discomfort with his wife. In spite of – or better, because of – the tensions and rivalries of personal relationships, the conclusion of *The Taming of the Shrew* presents us with an image of a society that conforms to all the members' individual desires. And the supreme example of eating his cake and having it too is Shakespeare: by transforming the traditional shrew story of a struggle for domestic mastery into a process of domestication, he manages to satirize the absurdities of social convention while simultaneously celebrating the human capacity to shape society to express individual values. By presenting Kate's transformation in a play-within-a-play, he also allows the unsettling implication that this happy reconciliation of individual freedom with repressive communal values is possible only in a work of art.

Part Two

Cultural Values and the Values of Culture

CHAPTER FOUR

Common Courtesy in *The Two Gentlemen of Verona*

> *'he being understood*
> *May make good Courtiers, but who Courtiers good?'*
> (John Donne, 'Satyre V')

Unlike *The Comedy of Errors* and *The Taming of the Shrew*, which build on contrasts between the civilized and the uncivilized, *The Two Gentlemen of Verona* and *Love's Labor's Lost* explore the manners and values of courtly society. In *The Comedy of Errors*, the physical danger threatening anyone outside the social group frames and conditions all the dramatic action. The violence of the physical world that originally dispersed the family, the Ephesian law that threatens aliens with death, and the harsh ministrations of Doctor Pinch that isolate transgressors produce the farcical confusions that can end only when everyone is recognized as belonging to Ephesian society. In *The Taming of the Shrew*, the contrasts between the savage and the civilized – between the bestial Christopher Sly and the aristocratic Lord, the wild Kate and the domesticated Kate – both describe and motivate the action. With *The Two Gentlemen of Verona* and *Love's Labor's Lost* our attention turns from the adventures of strangers and misfits in gaining a secure place in society to the activities, manners, and values of those securely at the top of the social hierarchy.

Although *The Two Gentlemen of Verona* has aroused little actual enthusiasm among critics, most commentators agree that by combining mockery of artificial conventions with lyric evocation of romantic love, *The Two Gentlemen of Verona* prepared the way for the great comedies to follow. Only the climactic final scene has presented an interpretative crux and provoked almost universal condemnation. In the last scene, immediately after saving his beloved Silvia from being raped by his treacherous friend Sir Proteus, Valentine accepts without question Proteus' protestations of remorse and offers to withdraw his own suit in favor of Proteus', saying:

> And that my love may appear plain and free,
> All that was mine in Silvia I give thee. (V.iv.82-3)

Critics who see the play primarily as a celebration of romantic love are understandably perplexed when the romantic hero suddenly offers the heroine to his rival. From this point of view, Shakespeare has violently contradicted the premises of his own romantic comedy, transforming his young lover into an insensitive brute. Another standard approach places the play in the Renaissance tradition that exalts friendship over love. From this perspective, the scene, far from undermining the basic conventions of its own fictional world, is 'the germ or core of the play' and Valentine's offer to give up Silvia to Proteus is not boorish but generous, the magnanimous sacrifice of love to friendship.[1]

From either point of view, the exchange between Proteus and Valentine is an artistic failure. If *The Two Gentlemen of Verona* is a celebration of the experience of falling in love – the absurdities and joys of youthful passion – the hero's cheerful offer of his mistress to the man who has just tried to rape her is certainly a blunder. On the other hand, if Valentine is intended as a model of selfless generosity according to Renaissance conceptions of ideal friendship, he is a remarkably weak exemplar of the tradition. In Sir Thomas Elyot's story of Titus and Gisippus, which apparently served as a source for the Valentine-Silvia-Proteus triangle, Gisippus relinquishes his betrothed to Titus, who marries her. Years later, when Gisippus is threatened with execution for murder, Titus confesses to the crime in an effort to die in his friend's place.[2] But in Shakespeare's play, neither Valentine nor Proteus actually sacrifices anything for friendship. After all, Valentine runs little risk that the repentant Proteus will take him up on his offer and even less that Silvia would accept him if he did.[3]

Without denying weaknesses and confusions in the early comedies, I think we should be suspicious of any critical position that convicts Shakespeare of inept bungling. It is not unthinking bardolatry to assume that even as an apprentice playwright Shakespeare would not construct a dramatic climax that signally fails to resolve and clarify any of the emotional or intellectual issues at stake. If the resolution of *The Two Gentlemen of Verona* does not illuminate the relationship of love to friendship, it is probable that interpretations emphasizing the triumph of one or the other are askew. Indeed, in the play itself only Proteus refers to a conflict between the claims of love and those of friendship, and he uses this formulation to justify betraying Julia's love as well as Valentine's friendship.

Although critics have been misled by Proteus' pat generalizations ('In love / Who respects friend?' [v.iv.53–4]), they have also responded to the ideas and values that recur throughout the play. For example, Sir Arthur Quiller-Couch denounces Valentine's offer of Silvia to Sir Proteus in these terms: 'there are, by this time, *no* gentlemen in Verona.'[4] And M.C. Bradbrook defends the same action as 'displaying in transcendent form the courtly virtue of Magnanimity, the first and greatest virtue of a gentleman.'[5] While Quiller-Couch and Bradbrook obviously disagree over how a gentleman should act in Valentine's awkward situation, they both assume that the play directs us to evaluate Valentine's action in terms of the conduct appropriate to a gentleman. Valentine's gesture, like Averagus' offer of his wife to her suitor in Chaucer's *The Franklin's Tale*, expresses a particular conception of 'gentilesse' that has provoked variously admiration and censure.[6] *The Two Gentlemen of Verona* is less an evocation of what it feels like to fall in love than a comic exploration of the nature and function of a gentleman.

Quiller-Couch's outraged denunciation of fictional characters of whom he disapproves as '*no* gentlemen' may strike us today as a quaint expression of his own Edwardian values, but we should remember that the scanty biographical knowledge we have suggests that the status of a gentleman was a subject Shakespeare personally took seriously enough. In the sixteenth century, moreover, the education, qualities, and functions of the gentleman were issues of considerable political and cultural importance.[7] Works as popular and significant as Castiglione's *The Book of the Courtier*, Sir Thomas Elyot's *The Book Named the Governor*, and Edmund Spenser's *The Faerie Queene* demonstrate the lasting interest and significance of Renaissance discussions on how to fashion a gentleman. *The Two Gentlemen of Verona* draws on and contributes to this tradition.

The opening scene introduces us to the play's unifying theme – the question of the proper behavior for a young gentleman – and to its dominant verbal mode – the indirections of polite discourse. Valentine, excited by his imminent departure 'To see the wonders of the world abroad' (I.i.6), and Proteus, 'over boots in love' (I.i.25) with Julia, are engaged in conventional activities for two young gentlemen of Verona, or of London. They debate the merits of their respective choices – foreign travel and love – with the verbal wit of the young gallant. For example, Valentine's taunting of Proteus with the follies of love leads to the following exchange:

> **Pro.** Yet writers say: as in the sweetest bud
> The eating canker dwells, so eating love
> Inhabits in the finest wits of all.
> **Val.** And writers say: as the most forward bud
> Is eaten by the canker ere it blow,
> Even so by love the young and tender wit
> Is turn'd to folly, blasting in the bud,
> Losing his verdure, even in the prime,
> And all the fair effects of future hopes. (I.i.42–50)

Valentine might have been reading in Castiglione's *The Courtier* of the 'merry conceites and jestes' that may appropriately grace the conversation of the perfect courtier: 'among other merry sayings, they have a verie good grace, that arise when a man at the nipping talke of his fellow, taketh the verie same words in the self same sense, and returneth them backe againe, pricking him with his owne weapon ... Also merry sayinges are much to the purpose to nippe a man ... so the metaphors be well applyed, and especially if they be answered, and he that maketh answere continue in the self same metaphor spoken by the other.'[8] Although the form of their speech, nipping and pricking at each other, implies opposition, Valentine and Proteus are actually in total agreement. For all his scorn at love's folly, Valentine does not seriously attempt to dissuade Proteus from loving; he wishes his friend well in love, acknowledging that in time he too expects to fall in love:

> But since thou lov'st, love still, and thrive therein,
> Even as I would, when I to love begin. (I.i.9–10)

And Proteus expects a friend's feelings of vicarious pleasure and protective concern from Valentine's travels:

> Wish me partaker in thy happiness

When thou dost meet good hap; and in thy danger
(If ever danger do environ thee)
Commend thy grievance to my holy prayers. (I.i.14–17)

Privately he concedes Valentine's point: love has made his 'wit with musing weak' (I.i.69). Ostensibly denoting rivalry, their wit actually expresses affectionate concord.

The wordplay that signals the young men's pretensions to courtly elegance also indicates their youth and inexperience. Valentine and Proteus, like Romeo and Mercutio or Beatrice and Benedick, use puns and ripostes and ironies to impress others with their mental and verbal agility and to give themselves a sense of control over their world as well as to express their high-spirited exuberance and to exercise their developing powers for sheer enjoyment. Their linguistic ingenuity is not the effortless command of language that expresses unselfconscious ease and assurance in a social situation but rather the ostentatious display of wit that indicates vulnerability and insecurity. When Valentine and Proteus are together, like-minded friends who understand and respect each other, mocking repartee is subsumed within the context of frank and open talk, and their conversation has some claim to grace as well as to vitality. In other situations, they are less able to balance rhetorical indirections with straightforward communication and consequently appear noticeably more awkward.

In the dialogue between Proteus and Speed that follows Valentine's exit, for example, repeated quibbles on 'ship,' 'sheep,' and 'mutton' grow tiresome. Since Proteus fails to get a clear report of the delivery of his message to Julia, while Speed does succeed in exacting his tip, Proteus emerges the loser in this contest of wits with his friend's servant. In his next appearance Proteus' language is even more completely at variance from literal truth, and his ingenuity is utilized to more disastrous – and comic – effect. In scene three, Proteus is exulting in a letter from Julia – 'her oath for love' (I.iii.47) – when his father interrupts to ask what he is reading. Proteus replies that his letter is from Valentine:

> he writes
> How happily he lives, how well-belov'd
> And daily graced by the Emperor;
> Wishing me with him, partner of his fortune. (I.ii.56–9)

Ironically, the lie designed to hide and protect his relationship with

Julia precipitates his separation from her by reinforcing his father's decision that Proteus should join Valentine to complete his education. The adolescent's instinctive impulse to hide his love letter from his all-too-solicitous parent should not be interpreted as evidence of a basically duplicitous character, but the spectacle of Proteus blundering into a trap he has set for himself certainly provokes amusement at his expense.

The same type of youthful gaucherie is the source of humor in both the preceding and the following scenes. In the preceding scene Julia indignantly scolds her maid, Lucetta, first for delivering Proteus' letter and then for interpreting her angry words literally instead of understanding them as conventional expressions of maidenly modesty:

> What 'fool is she, that knows I am a maid,
> And would not force the letter to my view!
> Since maids, in modesty, say 'no' to that
> Which they would have the profferer construe 'ay.' (I.ii.53–6)

After another round of verbal sparring with Lucetta, Julia histrionically tears the letter in pieces and finally is reduced to searching the ground for the precious fragments to piece together. Although subsequently Proteus' fickleness contrasts with Julia's constancy, in Act I it is their similarity that is most striking. Both feel the need to protect the privacy of their new, tender emotions, and both are comically inept in their attempts at dissimulation.[9]

Valentine too finds himself out of his depth in the emotional subtleties and linguistic indirections of polite society. While Proteus and Julia betray their naïveté through their bungling attempt at dissimulation, Valentine displays his through his literal-minded incomprehension. When the scene shifts to Milan we discover that Valentine, the scoffer at love, has fallen in love with Silvia, the Duke's daughter, and is suffering all the paradoxical pain and ecstasy, exaltation and humiliation of the conventional courtly lover. He has even complied with Silvia's request that he write a letter for her to 'one she loves' (II.i.88). Silvia then feigns anger at Valentine's reluctance to send her love to another and tells him to keep the lines of love he has written for himself:

> But I will none of them; they are for you.
> I would have had them writ more movingly. (II.i.127–8)

And, to Valentine's offer to repeat his effort:

And when it's writ, for my sake read it over,
And if it please you, so; if not, why, so. (II.i.130–1)

Although Silvia's jest, as Speed says, is as 'unseen, inscrutable; invisible, / As a nose on a man's face' (II.i.135–6), Valentine fails to understand that she is teaching him to court her in earnest.

Silvia, in fact, is instructing Valentine in just the kind of courtly wit and elegant discourse the young gentlemen from Verona have come to Milan to learn. When Proteus' father and uncle worry that he is wasting his time at home, they canvas the alternatives open to a well-born young man:

> Some to the wars, to try their fortune there;
> Some to discover islands far away;
> Some to the studious universities. (I.iii.8–10)

Apparently on the basis of the paramount importance of acquiring the social graces, they decide to send Proteus to court where he will be able to

> practice tilts and tournaments,
> Hear sweet discourse, converse with noblemen,
> And be in eye of every exercise
> Worthy his youth and nobleness of birth. (I.iii.30–3)

Several critics have condemned this courtly behavior as trivial or even corrupt, an unworthy goal that Valentine and Proteus must discard before real education can take place.[10] J.A. Mazzeo's defense of Castiglione's *The Courtier* from similar criticism illuminates, I think, the attitude to courtly sophistication in Shakespeare's play. Mazzeo acknowledges that the 'attention Castiglione gives to gesture, manner, games, jokes, and anecdotes might seem to some of his readers an extraordinary trivialization of the ideals of true education.' But, he argues, by neglecting these 'non-verbal modes of communication and expression, or the non-referential uses of language,' modern education often produces narrow specialists,

> 'experts' with extraordinary capacities in certain well-defined areas and no grasp of the meaning of human actions, activities, gestures, or of the varieties of emotional expression. Such are those who cannot distinguish between what men say and do and what they mean by what they say and do, who cannot truly understand speech because speech is much more than the words it uses. What the modern

reader may see as trivia in Castiglione's program of education are after all the vehicles of those subtle and feeling interchanges between people which do as much as anything to give them the sense that they are really alive.[11]

Castiglione's emphasis on style and gesture, on jokes and games, is essential to his subject, 'the creation of the self as a work of art through education' (Mazzeo, 149), and to his concept of individual perfection as a balance and harmony of all important human capacities without excessive development or suppression of any. This attempt to delineate human perfection in an ideal courtier links *The Courtier* to the important cultural impulse in the Renaissance that produced so much utopian literature and so many books outlining ideal social forms of various kinds (Mazzeo, 134–5). In addition, the popularity of *The Courtier* and other courtesy books reflects concern with social cohesion as well as with individual development. The courtesy books all agree that public service is the gentleman's primary function and that the end of his education in the ways of society is his ability to advise his ruler effectively.[12] The qualities of behavior that characterize the gentleman are those that bind people together in social harmony.[13] Thus, according to Edmund Spenser, the courtly virtue of courtesy is the source of all 'goodly manners' and 'civill conversation' (*The Faerie Queene*, VI.i.1).[14] It includes not only personal appearance and manner – 'all gracious gifts ... / Which decke the body or adorne the mynde' – but also 'friendly offices that bynde' and correct social behavior:

> how to each degree and kynde
> We should our selves demeane, to low, to hie;
> To friends, to foes, which skill men call Civility.
> (*FQ*, VI.x.23)

In this context, we can see that when Antonio worries that his son Proteus 'cannot be a perfect man' (I.iii.20) without more experience in the world, he is not identifying himself as a Neo-Platonic philosopher striving towards perfection, but neither is he betraying hopelessly superficial values. He endorses an educational program similar to Castiglione's when he chooses life at court as most suitable to his son's 'youth and nobleness of birth.' The play's early scenes have demonstrated clearly that young gentlemen need social tact, verbal dexterity, even some adeptness at polite dissimulation in order to get along harmoniously with servants, fathers, and women. In the first court scene, Silvia uses the letter as an 'excellent device' (II.i.139) to express her own desires and to help Valentine overcome his timidity without violating social decorum. By calling on the 'clerkly' skills of her 'gentle servant' (II.i.108), she utilizes Valentine's gentlemanly accomplishments of the most artificial and conventional kind – courtly love conventions and literary skills – in order to liberate real feelings.[15] The grace and wit with which she employs the artifices of sophisticated society in order to circumvent the obstacles erected by conventions of rank and sex role are no mean accomplishments.

While *The Two Gentlemen of Verona* presents courtly elegance as a positive value, it also shows how fragile and easily corrupted this ideal is. Superficially trivial manners are the necessary texture of a humane society that encourages people to develop their full potential and that fosters a variety of subtle feelings and relationships among people, yet these same manners may degenerate into hypocrisy or cynical intrigue. The courtly ideal is a precarious balance of self-enhancement and social responsibility. The aristocratic code blends strict devotion to truth (so that proverbially a gentleman's word is his bond) with an elegant grace of manner that involves artifice and pretense, the art of concealing art.[16] Sir Calidore, Spenser's knight of courtesy, for example, 'loved simple truth and stedfast honesty' (FQ, VI.i.3), but the 'friendly offices' he performed sometimes required deception.[17] *Sprezzatura*, the graceful nonchalance that Castiglione recommends for the ideal courtier, may degenerate into the disdain and contempt that, according to Mazzeo, are 'vaguely present' in the concept.[18] Gentlemanly dignity may degenerate into cold arrogance or ostentatious self-display, and playful wit into either irresponsible frivolity or malicious deceit.[19]

The plot of *The Two Gentlemen of Verona* unfolds out of Valentine's and Proteus' acquisition of courtly values and style. Not surprisingly, superficial manners prove to be more easily learned than the ability to use them to develop well-rounded individuality and social harmony. Valentine, who initially cannot distinguish between what Silvia says and what she means, readily picks up the art of courtly circuitousness and dissimulation. The next time he appears he courts Silvia indirectly by bandying insults with another suitor. His language in this scene demonstrates both the social utility and the danger of courtly linguistic conventions. By rejecting Speed's advice that his hated rival Sir Thurio should be 'knock'd' (II.iv.7) and instead expressing his hostility in what Silvia commends as 'A fine volley of words' (II.iv.33), Valentine acts out sexual rivalry with wit and gaiety rather than brutality. But when he adopts the language of courtly love without Silvia's ironic detachment from it, his perceptions are blunted rather than refined by the conventions. By acknowledging that 'Love's a mighty lord' (II.iv.136) and by confessing the sorrow and joy of love's service, Valentine joins in civilized humanity's transformation of sexual appetite into love. But he betrays self-deceit and insensitivity when he insists that Proteus acknowledge Silvia as 'divine,' not earthly, and when he refers to Julia, Proteus' beloved, with gratuitous contempt:

> She shall be dignified with this high honor –
> To bear my lady's train. (II.iv.158-9)

The contradictory tensions inherent in the sixteenth-century idea of gentlemanly behavior become even more evident in Valentine's scheme to elope with Silvia. By planning to release Silvia from the tower where her father locks her and from marriage to the rich but doltish Sir Thurio, Valentine is rescuing a damsel-in-distress in the best chivalric tradition and insisting on the dignity and delicacy of love and marriage. Yet he is also violating the Duke's parental right and abusing his hospitality. When Valentine first confides his plan to Proteus, considerations of the first sort combine with the conventional comic endorsement of youth and love against age and law to direct the sympathy of the audience towards the lovers. The irresponsibility of the plot comes more forcibly to mind later, when the Duke, under the guise of seeking love-advice himself, tricks Valentine into revealing his plan. In this scene, Valentine hypocritically praises Thurio as a match for Silvia, cynically explains that women reject men's advances only in order to egg them on and that any woman can be won with gifts and flattery, and proposes a rope ladder to gain access to a woman whose friends have promised her to someone else. The Duke's reply,

> Now as thou art a gentleman of blood,
> Advise me where I may have such a ladder, (III.i.121-2)

reminds us that Valentine is fulfilling his gentleman's duty to advise and serve his ruler in a particularly tawdry way. In this context, we watch with amusement rather than anxiety as the Duke outwits Valentine, discovering the ladder and the incriminating letter to Silvia hidden under his cloak.

In Valentine, then, we can discern the danger that aristocratic self-assurance will become pride and that delicacy and subtlety will become duplicity. Proteus perverts the gentlemanly ideal even more radically. As we have seen, his family encourages him to strive to perfect himself. Valentine, who gracefully apologizes for his own failure to achieve 'angel-like perfection' (II.iv.66), praises his friend as a model gentleman:

> He is complete in feature and in mind
> With all good grace to grace a gentleman. (II.iv.73–4)

When Proteus joins Valentine at the court of Milan, this exemplar of the art of self-cultivation becomes the apologist for sheer selfishness. No sooner does he learn of Valentine's love than he determines to win Silvia himself, consoling himself for the loss of Valentine's friendship with the thought 'I to myself am dearer than a friend' (II.vi.23), and justifying the plot he immediately formulates to betray Valentine to the Duke and subsequently to slander him to Silvia:

> I cannot now prove constant to myself,
> Without some treachery us'd to Valentine. (II.vi.31–2)

While Valentine becomes guilty of disdain and deceit, it remains for Proteus to stoop to the even more contemptible practice of detraction and slander.[20] His attempts at self-justification are so absurdly sophistical, however, and his machinations to win Silvia so obviously self-defeating that the audience is again not so much morally outraged by his perfidy as amused by the mess he is getting himself into.

Thus, aristocratic values contain the seeds of their own destruction. In the process of developing the qualities of a gentleman both Valentine and Proteus lose their status as gentlemen: the Duke denounces Valentine for aspiring to his daughter as a 'base intruder, overweening slave' (III.i.157), and Proteus, even as he undertakes to destroy Silvia's love for Valentine by accusing him of 'falsehood, cowardice, and poor descent' (III.ii.32), admits that slandering his friend is 'an ill office for a gentleman' (III.ii.40). This breakdown of civilized manners extends even to Launce's dog Crab, who 'thrusts ... himself into the company of three or four gentleman-like dogs, under the Duke's table' and there disgraces himself (IV.iv.16–18).

The elegant courtly society that draws all the young people to it through the first two acts begins, in Act III, to self-destruct, literally and physically as well as figuratively and spiritually. Valentine's introduction to courtly love and dissimulation culminates in his banishment from court. His exile precipitates Silvia's flight, which in turn causes the Duke, Proteus, and Thurio to pursue her, while Julia, disguised as a page boy, follows Proteus. By the end of Act IV, all the major characters have abandoned the court of Milan with its dangers and frustrations and have fled to the lawless and dangerous forest.

This contrary motion towards and away from the court suggests that the very qualities that bind people together in civilized society also threaten to fragment and dissolve those bonds. The aristocratic insistence on excellence as a standard and on perfection as a goal encourages individual fulfillment in a complex and humane society, but it is also inherently competitive. This paradox underlies the pattern in Shakespeare's portrayal of love discerned by René Girard, in which imitative desire produces increasing violence. Girard argues that the confusions of *A Midsummer Night's Dream* arise out of the young lovers' aspirations for sexual dominance deriving from an erotic ideal:

> they all worship the same erotic absolute, the same ideal image of seduction which each girl and boy in turn appears to embody in the eyes of the others. This absolute has nothing to do with concrete qualities; it is properly metaphysical. Even though obsessed with the flesh, desire is divorced from it; it is not instinctive and spontaneous; it never seems to know directly and immediately where its object lies; in order to locate that object, it cannot rely on such things as the pleasure of the eyes and the other senses. In its perpetual *noche oscura*, metaphysical desire must therefore trust in another and supposedly more enlightened desire on which it patterns itself.[21]

Thus, Helena, Hermia, Lysander, and Demetrius all 'choose love by another's eyes' (*MND*, I.i.140), according to Girard. The 'crucial point' about this mimetic desire is 'the necessarily jealous and conflictual nature of mimetic convergence on a single object. If we keep borrowing each other's desires, if we allow our respective desires to agree on the same object, we, as individuals, are bound to disagree ... Metaphysical desire is mimetic, and mimetic desire cannot be let loose without breeding a midsummer night of jealousy and strife' (191–2).

Conflicts arising from this kind of romantic passion that is not a spontaneous response to a desirable and desired other but primarily an imitation of a model are more clearly evident in *The Two Gentlemen of Verona* than in *A Midsummer Night's Dream*. When Valentine insists that Silvia is the ideal woman 'whose worth makes other worthies nothing' (II.iv.166), he teaches Proteus to forsake Julia and make Silvia the object of his desire. Even Proteus admits that 'Valentinus' praise' has as much to do with his passion as his own perception of Silvia's perfections (II.iv.196–8). And we realize that for him Silvia 'excels each mortal thing' (IV.ii.51) primarily *because* 'all our swains commend her' (IV.ii.40). Proteus' sudden desire for Silvia destroys the social group through betrayal and banishment and also undermines his sense of his own identity. As Girard explains, a metaphysical, mimetic passion is necessarily self-destructive: it is 'destructive not only because of its sterile rivalries but because it dissolves reality: it tends to the abstract, the merely representational' (193). It feeds on rejection and failure: 'The impossible is always preferred to the possible, the unreal to the real, the hostile and unwilling to the willing and available' (195). Although the aspiration to an erotic ideal is basically self-elevating, the worship of an unattainable idol results in the lover's self-abasement expressed in animal images: 'far from raising himself to the state of a superman, a god, as he seeks to do, the subject of mimetic desire sinks to the level of animality. The animal images are the price the self has to pay for its idolatrous worship of otherness' (197).

Thus Proteus complains that:

> spaniel-like, the more she spurns my love,
> The more it grows, and fawneth on her still. (IV.ii.14–15)

He begs for a picture of Silvia, announcing that since he cannot possess 'the substance of [her] perfect self,'

> I am but a shadow;
> And to your shadow will I make true love. (IV.ii.123–5)

And Silvia agrees that it is entirely appropriate for false Proteus 'To worship shadows and adore false shapes' (IV.ii.130). Even for Valentine the consequence of worshipping a human idol is dissolution of a sense of self-integrity:

> To die is to be banish'd from myself,
> And Silvia is myself: banish'd from her
> Is self from self, a deadly banishment.
> ...

> She is my essence, and I leave to be,
> If I be not by her fair influence
> Foster'd, illumin'd, cherish'd, kept alive. (III.i.171–3, 182–4)

Sending Valentine and Proteus to court to learn to act like perfect gentlemen by observing the best models ironically results in loss of a sense of self and destruction of social cohesion, but the play also makes clear that refusal to emulate models of decorum can have equally disastrous consequences, as Launce complains to Crab: 'I remember the trick you serv'd me, when I took my leave of Madam Silvia. Did not I bid thee still mark me, and do as I do? When didst thou see me heave up my leg and make water against a gentlewoman's farthingale? Didst thou ever see me do such a trick?' (IV.iv.34–9).

The genteel lovers experience the disadvantages of life without the restraints of civilization when they flee from court to the lawless wilderness. By escaping from the capricious dangers of courtly hypocrisy and ducal tyranny, they become vulnerable to physical brutality, threatened with robbery, murder, and rape. In the woods outside Milan they learn the worth and limitations of their conception of gentility.

In this first example in Shakespearean comedy of a rural retreat where courtly lovers overcome their difficulties and adjust their values before returning to civilization, the sylvan setting is far from being a pastoral world of innocence and peace. The woods are inhabited by society's outcasts, outlaws banished for murder and 'such like petty crimes' (IV.i.50), who live by terrorizing and robbing hapless travelers. In this setting, Proteus' frustrations erupt in violence. When Silvia continues to reject him and to condemn him after he rescues her from the outlaws, he tries to rape her.

But if the woods are a setting for violence and uncontrolled passion, they do not represent a state of nature free from social distinctions and hierarchy. The outlaws are absurdly proud that some of them are gentlemen by birth and feel acutely the need for a leader to command them. Rather than the possibility of an egalitarian society they embody an alternate and older idea of the gentleman, that is, the aristocrat as armed warrior. Fiercely loyal to their own band, sensitive to slights on their honor, they recognize no authority or social obligation beyond the immediate group. Their recognition of Valentine as their natural leader on the basis of his general deportment and linguistic ability is Shakespeare's comic rendition of actual historical process. The chivalric armed warrior, though romantically appealing, makes way for the educated, accomplished courtier.[22] Given the choice of joining the outlaws as their leader or of being killed for insulting them with his refusal, Valentine accepts an offer he cannot very well refuse. But he soon understands the undesirability of living with men who 'make their wills their law' (v.iv.14). He finds the 'unfrequented woods' a better place to lament his loss of Silvia than 'flourishing peopled towns' (v.iv.2-3), but he knows that total isolation is not possible. He must perforce relate to other people in some kind of social structure, if not as a lawful subject in a civilized community, then as a member of a faction of outlaws whose 'uncivil outrages' (v.iv.17) he can restrain only with difficulty.

In this situation, when Valentine witnesses Proteus' solicitation and attack on Silvia, his response reflects his developed understanding of the individual's relation to society as well as his personal hurt:

> Ruffian! let go that rude uncivil touch,
> Thou friend of an ill fashion!
> ...
> Thou common friend, that's without faith or love,
> For such is a friend now! (v.iv.60-3)

Proteus' treachery epitomizes the point at which the selfishness and shallow hypocrisy of courtly fashion are indistinguishable from uncivilized savagery, a paradox expressed in the ambiguous epithet 'common': by adopting the debased manners of the fashionable world, Proteus forfeits his claim to being a true gentleman. Betrayal by his most trusted friend forces Valentine to see feelingly that total disillusionment both with the manners of society and with their rejection, instead of allowing him a superior position of intellectual detachment, leads to the terrifying isolation of complete alienation:

> Who should be trusted, when one's right hand
> Is perjured to the bosom? Proteus,
> I am sorry I must never trust thee more,
> But count the world a stranger for thy sake. (v.iv.67-70)

Shocked into realizing what he has become, Proteus repents. Valentine accepts his apology both because he believes that forgiveness is at once naturally human and imitative of divinity and because for him the alternative to trusting Proteus is to trust no one. Valentine and Proteus have glimpsed a world of sheer brutality and total cynicism, and together they draw back from the abyss. Their reconciliation fills personal emotional needs and indicates their renewed acceptance of their place in civilized society where men are bound together by mutual trust as well as by civil authority. Valentine's speech accepting Proteus' repentance marks his return to a world where a gentleman's word is his bond but where gentlemen characteristically communicate through indirection. It modulates from the plain statement of the terms of their relationship – 'Then I am paid; / And once again I do receive thee honest'(v.iv.77–8) – to the elegant indirection of offering to give up Silvia. Because he accepts Proteus as honestly repentant, he has faith that his friend will not renew his pursuit of Silvia. His offer is a courteous gesture that will give Proteus a chance to be his best self.

At this point, the play averts the threatened bathos of repeated, elaborate gestures of repentance and forgiveness and re-establishes the prevailing comic tone by having Valentine's attempt at sophisticated indirection miscarry once again. Although his gesture demonstrates love and trust in Proteus with considerable tact and subtlety, he has no way of considering the effect on the disguised Julia. For her it is the last straw: she faints, revives, and immediately reveals her identity and her claim to Proteus' love and fidelity. Indeed, the happy ending is possible not only because Valentine and Proteus have gained a more complex understanding of themselves and their relation to other people, but because Julia and Silvia have always had a more balanced view. Both women defy convention and abandon society's protection in pursuit of love, but they struggle to preserve whatever decorum is possible. They do not choose love by others' eyes. Silvia is impervious to slander against Valentine and to praise of Proteus and Thurio. Julia justly resents Proteus' eulogizing of Silvia without learning to despise herself. Because they are confident of their own worth and their own judgment of the men they love, without claiming perfection for either, they can meet the situation that pushes them toward rivalry and conflict with mutual sympathy.

The re-establishment of the bonds of civilization begun with the reconciliation of the friends and lovers is completed by the entry of the Duke and by Valentine's deference to him. The Duke confirms the 'new state' of things, announcing, 'Sir Valentine, / Thou art a gentleman and well deriv'd' (v.iv.144, 145–6) and blessing his union with Silvia.[23]

The play has not, however, merely come full circle back to a celebration of courtliness and conventionality. If the outlaws and Proteus have discredited the image of the noble brigand, the gentleman simply as courtier and courtly lover has also proved inadequate. Silvia has trusted to the protection of Sir Eglamour on the grounds that he is a gentleman (IV.iii.11–13) and suffered for her folly when he is unable to save her from the outlaws. Thurio, the Duke's choice for son-in-law, proves to be a coward. Valentine no longer relies on indirection and subterfuge to win Silvia but directly warns off Thurio with violent threats. He wins the Duke's favor and reappraisal of his social rank, not by his obedience, but by his high spirit. And for the first time Valentine explicitly mentions serving the state as the gentleman's true vocation, urging the Duke to pardon the outlaws for they are 'fit for great employment' (V.iv.157). Indeed, the secret of Valentine's success is his flexibility – witty and courtly with Silvia, respectful to the Duke, contemptuous and then trustful of Proteus. Valentine's flexibility is the benign counterpart of Proteus' inconsistency; together they demonstrate contrasting possibilities inherent in human adaptability and potential for shaping individual identity.[24]

The Two Gentlemen of Verona ridicules the inadequacies of the elegant courtly lover, reckless adventurer, and sycophantic courtier, but the ideas of the gentleman current in the sixteenth century – as polished courtier, scholar, soldier, and statesman – all contribute to the unattainable ideal it suggests. By the end of the play, we feel that Valentine has proved himself a gentleman through an elusive combination of courtliness, high-spirited courage, social responsibility, and faithful love and friendship. If the play hints darkly that both pursuit of an external standard of perfection and lawless self-will are destructive of social cohesion and civilized life, it also celebrates the communal happiness possible when people combine idealism with realistic understanding of human imperfection and join self-cultivation and self-assertion with respect for other people. Proteus may be right that 'were man / But constant, he were perfect' (V.iv.110–11), but in a world of imperfect men the play prescribes a virtue closer to what Spenser calls courtesy:

> how to each degree and kynde
> We should our selves demeane, to low, to hie;
> To friends, to foes, which skill men call Civility.
>
> (*FQ*, VI.x.23)

CHAPTER FIVE

Learning and Language in *Love's Labor's Lost*

'society, saith the text, is the happiness of life' (IV.ii.162–2)

While in *The Two Gentlemen of Verona* scenes set in the woods represent lawlessness beyond the reach of civilized values, *Love's Labor's Lost* presents no alternative to its courtly milieu. The major characters are the King of Navarre with his retinue and the Princess of France with hers. The characters less exalted in the social hierarchy – Holofernes, Nathaniel, and Armado – share courtly values and are in the service of the court. And even more humble characters – Constable Dull, Costard, and Jaquenetta – have no existence independent of their relations to the court. The courtly activities of the dance, the masque, the pageant, the reception of foreign dignitaries, and the hunt comprise the action. The play is not only *about* but also *for* an elitist audience. The 1598 quarto presents a 'Newly corrected and augmented' text 'as it was presented before her Highnes this last Christmas, and in 1604 the play was performed before King James as part of the celebrations of the Earl of Southampton's release from prison. The play, that is, actively participated in the courtly entertainments that it represents. Considerable evidence also suggests that *Love's Labor's Lost* alludes to contemporary figures and topics that would have been immediately recognized by those familiar with courtly gossip.[1] There is an unmistakable parallel between Shakespeare's King of Navarre, who sets up a scholarly academy and takes a vow that he subsequently breaks, and the actual King of Navarre, who was known for his interest in and encouragement of letters and became even more notorious in England for abjuring Protestantism in order to become King Henry IV of

France. The names of the other members of the court, Berowne, Longaville, and Dumain, also derive from actual people. The Duc de Biron, the Duc de Longueville, and the Duc de Mayenne figured prominently in the news from France. The visit by the Princess of France to the court of Navarre may also be based on an actual event. In 1578 the Queen of France, Catherine de Medici, and her daughter, Marguerite de Valois, accompanied by a group of ladies-in-waiting, visited Henry's court, where negotiations over Aquitaine were conducted amid a notably brilliant display of courtly games and entertainment.

Even more intriguing are suggestions that the play originates in and refers to English literary and political rivalries. The exchanges between Moth and Armado, for example, have been seen as references to the quarrel between Gabriel Harvey and Thomas Nashe. A satiric portrait of Sir Walter Ralegh has been traced in both Armado and Holofernes, and the latter has also been linked with John Florio, George Chapman, Thomas Harriot, and Harvey. Frances Yates even argued that *Love's Labor's Lost* had its genesis in the rivalry at court between the Earl of Essex and Sir Walter Ralegh. According to Yates, the Earl of Southampton enlisted Shakespeare on the side of Essex and his friends, and the play's satire of intellectual and literary pretensions is directed at Ralegh's intellectual circle. In Yates' account, the play is permeated with allusions to the interest in esoteric studies, the celebration of the contemplative over the active life, and the misogyny of such men as George Chapman, John Florio, Giordano Bruno, and the Earl of Northumberland. Navarre's shortlived academy, she proposes, 'can be interpreted as representing either the Ralegh group, immersed in their studies, or the Essex-Southampton group who laugh at schemes of that kind.'[2] The French and English theories, moreover, are not necessarily separate. Essex and Southampton admired Henry of Navarre and fought for him as the champion of Protestantism in France.

Scholarly reactions to these arguments range from disdainful dismissal to guarded acceptance. On the one hand, Anne Barton, in the Riverside edition, objects that there is no proof for such topical allusions and that it would not matter very much if there were: 'Contemporary references of this kind, if and where they exist, are ultimately less important than the nature of *Love's Labor's Lost* as a complex and quite autonomous work of art.'[3] On the other hand, Richard David, in the Arden edition, while skeptical of some proposed historical identifications, is persuaded that 'the evidence ...

goes to show that *Love's Labour's Lost* was a battle in a private war between court factions.'⁴ Shakespeare, he concludes, 'intended his audience to recognize some living people of the time – Harvey, Chapman, Florio, Thomas Harriot's "schoole", and its patron, Sir Walter Ralegh. If these are the enemy, it is clear on whose behalf the play must have been written: Essex, and the young noblemen of his party, Bedford, Rutland, and Southampton' (xli).

The evidence for specific references to contemporary people and events is inconclusive. Although the setting and some names obviously derive from French history, the correspondences are inexact. The historical King of Navarre was named Henry, not Ferdinand.⁵ The Duc de Mayenne was an enemy, not a follower of Henry of Navarre. The Duc de Biron and the Duc de Longueville were supporters of Henry but not members of his academy. Henry was in fact already married to and separated from Marguerite de Valois, the French Princess who visited his court in an atmosphere of courtly gallantry in 1578. The interpretative significance of the French connection is more seriously obscured by the uncertain date of *Love's Labor's Lost*. Although most scholars now believe that the play was originally written in 1593 or 1594 and revised in 1597 or 1598, others favor the late 1580s as the date of original composition. David Bevington argues for the earlier date, when the kingdom of Navarre would have been a 'charmingly appropriate' setting for Shakespeare's dramatization of courtly aspirations and activities. After 1589, when Henry and his followers were embroiled in a bloody civil war, and especially after 1593, when Henry renounced Protestantism, references to current events in France, he reasons, would have been 'distastefully controversial.'⁶ Even if we doubt that Shakespeare and his original audiences found controversy distasteful, in the absence of a firm date we do not know whether Shakespeare, by identifying his fictional character as the King of Navarre, is most likely to have evoked associations with idyllic seclusion, the militant championship of Protestantism, or the abjuration of Protestantism for political power. Trying to understand how *Love's Labor's Lost* relates to its historical context, then, induces a kind of scholarly vertigo in which we date the play on the basis of topical allusions while interpreting the allusions on the basis of those dates.

The evidence for references to figures prominent in the intellectual and political life of Elizabethan London is even more tenuous, consisting primarily of explanations for a few verbal cruxes and a coincidence of interests and activities. The multiple candidates proposed as prototypes for each character tend to weaken the case for any one identification, as does the fact that the characters that seem most susceptible to identification with actual people are also the most clearly conceived of as conventional literary types.[7] Speech headings sometimes identify characters as Holofernes, Armado, or Nathaniel, and sometimes as the pedant, the braggart, or the curate. Even Berowne derisively lists the actors in the Pageant of the Worthies as 'The pedant, the braggart, the hedge-priest, the fool, and the boy' (V.ii.542–3). That *Love's Labor's Lost* was included in the celebrations of Southampton's release from imprisonment for his part in Essex's rebellion (nicely balancing the performance of *Richard II* on the eve of the rebellion) suggests that the play had special personal or political significance for Southampton and his friends. But it does not tell us *what* it meant to them. The gentleness of the satire and the ambivalence of the ending would seem to preclude seeing the play either as a devastating attack on one's enemies or as a satisfying compliment to one's own party.

My own guess is that members of the play's original audiences reacted very much as modern scholars do, generating mutually contradictory hypotheses from their various perspectives on the simultaneously typical and topical personalities and practices represented on stage. *Love's Labor's Lost* employs satire's traditional strategy of exploiting the intense interest aroused by topics of current debate and gossip while, in today's political jargon, preserving deniability. Although the King of Navarre's aspiration to 'study's godlike recompense' (I.i.58) *may* resemble the celebration of contemplation and study in Chapman's *Shadow of Night*, Shakespeare's group of aristocratic scholars is *certainly* inspired by the widespread humanist ideal of the gentleman scholar. Berowne's ingenuity in displaying 'How well he's read, to reason against reading' (I.i.94) or in providing a 'salve for perjury' (IV.iii.285) for himself and his friends may have reminded contemporaries of some particular wit at court, but it also illustrates Francis Bacon's generalized description of those who 'in their discourse desire rather commendation of wit, in being able to hold all arguments, than of judgment, in discerning what is true.'[8] This tension between topicality and generality is, I suspect, the point of the joke. Ralegh, or Chapman, or whoever, by presuming to distinguish himself in the exalted terms of humanist ideology, can be seen as in fact conforming to the recognizably reductive pattern of the pedant.

Group values and ideals, rather than individual temperament or actual behavior, are the play's central concern. If the stage action mirrors real controversies among aristocratic factions, it reflects a conspicuously selective image of such rivalries, omitting the violence that eventually destroyed both Essex and Ralegh. The play scrutinizes not what is, but ideas about what ought to be, the value system of the dominant social group. Like *The Two Gentlemen of Verona*, *Love's Labor's Lost* begins with a scene in which young men debate the values they should live by, but whereas in Verona, Valentine and Proteus agree to disagree, in Navarre, the King imposes values on the whole society. He has proclaimed a rule of asceticism to be enforced by the power of the state, with punishments devised to fit the crime and the offender's position in the social hierarchy. Thus 'no woman shall come within a mile of my court ... on pain of losing her tongue' (I.i.119–24), but 'If any man be seen to talk with a woman ... he shall endure ... public shame' (129–31), while 'a year's imprisonment' is the punishment proclaimed for being 'taken with a wench' (I.i.287–8). The punishments actually imposed are a good deal less severe than those threatened, of course. Berowne, who challenges the King's ideals, is brought into line with the threat of social ostracism. When the King stops arguing with him and dismisses him – 'Well, sit you out; go home, Berowne; adieu' (I.i.110), Berowne immediately yields to the will of the group. Reminded that the Princess of France is arriving to confer with him, the King decides to 'dispense with this decree' (I.i.147) rather than to execute it. And Costard, who is 'taken with a wench,' is sentenced to 'fast a week with bran and water' (I.i.301) under Don Armado's supervision (a sentence apparently later transmuted to fasting three days a week [I.ii.129–30] and then suspended altogether [III.i.127–9]). Still, although Berowne avoids shame, the Princess is in no danger of having her tongue cut out, and Costard does not suffer long in durance vile, unquestionably the values of the King and his courtiers define the conditions in which everyone in Navarre will live.

The opening scene of the play, then, is wholly concerned with defining the values of the courtly elite and their imposition on the whole society. Throughout the subsequent action our attention is focused on group, rather than individual, behavior. The comic characters are representative figures of both psychological and social types. Armado, for instance, combines the traditional braggart with the impecunious gentleman, and Nathaniel is both toady and parson. Together, Armado, Holofernes, Nathaniel, and Moth represent a group socially inferior to the aristocrats, while Dull, Costard, and Jaquenetta constitute a group still lower in the social hierarchy. The aristocrats are no more highly individualized. Again, comparison with *Two Gentlemen* is illuminating. After Proteus and Valentine decide to part ways ('He after honor hunts, I after love' [*TGV*, I.i.63]), the plot develops through the contrast between their parallel educations in pursuit of courtly honor and love. In *Love's Labor's Lost*, after securing conformity in the first scene, the characters act in unison as members of a group. The four gallants fall in love simultaneously, court the women they desire together, and together receive comparable penances from the women. The symmetrical action and pairing of characters forestall interest in individual character. Two pairs of lovers can function effectively to create complication and contrast, as in *Two Gentlemen*, *The Taming of the Shrew*, or *Much Ado*, but four pairs of lovers acting in unison can be perceived only as elaborate pattern with blurred individuality.[9] The King and the Princess stand out as distinctive not because of their individual characters but because of their political positions. The emphasis on their political positions is reinforced by the absence of given names. The Princess has none, and the King's is never used. Berowne gives us a sense of greater complexity, not because he has distinctive personal values or undertakes individual action, but because he articulates the inconsistencies and absurdities of group behavior. He acts as his friends do, and they come to think as he does. Even Don Armado, the fantastical Spaniard, conforms to the prevailing pattern, swearing to a life of study and abstinence, shaming himself by falling in love, suffering exposure and humiliation, and accepting a penance with the hope of gratified love to come in time.

Our attention focuses on groups rather than single characters not only because blocks of characters acting together make up the dramatic action, but also because they consciously articulate their identities as members of groups. All the inhabitants of Navarre have a strong sense of solidarity with their fellows. In this, as in other things, the King and his little band of courtiers set the tone. Although they compete among themselves, their competition serves to strengthen, rather than to weaken, the bonds that unite them. The King's odious comparisons between his beloved and Berowne's ('My love (her mistress) is a gracious moon, / She (an attending star) scarce seen a light' [IV.iii.226–7]) do not lead to the deadly treachery and rivalry that Valentine's praise of Sylvia at Julia's expense does.[10]

The ensuing banter, in which Berowne praises and the others insult Rosaline, clearly expresses their mutual exhilaration at the emotional release of confessing their secret loves, rather than any serious rivalry. And they soon abandon what the King calls 'this chat' (IV.iii.280) to concentrate on their common problem – how to justify their infatuations. Similarly, the visitors from France spar verbally among themselves, but they enunciate no conflicts of interest or of points of view. Their badinage is 'a set of wit well played' (V.ii.29), and after the Princess calls on them to suspend their 'civil war of wits' (II.i.226) in order to focus on their real enemy, they direct their wits against Navarre and his friends as a team sport.

The humbler characters share the aristocrats' dependence on and delight in the social group. Even Armado, ridiculed by the aristocrats and condemned by Holofernes as 'too odd' and 'insociable' (V.i.13, 18), is eccentric only in his over-zealous performance of communal values. He thinks of himself as a member of the court and addresses the world proudly as the King's 'very good friend' (V.i.96). Holofernes, Nathaniel, and Dull argue about whether the Princess shot a deer, a pricket, or a doe, but the argument is without rancor or significance. Like the courtiers' repartee, it is primarily an occasion for exhibiting their knowledge and verbal virtuosity for their friends' delectation. Nathaniel is gratifyingly appreciative of Holofernes' talents, and Holofernes reciprocates by extending his invitation to dine with his pupil's family to include Nathaniel and Dull. Nathaniel accepts because, as they agree, 'society ... is the happiness of life' (IV.ii.161–2). Moreover, they can depend on one another for help and protection in a crisis as well as for the pleasures of society. When Nathaniel crumbles under ridicule during the Pageant of the Worthies, Costard speaks up for him: 'He is a marvellous good neighbor, faith, and a very good bowler; but for Alisander – alas, you see how 'tis – a little o'erparted' (V.ii.582–4). Costard, indeed, speaks before the royal party not only as Nathaniel's apologist and neighbor, but also as Jaquenetta's champion, charging Armado 'unless you play the honest Troyan, the poor wench is cast away' (V.ii.675–6).

Even more conspicuous in Shakespeare's Navarre than conscious identification with a group is the intense and widespread dedication to education. The plan to transform the court into 'a little academe' (I.i.13) is the fundamental given of the play. Even Berowne, the sole dissenting voice at court, objects to the strictness of the proposed regime of study, not to the goal. When he argues that there is more knowledge to be gained from women's eyes than from books, his friends understand fully that such arguments are paradoxes, which, like John Donne's forays in the genre, are 'alarums to truth' designed to provoke 'better reasons against them.'[11] Thus the King acknowledges that Berowne has shown 'How well he's read, to reason against reading!' (I.i.94), and Berowne boasts that 'I have for barbarism spoke more / Than for that angel knowledge you can say' (I.i.112–13). Clearly, Berowne is contemptuous of barbarism and respects knowledge, whatever his doubts about the tactics proposed. Holofernes, the schoolmaster, and Nathaniel, the curate, are no less devoted (and certainly more faithful) to the cause of learning than the aristocrats. And Don Armado, although he presents himself as a soldier not a scholar, is more noted for his prose style than for his way with a rapier. Like his compatriot Don Quixote, Armado is a notably bookish knight.

This enthusiasm for learning that is so noticeable a feature of life in Navarre clearly depends on belief in the power of language. The life of the mind inspiring Navarre's 'little academe' is book-learning, the study of the written word. Holofernes' devotion to pure Latin, Armado's delight in 'high-borne words' (I.i.172), and Costard's excited adoption of new words also testify to faith that the 'angel knowledge' appears to men in verbal form. When Costard, for example, learns that the tip Armado has given him can be called 'remuneration,' he feels that acquiring the new word has changed his life: 'Remuneration: why, it is a fairer name than French crown! I will never buy and sell out of this word' (III.i.140–2).

A primary function of the intense interest in language and learning that animates the entire society from king to clown is to nurture the pervasive group consciousness. The characters pride themselves on their learning less as an individual distinction than as a joint endeavor. The King pursues fame and honor with his 'fellow scholars' (I.i.17). The schoolmaster and the curate also enjoy learning as a communal activity. When Holofernes displays his talents for Nathaniel, he confidently expects an appreciative audience, and Nathaniel, by praising his friend's performance, exhibits his own credentials as a connoisseur of rhetorical skill: '**Nath**. ... Your reasons at dinner have been sharp and sententious: pleasant without scurrility, witty without affection, audacious without impudency, learned without opinion, and strange without heresy' (V.i.2–6). Nathaniel defers to Holofernes' scholarship, but he identifies with the schoolmaster as an educated man: 'we of taste and feeling' (IV.ii.29). In Navarre, a display of learning is not so much a way to distinguish oneself as to establish one's place among the educated. Thus Holofernes' search for words to express his contempt for ignorance culminates with the concept of uncorroborated singularity: 'undressed, unpolished, uneducated, unpruned, untrained, or rather unlettered, or ratherest unconfirmed' (IV.ii.16–18).

Although language provides a field for competition, then, it also functions to unite members of a social group. Verbal games join characters as participants rather than pit them against each other as serious antagonists, and exchanges of wit can temporarily link natives with strangers, men with women, and nobles with commoners. Thus Costard joins the young women from France in sparring with Boyet and exults in the pleasures of participating in the gentry's favorite sport:

> By my soul, a swain, a most simple clown!
> Lord, Lord, how the ladies and I have put him down!
>
> (IV.i.140–1)

Costard even puts words into the mouth of the king himself:

> **King** Peace!
> **Cost.** – be to me, and every man that dares not fight!
> **King.** No words!
> **Cost.** – of other men's secrets, I beseech you. (I.i.226–30)

In this kind of wordplay, as Jane Donawerth contends, 'despite the denial of the original intention, two people together make the sentence, and the sharing of new meaning works as a social bond.'[12]

In Shakespeare's Navarre, the almost universal delight in the powers and possibilities of language is expressed in verbal elaboration that creates the impression of a homogeneous culture. Although critics have distinguished among the characters on the basis of their attitudes towards and uses of language,[13] for me, and I would argue for most of the theater audience – even an Elizabethan audience more familiar with subtle rhetorical patterns than we are – the primary effect is stylistic similarity rather than variety. Admittedly Armado looks for precedents in a ballad while Nathaniel cites scripture, and Berowne surpasses Holofernes in verbal grace and dexterity. But they are all eager to demonstrate their facility with puns and quips, figures of sound and sense, aphorisms, allusions, foreign words and phrases, and citations of learned authorities. The 'sweetly varied' epithets that Nathaniel so admires in Holofernes' speech – '*caelo*, the sky, the welkin, the heaven ... *terra*, the soil, the land, the earth (IV.ii.5–7) – and cultivates in his own – 'intituled, nominated, or called' (V.i.7–8) – are only slightly less absurd than Don Armado's elaborate synonyms – 'a child of our grandmother Eve, a female; or for thy more sweet understanding, a woman' (I.i.263–5). And the same delight in elegant variation inspires Berowne's epithets for Cupid, which differ in quality of inventiveness rather than in kind:

> This wimpled, whining, purblind, wayward boy,
> This senior-junior, giant-dwarf, Dan Cupid,
> Regent of love-rhymes, lord of folded arms,
> Th'anointed sovereign of sighs and groans,
> Liege of all loiterers and malecontents,
> Dread prince of plackets, king of codpieces,
> Sole imperator and great general
> Of trotting paritors ... (III.i.179–86)

Unlike the Venice where Shylock's alien status and values are embodied in spare, guarded speech that contrasts with the expansive speech patterns of the dominant culture, Navarre has a single ideal of verbal elegance and elaboration.

In this representation of a society swept by enthusiasm for education, Shakespeare is responding to significant developments in contemporary English society. Historians of early modern England agree that there was an unprecedented expansion of education and spread of literacy during the late sixteenth and early seventeenth centuries, a 'change of such magnitude,' according to Lawrence Stone, 'that it can only be described as a revolution.'[14] In addition, by giving dramatic emphasis to the unifying effect of education, Shakespeare strikingly anticipates conclusions recent historians have reached about the impact of education on English society in the late sixteenth century. Keith Wrightson, for example, suggests that 'a greater degree of cultural cohesion among the English ruling class,' the 'incorporation of literacy into the popular culture,' and the 'expansion of the cultural horizons' among the common people were significant consequences of the remarkable educational expansion during the period.[15]

The educational enthusiasms in Navarre clearly derive from ideas current in English society. The King and his courtiers express the humanists' faith in the value of education and banish women from court not as Christian ascetics avoiding fleshly temptation but as humanist scholars rejecting the lower passions in favor of reason. In their plan to learn things 'hid and barr'd ... from common sense' (I.i.57) they are pursuing a program of Neo-Platonic philosophical inquiry. Holofernes, the schoolmaster who is honored as 'a good member of the commonwealth' (IV.ii.76-7) for teaching the neighborhood children, exemplifies contemporary faith in the social benefits of education. To the founders of the many new schools during the period, Wrightson explains, education provided: 'both an answer to society's ills and a guarantee of social well-being. It would train up good men, virtuous rulers and useful citizens in accordance with the ideals of the humanists. It would advance the Protestant Reformation by banishing ignorance and implanting knowledge of the truth. It would provide opportunities for the advancement of talented children from humble origins in an orderly process of social mobility. It would promote the prosperity of the commonwealth and strengthen the bonds of the social order' (Wrightson, 185). Nathaniel, the Protestant clergyman, reflects the close connection between educational expansion and the Reformation. Protestant emphasis on the individual Christian's knowledge of scripture fostered education as a means of eradicating ignorance and superstition among laymen and of enabling the clergy to perform their pastoral duties. Costard's verbal enthusiasms and his adoption of the linguistic manners and forms of his social superiors dramatize the spread of the new learning among the common people. According to Wrightson, 'even among the less fortunate, there is evidence enough of the development among some of a passion for print, an intoxication with the world of information and ideas opened to them by literacy' (196). 'Gardon! Remuneration!' (III.i.172-3).

Navarre also parallels actual conditions in Elizabethan England in the distribution of education among the population. While the expansion of education undoubtedly changed English society as a whole, the impact of this 'educational revolution' was not uniform. Even in urging its importance, Stone makes a significant qualification: 'So great was the boom – much greater than has hitherto been recognized – that all classes above a certain level took their part ... Everyone was included except the very poor (who probably embraced the majority of the population)' (68). In spite of the many new schools and scholarships open to the poor, they were not everywhere available. Even in areas provided with educational facilities, the majority of the poor could not afford to take advantage of such opportunities. Thus, as Wrightson warns: 'Educational provision expanded certainly; access to education, however, remained limited. Above all it diminished as the social scale descended' (186). For women, educational opportunities were, predictably, 'doubly discriminatory.' By the 1640s most of the male English gentry were literate, considerable progress in literacy had been made among yeomen and tradesmen, but lower social ranks and women still could not read or write. 'Educational expansion had produced not a literate society, but a hierarchy of illiteracy which faithfully mirrored the hierarchy of status and rank' (190).[16]

Love's Labor's Lost reproduces this pattern. The aristocrats who plan to devote three years exclusively to study as a means of self-cultivation have the freest access to education. Holofernes and Nathaniel are the sort of people who benefited most from the education boom, men from the middle ranks of society for whom education provided professional advancement.[17] For all the faith in education shown by the king, the schoolmaster, and the curate, however, Navarre is not a literate society. Dull, Costard, and Jaquenetta are illiterate. Their inability to read, moreover, is neither an incidental fact nor an isolated joke, but a recurrent topic of dialogue and contributor to events. Because Costard cannot decipher the addresses of the messages he carries and Jaquenetta cannot read the letter she receives, together they unintentionally engineer Berowne's humiliation. More personally, Costard is the subject of Armado's letter to the King. His repeated interruptions as the King tries to read the letter and the formal language of his confession ('The matter is to me, sir, as concerning Jaquenetta: the manner of it is, I was taken with the manner' [I.i.201–3]) may suggest his sense of vulnerability to a legal system that rewards literacy. Lawrence Stone, noting that the ability to read a sentence from the Bible could mean the difference between life and an agonizing death, quotes this judicial record of the sentencing of two thieves: 'The said Paul reads, to be branded; the said William does not read, to be hanged' ('Educational Revolution,'43).

In spite of the unifying effects of educational expansion, then, the educational revolution also contributed to a profound polarization of English society. In the middle of Elizabeth's reign, most English people were illiterate and shared a common culture. One hundred years later illiteracy was a characteristic of the poor, who 'had become not simply poor, but to a significant degree culturally different' (Wrightson, 221). 'The spread of popular literacy and the progress of the Reformation,' Wrightson argues, had increased opportunities for a significant minority of the common people, but had also 'brought about a widening fissure between polite and plebeian culture, the informed and the ignorant, respectability and the profane multitude' (220).

So too education has a divisive as well as a cohesive effect in Shakespeare's Navarre. The obverse of the sense of camaraderie generated by shared learning is disdain for the uneducated.[18] The pride that Armado has in his own cultivated eloquence is matched by contempt for the 'base and obscure vulgar' of the 'rude multitude' (IV.i.68–9, V.i.89). He contemptuously dismisses the illiterate Costard as an 'unlettered small-knowing soul' (I.i.250). To Holofernes even literacy is an inadequate standard. He equates Costard's lack of Latin with ignorance and condescendingly praises his wit in spoken English as 'pearl enough for a swine' (IV.ii.89). Armado will associate with Holofernes as an 'Arts-man,' but he and the schoolmaster agree in wanting to be 'singuled from the barbarous' (V.i.81–2). Armado, Holofernes, and Nathaniel consistently speak as initiates in a fraternity of the learned – a fraternity where membership is valued for its exclusivity. For example, Nathaniel's assertion of solidarity with Holofernes significantly occurs in the context of explaining the depths of Costard's ignorance:

> Sir, he hath never fed of the dainties that are bred in a
>   book;
> He hath not eat paper, as it were; he hath not drunk ink;
> his intellect is not replenished; he is only an animal, only
>   sensible in the duller parts;
> And such barren plants are set before us, that we thankful
>   should be –
> Which we of taste and feeling are – for those parts that do
>   fructify in us more than he.
>
>   (IV.ii.24–9)

To Nathaniel, the uneducated are sub-human creatures that exist solely to increase the self-satisfaction of educated men like himself. The absurd exaggerations of the comic characters, moreover, reveal the characteristics of the aristocrats. Significantly, the only recreation scheduled for Navarre's monastic retreat is the courtly scholars' mockery of their inferiors: their plan to use Armado and Costard for 'our sport' (I.i.179).

Although the irrepressible Costard may enjoy expanding his cultural horizons by a remuneration and exchanging witticisms with courtiers, most of the common people are excluded from the intellectual ferment among the gentry. Characters like Dull and Jaquenetta, moreover, are not only unassimilated into the literate culture but actively suspicious of it. Jaquenetta's responses to Armado's boorish condescension are sullenly sarcastic:

> **Arm.** I will visit thee at the lodge.
> **Jaq.** That's hereby.
> **Arm.** I know where it is situate.
> **Jaq.** Lord, how wise you are! (I.ii.135–8)

Dull is respectful to Nathaniel and Holofernes but is intransigent in his claim that he knows better than they what kind of deer the Princess killed. Admittedly, he is not completely immune to the seductions of what Armado calls the 'Sweet smoke of rhetoric' (III.i.63). Like Costard, he tries his hand at word games and blunders into malapropisms by picking up new words from Holofernes. But there is a note of hostility in his verbal sallies. After Holofernes and Nathaniel volubly decry the monstrosity of his ignorance, Dull defiantly challenges the wits of the two 'book-men' with a riddle. When Nathaniel exclaims on Holofernes' 'rare talent,' Dull mutters, 'If a talent be a claw, look how he claws him with a talent' (IV.ii.62–64). Dull's resentment, moreover, is directed not simply at the pretentiousness of pedantry but at its unintelligibility. When Holofernes comments on Dull's silence during a later episode, 'Via, goodman Dull! thou hast spoken no word all this while,' Dull dryly agrees, 'Nor understood none neither' (v.i.149–51). The pedantry that unites Holofernes and Nathaniel makes them incomprehensible to Dull. Similarly the wordplay that entertains the court merely confuses the Forester when the Princess tries to engage him in witty, flirtatious badinage as she sets out on a royal hunt:

> **For.** Hereby, upon the edge of yonder coppice,
> A stand where you may make the fairest shoot.
> **Prin.** I thank my beauty, I am fair that shoot,
> And thereupon thou speak'st the fairest shoot.
> **For.** Pardon me, madam, for I meant not so.
> **Prin.** What, what? First praise me, and again say no?
> (IV.i.9–14)

Cultivated, educated discourse, as it is represented in *Love's Labor's Lost*, creates a sense of aristocratic cohesiveness that goes beyond consciousness of common social and economic status, but these very ways of thinking and talking render the community of the educated alien and incomprehensible to the rest of society.

Love's Labor's Lost, then, which in some ways seems the least realistic of plays – a tour de force whose delightful flashes of wit consume themselves in self-referential acknowledgements of their own artificiality – is equally impressive for its acute observation of social behavior. More interesting and significant than the possibility of teasingly ambiguous references to actual people is the play's treatment of the impact of humanistic education on an hierarchical society. Although many critics have analyzed the play's contribution to contemporary debates about language and learning, few have discussed its portrayal of the social and political consequences of the debate itself. Early in the period described by historians like Stone and Wrightson, Shakespeare was focusing attention on the simultaneously unifying and divisive effects on contemporary social life of educational expansion and the spread of literacy.

Of course, the way in which specialized learning can create cohesion among its adherents while alienating them from outsiders is not an exclusively sixteenth-century phenomenon. While speculating about how twentieth-century undergraduate elitism might have contributed to alienation from mainstream British society, Noel Annan has commented on the intensity of some undergraduate friendships: 'The Apostles were devoted to each other because they felt they were discovering truths hitherto unknown.'[19] The experience of Anthony Blunt and Guy Burgess at Cambridge sounds rather like the search for 'Things hid and barr'd ... from common sense' at Navarre. Intellectual cliques contemptuous of and incomprehensible to outsiders are also common in areas closer to most students of Shakespeare than either Cambridge elitism or international espionage. Consider Edward Said's observation that recent movements in literary criticism became increasingly exclusive and exclusionist: 'In time the guild adversarial sense grew as the elaborate techniques multiplied, and an interest in expanding the constituency lost out to a wish for abstract correctness and methodological rigor within a quasi-monastic order.'[20] In addition, as Said argues, the cult of expertise in scientific, social, and political areas is a conspicuous feature of our culture.

Intellectual elitism obviously can take varied forms. The kind Shakespeare portrays in his representation of a French academy produces neither treason nor competitive careerism, but it does pose some social danger – a social irresponsibility stemming from a narrowing of interests and sympathies. Most absurdly, Armado disdains knowing basic arithmetic because 'it fitteth the spirit of a tapster' (I.ii.40–1). More significantly, the King's academic aspirations cause him to neglect his public responsibilities. In proposing to transform his court into 'a little academe, / Still and contemplative in living art' in opposition to both personal 'affections' and 'the world's desires' (I.i.9–14), Navarre invokes the traditional choice among the *vita contemplativa* or life ruled by intellect, the *vita activa* or the active life in pursuit of power and wealth, and the *vita voluptuosa* or the life of love and pleasure.[21] Most Renaissance humanists either stressed the importance of the active life or advocated a balance of all three. For example, in La Primaudaye's *French Academie*, a popular account of a philosophical retreat that probably influenced the composition of *Love's Labor's Lost*,[22] study and contemplation are presented not as an alternative to, but as preparation for a life of public service. La Primaudaye, for example, credits 'Divine Plato' with 'joining action with contemplation in a happie and perfect life' and saying that 'next to the glorie of God we must have regard to do that which is profitable for the Common-wealth.'[23] Of course, Navarre's choice of the contemplative life has venerable precedents in Aristotle's *Nicomachean Ethics* and in medieval religious thought. But even if there is nothing self-evidently wrong with his choice in the abstract, it soon becomes demonstrably impractical for a king. The banishment of women from court is, as Berowne points out, 'A dangerous law against gentility' (I.i.128). Navarre has forgotten the announced arrival of the French Princess to negotiate the disposition of Aquitaine. Also he apparently has the facts wrong. Although he initially rejects the Princess' request for the return of Aquitaine, she documents her case and wins her suit easily. Not only is the King unprepared as a negotiator, he insults his royal guest.

Within a few years of this dramatization of a meeting between the King of Navarre and a French Princess, a real-life French intellectual and public official noted the folly of praising men for qualities inappropriate to their calling, such as commending a king for artistic skills rather than for 'justice, and the skill to governe, and knowledge to direct his people both in peace & warre.'[24] Michel de Montaigne also speculated about 'The ceremony of interviews between Kings' referring to the usual French custom of going out to meet an honored guest as well as citing the opinion of Marguerite de Valois, the French Princess married to the King of Navarre, that 'it more agreeth with civility and respect, to stay for him at home' (23). In contrast, the fictional King of Navarre entertains the French Princess on an important diplomatic mission by assigning her to camp out in the field, a welcome, she pointedly reminds him, that is 'too base' for her (II.i.93).

The incivility of the Princess' reception in Navarre, moreover, is not accidental to, but inherent in, the courtiers' conception of their scholarly project. They are not idealistic young intellectuals who happen also to be contemptuous of women. The two impulses are intimately linked. Their sense of solidarity depends on their exclusiveness and their sense of honor on their superiority to others. Their proscription of women, like their mockery of Armado and Costard, expresses their contempt for outsiders. The extent to which they define themselves in terms of their superiority over others is suggested at the very beginning of the play in Dumaine's reply to the King's opening speech:

> My loving lord, Dumaine is mortified:
> The grosser manner of these world's delights
> He throws upon the gross world's baser slaves;
> To love, to wealth, to pomp, I pine and die,
> With all these living in philosophy. (I.i.28–32)

As Dumaine echoes the King's choice of the contemplative over the active and the voluptuary life, he makes clear that he measures the honor he hopes to gain through study by the disdain he feels for 'the gross world's baser slaves' who choose other ways of life.

The intellectual elitism of Navarre's courtly coterie affects the King's relations with his subjects as well as with visiting royalty. In this rigidly hierarchical society, disdain for ignorance soon becomes the contempt of the privileged for their social and economic inferiors. The aristocrats' contempt for commoners is evident but not much at issue in the play's early scenes; it becomes dramatically dynamic in the last act with the nobles' reactions to the Pageant of the Worthies. First, the King tries to forestall the performance for fear that its incompetence will shame him. His reluctance to accept his subjects' efforts to satisfy his request for an entertainment falls significantly short of the cultural ideal of kingly magnanimity. In *The French Academie*, for example, La Primaudaye's dedicatory epistle addressed to Henry III tells about a great monarch who graciously accepted from a poor man a gift of water, 'thinking it to be as great an act of magnanimitie to take in good part, and to receive cheerfully small presents offered with a hartie and good affection, as to give great things liberally ... ' (La Primaudaye, sig. Ajv). While Navarre is churlish, Berowne and the other courtiers are aggressively rude, ridiculing and mocking the actors. In telling contrast to the entertainment presented by the commoners for the aristocrats in the last act of *A Midsummer Night's Dream*, the pageant offered to entertain the Princess in *Love's Labor's Lost* is a fiasco, continually interrupted by the audience's heckling and disrupted finally with threats of violence. *The most lamentable comedie ... of Pyramus and Thisby* is a theatrical success in spite of the actors' incompetence because of the mutual good will of performers and audience. The Pageant of the Worthies is a failure because of the audience's contempt for the (relatively capable) performers.

Admittedly, the cohesive power of verbal and intellectual sophistication as well as its divisive power is evident in this final scene. The antagonism between Berowne and Boyet dissolves in their appreciation of each other's wit. When Boyet follows Berowne in interrupting Costard's first speech and supplies a rhyme for Berowne's interruption, Berowne applauds Boyet: 'Well said, old mocker. I must needs be friends with thee' (V.ii.549). But if the sport of mockery can expand fractionally the perimeters of an aristocratic clique, its most powerful effect is divisive. Although the King has rescinded the 'dangerous law against gentility' and Berowne gestures towards 'russet yeas and honest kersey noes' (V.ii.413), Holofernes' judgment of his tormenters is irrefutable: the social discourse that unites the gentles 'is not generous, not gentle, not humble' (V.ii.629).

The coterie mentality that hampers Navarre's discharge of his public responsibilities and creates tensions between the aristocrats and commoners also complicates personal relationships and contributes to the barriers between men and women. Armado's attitude towards love demonstrates clearly a sense of superiority that conflates intellectual, sexual, and social attributes. He feels degraded by his love for Jaquenetta because love in itself is beneath his high heroic calling and because of Jaquenetta's humble birth: 'as it is base for a soldier to love, so am I in love with a base wench' (I.ii.58–9). With the help of Moth's classical learning that provides him with noble precedents, Armado reconciles himself to his weakness and professes his willingness to humble himself for love. But he continues to assert his superiority, and the threat of coercion is only thinly veiled. He woos Jaquenetta with the story of King Cophetua's love for a beggar girl: 'I am the king, for so stands the comparison; thou the beggar, for so witnesseth thy lowliness. Shall I command thy love? I may. Shall I enforce thy love? I could. Shall I entreat thy love? I will' (IV.i.78–82). And in case she should take the promise to entreat too literally he adds a postscript to his love letter:

> Thus dost thou hear the Nemean lion roar
> 'Gainst thee, thou lamb, that standest as his prey;
> Submissive fall his princely feet before,
> And he from forage will incline to play.
> But if thou strive, poor soul, what art thou then?
> Food for his rage, repasture for his den. (IV.i.88–93)

The French nobles express themselves less crudely, but their basic attitudes are similar. When Berowne falls in love, his sense of degradation at succumbing to an inferior is remarkably like Armado's:

> What! I love, I sue, I seek a wife –
> A woman, that is like a German clock,
> Still a-repairing, ever out of frame,
> And never going aright, being a watch,
> But being watch'd that it may still go right! (III.i.189–93)

Berowne assumes not only that women are intrinsically ill-made and irrational, but also that he loves a woman of unrestrained sexuality, 'one that will do the deed / Though Argus were her eunuch and her guard' (198–9). Curiously, he also raises the issue of social rank: 'Well, I will love, write, sigh, pray, sue, groan: / Some men must love my lady, and some Joan' (204–5). Since there is no indication that Rosaline's social rank is inferior to that of the other ladies-in-waiting, or, for that matter, to Berowne's, this line suggests the close association of social and educational levels. Berowne associates irrational sensuality with women and with humble birth and equates loving a woman with becoming entangled with a social inferior.[25] And, just as Berowne's ironically resigned capitulation to love is a less extreme version of Armado's feeling of degradation, so the military metaphors for love favored by the nobles recall Armado's predatory attitude to the peasant girl:

> **King.** Saint Cupid, then! and, soldiers, to the field!
> **Ber.** Advance your standards, and upon them, lords;
> Pell-mell, down with them! (IV.iii.363–5)

Love's Labor's Lost 93

In short, the peremptoriness of the young noblemen in love is only thinly disguised by the conventional self-abasement of their courting and not so very distant from their earlier repudiation of women.

When Navarre, Berowne, Longaville, and Dumain decide to become 'affection's men-at-arms' (IV.iii.286), they turn to the same erudition and verbal facility they had used to establish their superiority when they saw themselves as 'brave conquerors [of their] own affections' (I.i.8–9). Ironically both their predicament and their strategy for handling it reveal their kinship with Armado and Costard, whom they have treated with such derision. Armado asks Moth to name 'great men [who] have been in love' as 'authority' (I.ii.65, 67) to justify his desire for Jaquenetta; similarly, the nobles appoint Berowne to prove 'Our loving lawful, and our faith not torn' by providing 'some authority how to proceed' (IV.iii.281, 283). Berowne decorates his argument with classical references, even citing Hercules, the same authority Moth names for Armado. Earlier, Berowne had cited Hercules to express contempt for the spectacle of love's folly, the indecorum of grown men behaving like lovesick school boys:

> To see a king transformed to a gnat!
> To see great Hercules whipping a gig,
> And profound Salomon to tune a jig. (IV.iii.164–6)

Now, when he wants to argue that love fulfills rather than debases human nature, Herculean valor becomes an image of love's ennobling power:

> For valor, is not Love a Hercules,
> Still climbing trees in the Hesperides? (IV.iii.337–8)

Costard relies not on classical precedents but on verbal sleights of hand to deal with the practical and ethical problems presented by his encounter with Jaquenetta. When threatened with punishment for being 'taken with a wench,' Costard counters, 'I was taken with none, sir, I was taken with a damsel' (I.i.288–90). When the King insists that the proclamation included 'damsel,' Costard tries in turn 'virgin' and 'maid,' finally consoling himself with the image of himself as a martyr: 'I suffer for the truth, sir; for true it is, I was taken with Jaquenetta, and Jaquenetta is a true girl, and therefore welcome the sour cup of prosperity!' (I.i.291–313). Later, Longaville employs essentially the same strategy in a sonnet to Maria:

> Vows for thee broke deserve not punishment.
> A woman I forswore, but I will prove,
> Thou being a goddess, I forswore not thee. (IV.iii.61-3)

For all the differences between the courtly sophisticate and the country bumpkin, then, they share certain habits of mind and expression as well as natural affections. Berowne is contemptuous of Longaville's profane rationalization – 'This is the liver-vein, which makes flesh a deity, / A green goose a goddess; pure, pure idolatry' (IV.iii.72-3), but he too invokes the religion of love to justify their common perfidy, concluding his long speech with this bit of sophistry:

> It is religion to be thus forsworn:
> For charity itself fulfills the law,
> And who can sever love from charity? (IV.iii.360-2)

Although some critics are persuaded by Berowne's eloquence and see it as the thematic heart of the play, neither Berowne nor his fellows doubt for an instant that the speech is sheer sophistry and that they are forsworn. Indeed, Berowne's fear that Rosaline is a 'wanton' (III.i.196) seems to express his guilty sense that loving a promiscuous woman is what he deserves:

> Light wenches may prove plagues to men forsworn;
> If so, our copper buys no better treasure. (IV.iii. 382-3)

Berowne is only half right, of course. The men have indeed debased themselves by violating their oaths, but the women, far from being 'light wenches' are notably trustworthy and reliable. This contrast between conscientious, responsible young women and shallow, inconstant young men is the foundation of the dramatic structure. The critical terms usually proposed for analyzing the play – study and love, contemplation and action, or artifice and nature – describe the characters' range of experience and interests rather than the dramatic conflict. The standard interpretation of the action as the triumph of natural affection and love over sterile affectation sees the play too much from the male characters' point of view, misunderstanding the crucial opposition provided by the female characters. While the young scholars' absurd vow is defeated by the very presence of the women and their affected courtship in the Masque of Muscovites is baffled by the women's wit, the play does not present the men as representatives of affectation defeated by the women as representatives of love. The values the women embody are not artless spontaneity or emotional intensity. They do not speak 'russet yeas and honest kersey noes' (V.ii.413) any more than Armado or Berowne do, and they are not in love, although critics ingeniously supply motives to account for their failure to say that they are. The struggle between the Princess of France and her attendants and the King of Navarre and his is between a group of responsible young women who see themselves as part of a larger community and a group of self-absorbed young men who constitute an exclusive coterie.

In the early scenes, the contrast is evident in their respective manners of discharging the 'serious business' (II.i.31) of Aquitaine and in their attitudes to the vow. Berowne alerts us in the first scene to the men's rather cavalier attitude toward making and breaking oaths. Picking up the King's ruling that, in spite of the ban against women, the Princess 'must lie here on mere necessity' (I.i.148), Berowne predicts:

> Necessity will make us all forsworn
> Three thousand times within this three years' space;
> For every man with his affects is born,
> Not by might mast'red, but by special grace. (I.i.149–52)

Berowne's belief that human passions can be controlled only with the aid of divine grace is certainly theologically respectable, but his conclusion that the doctrine of grace absolves people of moral responsibility is not. After pointing out how conveniently the idea of necessity can be invoked to excuse any weakness, Berowne nevertheless proceeds to rely on it.[26] As he signs the oath, he plans his defense for breaking it:

> If I break faith, this word shall speak for me:
> I am forsworn 'on mere necessity.' (I.i.153–4)

The women, in contrast, consistently see the vow as morally binding. The Princess especially insists on the moral authority of the oath and the danger of violating it. She breaks off her first conversation with the King with the warning 'you'll prove perjur'd if you make me stay' (II.i.113), and when finally invited to Navarre's court, she declines:

> This field shall hold me, and so hold your vow:
> Nor God, nor I, delights in perjur'd men. (V.ii.345–6)

The Princess even articulates the theological basis for her attitude: the moral responsibility of the human will. She reminds Boyet, for example, 'All pride is willing pride, and yours is so' (II.i.36), and she warns the King that should he break his word, 'will shall break it, will, and nothing else' (II.i.100).

The suggestions that the men do not take their moral responsibilities quite seriously are confirmed when they fall in love. They are more disturbed by a sense of isolation than by guilt for violating their oaths. Berowne, for example, feels the degradation of lovesickness primarily as a contrast with his friends: 'The King he is hunting the deer: I am coursing myself. They have pitch'd a toil: I am toiling in a pitch,' and he admits, 'I would not care a pin, if the other three were in' (IV.iii.1–3, 18). Similarly, the King, overhearing Longaville's confession, welcomes 'sweet fellowship in shame' (IV.iii.47). In fact, they all, like Dumaine, 'in love's grief desir'st society' (IV.iii.126), and all share his belief that 'none offend where all alike do dote' (IV.iii.124). Now the men add irresistible female beauty to necessity and grace as factors limiting their moral responsibility. Although they admit that they are forsworn, they try to transfer blame to the women who have tempted them. Thus Longaville, writing to Maria, constructs a particularly tortuous argument that weaves a scientific explanation of the materiality of words together with a metaphorization of woman as sun:

> Vows are but breath, and breath a vapor is;
> Then thou, fair sun, which on my earth dost shine,
> Exhal'st this vapor-vow; in thee it is.
> If broken then, it is no fault of mine. (IV.iii.66–9)

More simply, the King defends himself from the charge of perjury by accusing the Princess:

> Rebuke me not for that which you provoke:
> The virtue of your eye must break my oath. (V.ii.347–8)

And while Longaville and Navarre may be simply trying to flatter their beloveds rather than to construct a serious moral argument, Berowne seems distressingly sincere when he presents the case more fully:

> For your fair sakes have we neglected time,
> Play'd foul play with our oaths. Your beauty, ladies,
> Hath much deformed us, fashioning our humors

> Even to the opposed end of our intents;
> And what in us hath seem'd ridiculous –
> As love is full of unbefitting strains ...
> Which parti-coated presence of loose love
> Put on by us, if, in your heavenly eyes,
> Have misbecom'd our oaths and gravities,
> Those heavenly eyes, that look into these faults,
> Suggested us to make. Therefore, ladies,
> Our love being yours, the error that love makes
> Is likewise yours. (V.ii.755–60, 766–72)

Unlike twentieth-century critics who applaud the young men's change of heart as a triumph of natural affection over sterile academicism, the objects of their affection see no radical break from earlier behavior in the elaborate courtship rituals. They interpret the poems, gifts, and entertainments as the witty courtiers' 'mockery merriment' and respond in kind, offering 'mock for mock' (V.ii.139–40). They may be mistaken in dismissing as 'courtship, pleasant jest, and courtesy' (V.ii.780) what the men intend as sincere protestations of love, but in light of the men's sudden repudiation of their solemn oaths, the women's judgment that their suitors are basically frivolous is unavoidable. From their point of view, the men's renunciation of their vows of celibacy is simply another form of the self-absorbed irresponsibility manifested in the original rash vows. For a king and his advisers to repudiate the obligations of hospitality and the responsibilities of governance is 'deadly sin,' as the princess had admonished Navarre at their first meeting, but, as she also warned him, the vow is morally binding, and it is equally 'sin to break it' (II.i.105–6). The women are totally unimpressed by their suitors' attempts to evade moral responsibility by attributing their sin to the power of female beauty. When Richard of Gloucester makes a similar argument in the more sinister atmosphere of *Richard III*, he is successful. Lady Anne begins to soften towards him when he pleads, ' 'twas I that stabb'd young Edward – / But 'twas thy heavenly face that set me on' (*RIII*, I.ii.181–2). In the comedy, the women are not caught off balance by this appeal to their sexual power. The Princess answers sharply the King's sally about 'the virtue of [her] eye' causing his transgression:

> You nickname virtue; vice you should have spoke,
> For virtue's office never breaks men's troth ...
> A world of torments though I should endure,

> I would not yield to be your house's guest:
> So much I hate a breaking cause to be
> Of heavenly oaths, vow'd with integrity.
>   (v.ii.349–50, 353–6)

Thus, the point at issue in the final scene is not primarily affectation or misunderstanding of love, but trust. Perjury has proved to be not only the impiety of taking God's name in vain but a subversion of the trust essential for human relationships. All human contracts and associations, from the settlement of territorial disputes such as that over Aquitaine to the 'world-without-end bargain' (v.ii.789) of marriage depend on being able to have faith in one another's word. According to La Primaudaye, moreover, while breach of faith is dishonorable for anyone, it is especially so for a king, 'because he is the formall Warrantie unto all his subjects, of that fidelitie which is amongst themselves: so that no fault is more detestable in a Prince than perjurie' (La Primaudaye, 417). In spite of their many genuine virtues, the King and his friends have shown themselves untrustworthy and have loosened the bonds of trust that hold society together.

The conventional comic celebration of love and marriage is precluded from the final scene of *Love's Labor's Lost* by this focus on the men's sins and by Mercade's arrival with word of the death of the Princess' father. Like Mercury arriving in Carthage to interrupt Aeneas' dalliance with Dido and to remind him of his civic mission, Mercade disperses the atmosphere of flirtatious gaiety and recalls the Princess to her familial and political responsibilities.[27] The men and women respond in character to this abrupt encounter with mortality. The men continue to assume that they can shape the world to their satisfaction, while denying their own accountability. The King single-mindedly continues his courtship, pressing for an answer from the grief-stricken Princess. Berowne laments the indignity of love and charges the women with responsibility. The women are more responsible and simultaneously more humbly responsive to the contingency of events and to intractable social and biological givens. The Princess immediately makes preparations for her return to France, courteously thanking the King for his hospitality and the settlement of her diplomatic mission. When she finally understands that Navarre is not playing one more courtly game but seriously proposing marriage, her response is severe:

> No, no, my lord, your Grace is perjur'd much,
> Full of dear guiltiness ...
> Your oath I will not trust ... (v.ii.790-1, 94)

But she does not reject him. The Princess, echoed by Katherine, Maria, and Rosaline, promises to marry her suitor on the condition that he serve a year's penance to atone for his guilt and to test his love.

Love's Labor's Lost is unconventional not just because the anticipated marriages are conditional and postponed but because the social group is dispersed rather than unified at the end of the play. In *The Two Gentlemen of Verona*, society is disrupted temporarily, but the characters' sociability, their need and desire for human relationships, finally controls aggressive individualism and re-establishes social bonds. In *Love's Labor's Lost*, although there is no corrosive envy, intense suffering, or threatened violence, the ending is bleaker, culminating not in 'One feast, one house, one mutual happiness' (*TGV*, V.iv.173), but in separation. Before a new, more expansive society can form, old obligations must be honored and the exclusive coterie that fosters disdain and irresponsibility must be dissolved. The Princess intends to 'shut / [Her] woeful self up in a mourning house' (v.ii.807–8). The King promises to withdraw into an 'austere insociable life' (v.ii.799). Rosaline condemns Berowne for the mocking disdain with which he has treated 'all estates' (v.ii.845), so while the King does penance for self-indulgent irresponsibility by suffering 'frosts and fasts, hard lodging and thin weeds' (v.ii.801), Berowne will correct his 'gibing spirit' by exhibiting his wit for the 'speechless sick,' rather than for the 'shallow laughing hearers' (v.ii.858, 851, 860) of his appreciative clique.

This dispersal of characters is unique among Shakespeare's comedies and creates a disturbing tone, but to interpret the play as wholly bitter and pessimistic would impoverish the experience it offers just as seeing it as wholly festive would. In this case at least, ambivalence is not a product of critical ingenuity; the play is genuinely open-ended. Even though the year's separation is, as Berowne says, 'too long for a play' (v.ii.878), the text points beyond itself to the future union that the women conditionally promise and that the King confidently predicts. The final songs of Winter and Spring both reassure that a year will pass and warn that time can bring betrayal as well as fulfillment. *Love's Labor's Lost* was selected for its 'wytt and mirthe' to celebrate the Earl of Southampton's release from prison,[28] perhaps because he identified with the portrayal of ambitious, idealistic young nobles or perhaps because he enjoyed satire of his old enemies at court. But insofar as the text points not merely into the fictional future but out into the world of actual people and events, it also recalls that the festivities celebrating the wedding of the King of Navarre with a French princess in 1572 ended in the bloody Massacre of St. Bartholomew's Day and a renewal of civil war. *Love's Labor's Lost* is less an expression of the spirit of aristocratic faction, as Frances Yates argued, than a warning that the insider/outsider mentality of factionalism may be even more detrimental to social cohesion than selfish individualism or malice.

Part Three

Change and Continuity

CHAPTER SIX

The Changes and Chances of Mortal Life in *A Midsummer Night's Dream*

'What change is this, / Sweet love!' (III.ii.262-3)

Among Shakespeare's plays, only *The Merry Wives of Windsor* is set in contemporary England; all others portray worlds temporally or geographically distant. Yet these fictional settings combine the foreign with the familiar. Shakespeare's versions of republican Rome in *Coriolanus*, medieval Scotland in *Macbeth*, or sixteenth-century France in *Love's Labor's Lost* are distinctive cultures, differing significantly from each other and from Elizabethan and Jacobean England, but they also exhibit social and political structures and processes familiar to Shakespeare and his contemporaries. The political career of Caius Martius Coriolanus was peculiar to the conditions of republican Rome, but Shakespeare's representation of it, while adhering to his source in Plutarch with unusual closeness, also illustrates electoral procedures in contemporary England with striking accuracy.[1] Macbeth's violent and sinister court could scarcely be more different from Navarre's little band of scholars cum lovers, but both exhibit ideas and attitudes current and controversial in England in the late sixteenth and early seventeenth centuries. Invariably, Shakespeare's fictional settings comment on aspects of his own culture rather than presenting for consideration alternative social organizations.

Even the comedies, whose generic predilection for ending happily encourages imaginative constructions of golden worlds, are no utopian fantasies of perfect worlds without disparities of wealth and power. On the contrary, all that Gonzalo would banish from his perfect commonwealth – trade, magistrates, letters, riches, poverty, servitude, inherited privilege, and individual property – are the very stuff of Shakespeare's comic societies. This characteristic blending of the familiar with the foreign is most noticeable in *A Midsummer Night's Dream*, where the mysterious and fantastic has a local habitation and a name while incidents and situations from common life appear strange and wonderful, where a legendary Greek hero presides over recognizably Elizabethan marital arrangements and an English artisan sleeps with a fairy queen. If the scholars who argue that the play was originally performed as part of the festivities celebrating an aristocratic wedding are right,[2] the wedding of Theseus and Hippolyta not only reinterprets a literary tradition transmitted through Plutarch and Chaucer, but also had immediate topical significance. Certainly the reference to 'a fair vestal throned by the west' (II.i.158) complimented Elizabeth, and the performance of *The most lamentable comedie ... of Pyramus and Thisby* identifies the on-stage representation of play-watching with the audience's present experience. Although the law sentencing a disobedient daughter to either death or life in a convent would have been scarcely less exotic to an Elizabethan audience in the 1590s than a marital quarrel over a stolen Indian prince, the quarrels between Hermia and Egeus and between Titania and Oberon presuppose Elizabethan notions of social stratification.[3]

This amalgam of past and present, near and far, has been popular with critics as well as with audiences. For Northrop Frye, *A Midsummer Night's Dream* is a paradigmatic green world comedy in which youth and passion triumph over age and law, and for C.L. Barber it is the first festive comedy in which release from societal repressions into the natural world clarifies relations between the human and the natural. To Jan Kott the lovers' experiences in the wood outside Athens demonstrate the cruel brutality of eroticism, and to René Girard the night in the woods reveals the destructive force of mimetic desire. More recently, the play has served Louis Montrose and Leonard Tennenhouse as a representative Elizabethan comedy presenting patterns of state and sexual politics.[4] In spite of profound differences in method, interpretation, and emotional response – Kott's revulsion from the spectacle of 'erotic madness' (Kott, 189) is at the opposite pole from Barber's delight in the 'unshadowed gaiety' (Barber, 161) with which the play makes fun of human folly – these critics all treat the remote and improbable in setting, plot, and character, not as imaginative inventions of other, unknown ways of being, but as symbolic representations of ordinary human experience. More specifically, they all note its emphasis on the forces controlling individual human experience. To Frye, Kott, and Girard, those forces are primarily internal – desires and passions, if not intrinsic to human nature, at least deeply inscribed in Western culture. Barber is more interested in specifically English communal traditions and in human responses to physical nature. Montrose and Tennenhouse, denying any essential human nature, analyze the social constructions of gender and power in terms of circumstances peculiar to late Elizabethan culture.

A Midsummer Night's Dream is the prototypical Shakespearean comedy for critics so diverse because it focuses less on the attitudes and values of particular characters than on patterns in human experience and on the powers that shape them. From the first scene, where Hermia's love is thwarted and the desires even of Theseus, the conquering hero, must wait on the passage of time, through the eruption of uncontrollable sexual attractions and aversions in the moonlit wood, to the final scene's focus on the deficiencies of the amateur actors, the action of the play consists in the subjection of individual characters to powers beyond their control. The situation that precipitates the plot is presented first as a conflict between individual will and social authority. By defying her father, Hermia challenges the whole social structure. Egeus claims 'the ancient privilege of Athens' (I.i.41) to dispose of his daughter as he wishes and asks Duke Theseus either to enforce his right or to punish Hermia's disobedience with death 'according to our law / Immediately provided in that case' (I.i.44–5). By qualifying Egeus' interpretation of the law only to the extent of allowing confinement in a convent as an alternative to death, Theseus makes clear that for Hermia to disobey her father is also to disobey the law and to defy her ruler. In response to these claims of the right to control her, Hermia opposes her desire to choose her own husband. Against the social norms that direct her to accept the husband her father has chosen for her, she asserts her personal desire: she does not want to. Athens, which had seemed a heaven, has become a hell to her, and she decides to flee from 'the sharp Athenian law' (I.i.162). Rejecting her father's choice of husband, she rejects Athens.

All Shakespeare's comedies exhibit conflict between the duty of submission and the desire for individual autonomy, but *A Dream* addresses the conflicting claims of the individual and the authority of society more directly than the earlier plays. Although Egeon in

The Comedy of Errors and Costard in *Love's Labor's Lost* run afoul of the law, in both cases our attention is directed towards particularities of their situations. Egeon's problem is that he is not a citizen of Ephesus; as soon as he is accepted as part of the group, the problem disappears. In *Love's Labor's Lost* the emphasis is on the silliness of the edict banishing women, a law the King himself finds impossible to obey; the appropriateness of the Prince's making laws or of his subjects' obeying them is uncontested. In contrast, much is done in *A Dream* to make us see Hermia's dilemma as an instance of a basic problem rather than to interest us in the merits of the individual case. The conflict between Hermia and Egeus explodes in the first scene without any prior introduction to individualize the characters. Instead of contrasting the rival suitors, the scene insists on their essential sameness in the eyes of society. No one denies Lysander's plea that he is 'as well deriv'd' and 'well possess'd' (99, 100) as Demetrius, nor does Hermia attempt to dispute the wisdom of her father's judgment by proving Lysander the better man. The problem, as all agree, is that Egeus has chosen Demetrius while Hermia has chosen Lysander. And when Hermia protests that Lysander is as worthy as Demetrius, Theseus replies:

> In himself he is;
> But in this kind, wanting your father's voice,
> The other must be held the worthier. (I.i.53–5)

The first scene, then, presents the quarrel between Hermia and her father as a conflict between an individual and the social norms and as a conflict between an inferior and a superior in a social hierarchy. In earlier comedies, the stratification of society is primarily a given rather than an issue. For example, *The Comedy of Errors* and *The Taming of the Shrew* call into question the subordination of women to men, but both Adriana's query ('Why should their liberty than ours be more?' [*CE*, II.i.10]) and Petruchio's parodic denigration of his wife ('My horse, my ox, my ass, my any thing' [*TS*, III.ii.232]) are responses to particular abuses – Antipholus' infidelities and Kate's shrewishness. Kate's subordination to Petruchio is part of the society she must come to terms with: she learns to obey her husband as she learns to appreciate civilized comforts and to control arbitrary social conventions. In *Love's Labor's Lost*, the aristocrats' scorn for their inferiors is treated as a lack of true civility, not as a problem inherent in the social order. Berowne and Costard point out that the King's edict is futile, since 'it is the manner of a man to speak to a woman' (*LLL*, I.i.209–10), but no one resents submitting to the King's authority. When Sylvia refuses to marry the man her father chooses and runs away to the woods to join her lover, her confrontation with her father is reported rather than dramatized, and we see her flight primarily in relation to the rivalry between the two gentlemen of Verona rather than to the conflict between Sylvia and her father.

A Midsummer Night's Dream, in contrast, stresses the hierarchy of power. In the opening scene, by basing his claim on the law and by appealing to Theseus for judgment, Egeus not only claims a father's power over his child but also acknowledges a citizen's subjection to Athenian laws and traditions and to his political superior. Duke Theseus lectures Hermia on her position relative to her father: 'To you your father should be as a god' (I.i.47). And he repeatedly threatens her with his legal power to force her 'Either to die the death, or to abjure / For ever the society of men' (I.i.65–6). For her part, Hermia is deferential, apologizing elaborately to Theseus for daring to speak in his presence:

> I do entreat your Grace to pardon me.
> I know not by what power I am made bold,
> Nor how it may concern my modesty,
> In such a presence here to plead my thoughts. (I.i.58–61)

She assumes too her subordination to her future husband, should she marry, announcing she will remain celibate rather than accept Demetrius, 'whose unwished yoke / My soul consents not to give sovereignty' (I.i.81–2).

Through this interplay of assertion and deference the opening scene focuses attention on the distribution of power without making it a topic of debate. Certainly Hermia is no political theorist proposing a concept of individual rights nor a proto-democrat challenging the hierarchical structure of Athenian political order. She is, nevertheless, an effective embodiment of the individual subject in two senses: she is subjected to patriarchal and political power, and she expresses the claims of individual subjectivity. She recognizes that she and her father see the world differently and accepts this difference as inevitable. Thus, while Lysander condemns his rival as 'this spotted and inconstant man' (I.i.110), Hermia makes no effort to discredit Demetrius. Her only objection to him is that he is not Lysander: she would refuse as well any other man her father chose for her. She wishes her father could see things her way – 'I would my father look'd but with my eyes' (I.i.56) – and sympathizes with anyone forced 'to choose love by another's eyes' (I.i.140), but she doesn't try to persuade either Egeus or Theseus to change his mind, assuming that since individual perceptions differ, rational argument is irrelevant. Like Hermia, Lysander makes no effort to challenge the legitimacy of Egeus' or Theseus' power. He accuses Demetrius of having made love to Helena, but he bases his 'right' (I.i.105) to Hermia on her subjective preference, arguing that not only does he equal Demetrius in terms of economic and social status, but also:

> (which is more than all these boasts can be)
> I am belov'd of beauteous Hermia. (I.i.103–4)

And he shows his confidence in the resistance of personal emotion to social force by jeering at his rival:

> You have her father's love, Demetrius,
> Let me have Hermia's; do you marry him. (I.i.93–4)

Hermia's quarrel with Egeus, then, demonstrates both the coercion inherent in the exercise of authority and the limits of such power. For her to obey her father would be not only to subject her will to his but to substitute his perception of reality for her own. Whatever her father's legal rights, however, she has the power to resist. She cannot be forced to see as her father sees or to love anyone to whom her 'soul consents not to give sovereignty.'

Even though the lovers do not dispute the legitimacy of the authority that condemns them, Egeus and Theseus are at pains to explain their position. Egeus carefully grounds his claim to power over Hermia in Athenian law. Theseus endorses Egeus' legal claim, advising Hermia that youthful perceptions should be guided by a father's mature judgment. In addition to recommending paternal authority pragmatically, he explains its theoretical basis. A father's power over his children, he tells Hermia, is analogous to a god's over his creation: 'To you your father should be as a god; / One that compos'd your beauties' (I.i.47–8). Theseus not only defends the law but he too defers to it, insisting that his judgment of the case is dictated by 'the law of Athens ... / (Which by no means we may extenuate)' (I.i.119–20). In addition to upholding specific Athenian laws and traditions, Theseus endorses society as such, counseling Hermia to consider her nature as a social being. The punishment for disobeying her father, he rules, is either 'to die the death, or to abjure / For ever the society of men.' And although he grants that there are exceptional women capable of the 'single blessedness' of a nun's life, he obviously recommends 'the society of men' over life as 'a barren sister' (I.i.65–78).

Although scene one presents individual desire and social authority as concepts for understanding the plot, these analytical categories do not correlate clearly with the dramatic action. Demetrius, for example, who bases his 'certain right' (I.i.92) to Hermia on the law, has attacked the integrity of such social contracts by violating his oath to Helena. Egeus and Theseus defend law and tradition, but they obviously use their espousal of communal values to assert their own will to power, demanding that Hermia 'fit [her] fancies to [her] father's will' (I.i.118). Egeus offers no more rational grounds for his choice of Demetrius than Hermia does for hers of Lysander, and his demand for the death of his disobedient daughter resonates discordantly with the references to his 'judgment' (I.i.57) and godlike creative power. Although Theseus defends paternal authority on biological grounds, he traces his authority over Hippolyta to physical force:

> Hippolyta, I woo'd thee with my sword,
> And won thy love doing thee injuries. (I.i.16–17)

His position is not necessarily self-contradictory, but his defense of the distribution of power on the basis of military force as well as on legal, biological, psychological, and moral grounds is too overdetermined to be convincing. His admission, moreover, that his own bride is a prize of war undermines his argument that the Athenian law governing marriage is natural, even sacred. And his later repudiation of the law in Act V confirms this hint that his posture of submission to the law which he interprets and executes is largely a matter of convenience.

Hermia and Lysander are proponents of individual perception and preference, yet their rebellion against constricting communal values consists of the substitution of one society and set of traditions for another. When they find themselves isolated by the combined force of Egeus, Demetrius, and Theseus, they take comfort in the thought that 'The course of true love never did run smooth' (I.i.134). When they find 'the sharp Athenian law' (I.i.162) cruel, they construct a law they can adhere to from the tradition of unhappy love. 'If then true lovers have been ever cross'd,' Hermia concludes their litany of the forces hostile to love,

> It stands as an edict in destiny.

> Then let us teach our trial patience,
> Because it is a customary cross,
> As due to love as thoughts and dreams and sighs,
> Wishes and tears, poor fancy's followers. (I.i.150–5)

And just as Lysander and Hermia examine what they have read or heard about love 'by tale or history' (I.i.133), Helena tries to understand her rejection by Demetrius by interpreting the traditional iconography of love:

> Love looks not with the eyes but with the mind;
> And therefore is wing'd Cupid painted blind.
> Nor hath Love's mind of any judgment taste;
> Wings, and no eyes, figure unheedy haste;
> And therefore is Love said to be a child,
> Because in choice he is so oft beguil'd. (I.i.234–9)

In a world bewilderingly transformed by love, then, the young Athenians try to get their bearings from their cultural traditions. When love alienates them from their society, they resist isolation by aligning themselves with lovers of story and history and look for reassurance even in tragedies of love. They are like the lovers in Navarre, who in 'love's grief [desire] society' (*LLL*, IV.iii.126). They have discovered, as John Donne puts it, that 'love, all love of other sights controules,' transforming a paradisal childhood home into a hell of repression, but for Hermia and Lysander, love does not make 'one little roome, an every where.' They are no Donnean lovers closing out the external world to become 'one anothers All.'[5] Lysander proposes fleeing Athens not to seek the melancholy solace Valentine finds in the 'unfrequented woods' (*TGV*, V.iv.2), but in order to reach the protection of his rich aunt, who can be counted on to treat him as her son and heir. He and Hermia leave Athens to 'seek new friends and stranger companies' (I.i.219).

The first scene of the play, then, presents intense personal feeling being contained and controlled by external social forces, but it does not pit characters representing communal values against those representing individual values. Instead, it shows each character as a site of struggle between desire for freedom and desire for the reassurances of community. Nor does the scene give the audience clear signals of how to evaluate and respond to this process. Egeus' murderous rage is restrained by Theseus, who acknowledges the joys of sexuality while advocating society's right to control it. Theseus recommends to Hermia socially sanctioned marriage over a barren celibacy and defers his own impatient desires to the solemnities of his wedding as a social occasion involving all Athens. But although he balances passion with social responsibility, his hope to transform the violence of his courtship into a communal celebration through 'pomp,' 'triumph,' and 'revelling' (I.i.19) reminds us that, while *his* desires are channeled by social conventions, *Hippolyta's* love has been compelled by his sword. His reference to his battle with the Amazons reminds us also of later events in the legend – his repudiation of his marriage to the Amazon queen and marriage to Phaedra, her love for Hippolytus, and Theseus' rash revenge on his and Hippolyta's son. Two scenes later, Oberon recalls other events in the Theseus legend – his rape of Perigenia and desertion of Ariadne, Aegles, and Antiopa. Clearly, neither the intemperate and vengeful father nor the ruler whose life is marked by perjury, lust, and violence is a totally persuasive spokesman for Athenian social order.

On the other hand, if the play does not unqualifiedly endorse the coercive power of authority in Athenian society, neither does it indicate wholehearted approval of resistance. The courageous dignity of Hermia's determination to live and die a virgin rather than submit to a husband she does not love and Lysander's witty jibe at his rival's reliance on parental coercion are attractive, but young love is presented also as irrational and self-absorbed, personally destructive and socially destabilizing. While Hermia thinks that the source of her troubles is that her father cannot see with her eyes, Helena articulates the traditional wisdom that love is blind. Of course, a strong dose of sour grapes flavors Helena's analysis of love, but plenty of evidence for her view is at hand. Her observation that 'Things base and vile, holding no quantity, / Love can transpose to form and dignity' (I.i.232–3) seems at least as plausible as Hermia's interpretation of love's transforming power:

> Before the time I did Lysander see,
> Seem'd Athens as a paradise to me;
> O then, what graces in my love do dwell,
> That he hath turn'd a heaven unto a hell! (I.i.204–7)

Helena's accusation that 'the boy Love is perjur'd every where' (I.i.241) is confirmed by Hermia's allusions to stories of love betrayed and by her jokes about broken vows as well as by Demetrius' melted oaths to Helena. Helena's declaration that, were the world hers, she would give it all away in exchange for Demetrius' love, Lysander and Hermia's actual decision to leave Athens forever, and Helena's decision to betray her friend's confidence in order to be able to spend a few hours with Demetrius – all portray romantic passion as an overpowering emotion that obliterates other loyalties and obligations. The tangled emotions of the young Athenians suggest not only that social norms mask coercion, but that adolescent romantic rivalries, uncontrolled by familial and social authority, could well have consequences intolerable to the lovers themselves as well as to the rest of society. After all, the withdrawal of Egeus' objections would not solve the problem that both Demetrius and Lysander love Hermia while no one loves Helena.

A similar play of forces animates the quarrel between Titania and Oberon. From one perspective, Titania's refusal to give up the changeling boy to Oberon, like Hermia's refusal to marry Demetrius, constitutes a flouting of established authority. Like Egeus and Theseus, Oberon responds to disobedience with power and punishment. He determines to 'torment [Titania] for this injury' and to 'make her render up her page to me' (II.i.147, 185). The punishment he devises, moreover, presupposes a conception of hierarchical order: he will make 'proud Titania' (II.i.60) dote on an inferior being: 'on lion, bear, or wolf, or bull, / On meddling monkey, or on busy ape' (II.i.180–1) – or, as it turns out, on an ass. He is ready for reconciliation with the Fairy Queen when he feels she has been sufficiently humiliated by her love for the assified Bottom and when he has successfully gained control:

> When I had at my pleasure taunted her,
> And she in mild terms begg'd my patience,
> I then did ask of her her changeling child;
> Which straight she gave me ...
> And now I have the boy, I will undo
> This hateful imperfection of her eyes. (IV.i.57–60, 62–3)

But while Oberon views Titania's defiance as a challenge to his authority to be resolved through the exercise of power, Titania looks at their quarrel in emotional rather than political terms. While he calls her 'proud' for her presumption, her epithet for him is not cruel or tyrannical but jealous (II.i.61). Oberon is jealous both in that he is possessive of Titania and in that he is envious of what she has that he has not. She claims that his accusations that she has loved Theseus 'are the forgeries of jealousy' (II.i.81), and Puck reports that

Oberon is 'passing fell and wrath' because Titania 'as her attendant hath / A lovely boy' (II.i.20–2),

> And jealous Oberon would have the child
> Knight of his train, to trace the forests wild;
> But she, perforce, withholds the loved boy,
> Crowns him with flowers, and makes him all her joy.
> (II.i.24–7)

Titania accuses Oberon of sexual jealousy and is explicit about her own, complaining that she knows all about Oberon's stealing away from fairy land to dally with 'amorous Phillida' (II.i.68) and charging that he has returned only to honor the wedding of 'the bouncing Amazon, / Your buskin'd mistress, and your warrior love' (II.i.70–1). She also talks of the changeling in terms of emotional bonds rather than of political authority. While to Oberon the object of contention is only 'a little changeling boy' (II.i.120) whom he wants to swell his train of attendants as knight or 'henchman' (II.i.121), to Titania the boy is a 'child' (II.i.122) whom she is raising out of love and loyalty to his dead mother.

From Titania's perspective the quarrel is resolved through changes in emotional attachment rather than in the re-establishment of order. Oberon, in a curious indulgence in the pathetic fallacy, interprets the dewy flowers with which Titania garlands Bottom's head as evidence of her shame and repentance:

> Her dotage now I do begin to pity ...
> For she his hairy temples then had rounded
> With coronet of fresh and fragrant flowers;
> And that same dew which sometime on the buds
> Was wont to swell like round and orient pearls,
> Stood now within the pretty flouriets' eyes,
> Like tears that did their own disgrace bewail. (IV.i.47, 51–6)

But in fact Titania gives him the changeling not because she has recognized the error of her ways but because she is totally engrossed in her love for Bottom. When Oberon applies the herbal antidote to her infatuated eyes, she, like Lysander, looks again 'with wonted sight' (III.ii.369), recoils from Bottom, and joins Oberon 'in amity' (IV.i.87), but she shows no sense of humiliation or deference to his authority.

From one angle, then, the quarrels are problems of power relations and from another, misaligned love relationships. The tensions of domination and the incompatibilities of subjectivity among both the Athenians and the fairies are brought to open conflict by the instability of material conditions, perception, and desire. Theseus has defeated the Amazons in battle, the mother of the changeling boy has died, Hermia and Helena have grown up, Demetrius has stopped loving Helena and fallen in love with Hermia. The problems these political, biological, and emotional changes have produced would not disappear with a less arbitrary or more conciliatory exercise of power by Egeus, Theseus, and Oberon or with more tractability or compliance on the part of Hermia and Titania. Because change is pandemic in *A Midsummer Night's Dream*, Hermia and Lysander do not escape their predicament by running away to the wood, and Titania does not escape hers by avoiding Oberon.

Critics have made much of the two settings of the play – Athens, the region of human society, law, and reason; the wood, the region of nature, unconstrained passion, and imagination – but these critical dichotomies are misleading. Events in the wood are a dreamlike distortion and heightening of experience in Athens rather than an alternative or complementary reality. Social norms constrain individual action in the wood as well as in Athens, while passion and imagination disrupt fixed order in both settings. If law and custom are points of reference in Athens, a standard of decorum is no less important in the wood. Puck disapproves of Lysander as a 'kill-courtesy' (II.ii.77), and Titania instructs her well-trained attendants to serve Bottom and 'do him courtesies' (III.i.174). The wood, of course, is not a city and in this sense represents the non-human world, but the language of the play, in which both Athens and the wood exist, continually blurs the line between the human and the natural. Wind, rain, moon, stars, flowers, and animals are continually personified or domesticated as human artifacts, while just as insistently the properties of the natural world are attributed to human characters. In the first scene, for example, the moon reminds Theseus of a 'dowager, / Long withering out a young man's revenue' (I.i.5–6), while to Hippolyta it is like 'a silver bow' (I.i.9) and to Lysander it is Phoebe admiring 'Her silver visage in the wat'ry glass' (I.i.210). Conversely, Theseus speaks of a married woman as a 'rose distill'd' in contrast to 'that which withering on the virgin thorn / Grows, lives, and dies in single blessedness' (I.i.76–8). Lysander speaks of the roses fading from Hermia's cheek and of human love, 'Brief as the lightning in the collied night' (I.i.145).

The commingling of the natural, the human, and the artificial is even more striking in the scenes set in the wood. Titania remembers sitting on the shore with her mortal votress watching the merchant ships:

> When we have laugh'd to see the sails conceive
> And grow big-bellied with the wanton wind;
> Which she, with pretty and with swimming gait,
> Following (her womb then rich with my young squire)
> Would imitate, and sail upon the land. (II.i.128–32)

The fairies, with their ambiguous ontological status, mediate between the natural and the human. Portrayed by human actors and capable of love affairs with humans, they are yet personifications of nature. The Fairy Queen is attended by Peaseblossom, Cobweb, Moth, and Mustardseed; 'cowslips tall her pensioners be' (II.i.10). Puck participates with equal ease in the fairy, natural, and human spheres, transforming himself into 'a filly foal,' 'a roasted crab,' or a 'three-foot stool' and playing his tricks on 'a fat and bean-fed horse' as well as on a human 'gossip' or 'wisest aunt' (II.i.45–52). Titania's account of the consequences of her quarrel with Oberon is an exposition of the interaction of the fairy, the natural, and the human. Oberon's brawls have disrupted the fairy dance, she laments,

> Therefore the winds, piping to us in vain,
> As in revenge, have suck'd up from the sea
> Contagious fogs; which, falling in the land,
> Hath every pelting river made so proud
> That they have overborne their continents. (II.i.88–92)

Nature, she explains, has reacted to the fairies' quarrel with humanlike revenge and pride and has affected human life directly:

> The ox hath therefore stretch'd his yoke in vain,
> The ploughman lost his sweat, and the green corn
> Hath rotted ere his youth attain'd a beard. (II.i.93–5)

The ox, the ploughman, and the young corn, in Titania's view, are not arranged hierarchically in a chain of being but are parallel victims of the unseasonable storms. The sequence of cause and effect moves from the human to the natural as well as from the natural to the human:

> No night is now with hymn or carol blest.
> Therefore the moon (the governess of floods),
> Pale in her anger, washes all the air,
> That rheumatic diseases do abound. (II.i.102–05)[6]

Thus, while the earlier comedies generally posit a contrast between human civilization and untamed nature, in *A Midsummer Night's Dream* the line between the human and the natural is blurred. This permeable boundary is crossed most spectacularly in Bottom's acquisition of an ass's head and in Lysander's and then Demetrius' herbally induced changes of affection, but everywhere 'nature shows art' (II.ii.104) and humans are inextricably involved in nature. The interaction of the human and the natural is figured most often in images of change. The roses fading from Hermia's cheeks, love flaring brilliantly and darkening in confusion like other 'quick bright things,' the 'wanton wind' making the sails 'conceive and grow big-bellied,' the references to a young 'changeling' – all suggest that despite attempts to analyze experience in terms of legal or political rights, human life is inescapably part of nature, and nature is always in flux. As C.L. Barber observed, the wood outside Athens is a 'region of metamorphosis, where ... things can change, merge and melt into each other.'[7] Although the first scene in Athens creates comedy and conflict out of the incommensurability of personal and social views of love, there too change is central. Egeus' power is the power to change. Thus Theseus explains to Hermia that her father is one

> To whom you are but as a form in wax,
> By him imprinted, and within his power,
> To leave the figure, or disfigure it. (I.i.48–51)

The scenes in the woods are an acceleration of rather than an antithesis to the life in Athens.

The fairies act as tutelary deities of change, altering shape at will and precipitating physical and emotional transformations at dizzying speed. Puck is an embodiment of wild, uncontrolled volatility who can 'put a girdle round about the earth / In forty minutes' (II.i.175–6) and turn himself into 'a horse ... a hound, / A hog, a headless bear, sometime a fire' (III.i.108–9). He delights in his Protean skills and in the preposterous shapes they produce. Oberon makes Titania forget her protestations of unswerving loyalty to her friend's memory and gloats in his power to change her joy in the changeling to dotage on an ass. But he is dismayed when his plan to change Demetrius' disdain into love misfires, producing a 'true love turn'd, and not a false turn'd true' (III.ii.91). Even his success in taking the changeling from Titania depends on the absurdly Pyrrhic victory of inducing his lady to love someone else. The Athenian tradesmen are yet more discomfited by the shifting shapes of the moonlit woods. Originally confident that they can transform themselves into convincing representations of anything from a raging lion to a plaster and loam wall, they flee in terror from Bottom's metamorphosis, while Puck misleads them through a wood suddenly turned strange and hostile. For the young lovers, change is most often painful. Already in the first scene the changes of love have subjected Hermia and Lysander to repression by social authority, Demetrius and Helena to rejection by the object of their affections, and tempted Helena to betray her friend's secret. In the woods their problems multiply chaotically.[8] Lysander's and then Demetrius' change of heart transforms friendship and love into treachery, bitter rivalry, humiliation, and violence.

In their bewilderment, Hermia and Helena look for stability in the continuities of unitary identity and in familiar social codes. When Helena follows Demetrius into the forest, she believes that her pursuit is futile ('bootless speed, / When cowardice pursues and valor flies' [II.i.233-4]) and unnatural (women 'should be woo'd, and were not made to woo' [II.i.242]). But she overturns conventional order deliberately: 'the story shall be chang'd: / Apollo flies, and Daphne holds the chase' (II.i.230-1), and she claims that subjective perceptions constitute reality for her: 'It is not night when I do see your face' (II.i.221); 'I'll follow thee and make a heaven of hell' (II.i.243). As the emotions around her take unexpected shapes, however, Helena increasingly tries to find steady footing on the firm ground of commonly perceived reality. When Lysander incredibly declares his love, even her rejection by Demetrius becomes somehow reassuring – painful but familiar, and she insists on its incontrovertible reality:

> Is't not enough, is't not enough, young man,
> That I did never, no, nor never can,
> Deserve a sweet look from Demetrius' eye,
> But you must flout my insufficiency? (II.ii.125-8)

She reproves Lysander, 'I thought you lord of more true gentleness' (II.ii.132), and reminds Hermia of their 'school-days friendship' (III.ii.202). When her friend seems to betray their 'ancient love' and 'to join with men' (III.ii.215-16) in mocking her, she finds an explanation in their common past: 'O, when she is angry, she is keen and shrewd! / She was a vixen when she went to school' (III.ii.323-4). Helena, who defied convention, lectures her tormentors for failures of civility and courtesy. That she is wrong about a conspiracy of mockery is a further indication of her inability to assimilate change.

Hermia accepts the suggestion that Lysander's declarations of love to Helena are merely jokes because she too clings to a familiar constellation of relationships and to a sense of stable identities: 'Am not I Hermia? Are not you Lysander? / I am as fair now as I was erewhile' (III.ii.273-4). When Lysander showers her with insults – 'Hang off, thou cat, thou bur! Vile thing, let loose' (III.ii.260), the mildness of her reply – 'What change is this, / Sweet love?' (262-3) – is a measure of the difficulty of integrating unexpected evidence into her perception of the real. When she tries to grasp the possibility that Lysander rejects her in earnest, she resorts to the same hypothesis her father had proposed for her inexplicable love for Lysander. Just as Egeus accused Lysander of having 'stol'n the impression of [Hermia's] fantasy' and of having 'filch'd [her] heart' (I.i.32, 36), so Hermia calls Helena a 'thief of love,' who has 'stol'n my love's heart from him' (III.ii.283-4).

Since the women remain constant in love, Lysander and Demetrius need to cope only with their own fickleness. They are notably less bewildered than the women, but no less determined to make sense of astonishing change by applying familiar categories of thought. Lysander solemnly explains his abrupt turnabout as the ineluctable operation of reason:

> The will of man is by his reason sway'd;
> And reason says you are the worthier maid.
> Things growing are not ripe until their season,
> So I, being young, till now ripe not to reason;
> And touching now the point of human skill,
> Reason becomes the marshal to my will. (II.ii.115-20)

Demetrius, with equal absurdity, finds in his capriciousness a pattern of natural consistency. His love for Hermia seems to him a temporary aberration, 'an idle gaud, / Which in my childhood I did dote upon' (IV.i.167-8) and his love for Helena 'my natural taste' (IV.i.174).

The Athenians' attempts to resist and rationalize the changes that overwhelm them indicate that their need for certainty and trust is as persistent as their subjectivities are inescapable, but the standards of decorum, legality, and rationality they invoke offer them as little stability in the wood as they did in Duke Theseus' court. If the play's movement towards a comic *telos* guarantees they will not come to permanent harm, it is not because morally enlightening experience cures them of individual sins and follies and produces reliable steadfastness. Rather, it is change that resolves the confusions it has created. The transformations of fairy magic deprive Titania of her loved boy, disrupt the tradesmen's rehearsal, and further complicate the already tangled love lives of the aristocrats, but they also reconcile Titania and Oberon, restore Bottom to his friends, and return Demetrius' love to Helena and Lysander's to Hermia. The satisfactions of these returns, of course, would be impossible without some continuity. Bottom's 'mortal grossness' proves too intractable for Titania's efforts to transform him so that he can 'like an aery spirit go' (III.i.160–1). He returns to Athens essentially unchanged, ready to play his part on cue. Helena and Hermia remain constant in love, despite their lovers' fickleness. Like all narratives, the plot of *A Dream* requires some degree of continuity, but in its representation of experience, change is the only sure thing. When Puck is reprimanded for anointing the eyes of the wrong Athenian, he invokes an external power in a way similar to Hermia's explanation of her problems as due to 'an edict in destiny.' To Oberon's complaint that his mistake has turned true love false, Puck replies:

> Then fate o'errules, that one man holding troth,
> A million fail, confounding oath on oath. (III.ii.92–3)

While Hermia reasons that love's trial teaches patience because 'it is a customary cross' (I.i.153) and Puck uses fate to excuse the proliferation of infidelity, they both find a principle of instability and transience in the action of fate.

Events in the wood near Athens represent not only a Heraclitan world of perpetual change but also the achievement of permanence through change. Since by Act III both Lysander and Demetrius have promised eternal love to both Hermia and Helena, only by confounding oath on oath can Oberon sort out the lovers and send them back to Athens in couples 'whose date till death shall never end' (III.ii.373). Lysander and Titania, who have changed their loves through the operation of love-in-idleness, are also susceptible to the remedy that restores their delight in former loves, so that finally, in Puck's proleptic summary, 'Jack shall have Jill; / Nought shall go ill' (III.ii.461–2).

These pairings fulfill a prescribed pattern, but although the characters find true love by 'turning to themselves at length againe' through their various transformations, the harmony reached through change in *A Dream* is too contingent to constitute a Spenserian vision of dilation resting steadfastly on 'pillours of Eternity.'[9] The arrest of the giddy changes of love at the moment when Demetrius is charmed by Cupid's flower and Lysander and Titania are freed from error by Dian's bud is too arbitrary to figure as the providential working out of the perfection of their being. For the play's happy ending, the necessary complement to the capacity for change is Oberon's intervention. Although the wood offers no asylum from the changes and chances of mortal life, it is in the intersection of the fairy and the mortal worlds that the problems are resolved. Although the fairies often are interpreted as symbolic projections of the human characters' internal qualities, surely they function primarily as beings of a similar but distinct kind whose activities and emotions overlap without coinciding totally with human behavior. They dance, hunt, and quarrel; they feel love, jealousy, and anger. But they can travel faster than the wind and become invisible at will. 'Mortal,' their epithet for people, suggests that they themselves are immune to death. Still, they must confine their activities to the hours between sunset and sunrise. They have a king and queen, but how closely their political and familial structures duplicate human arrangements is unclear. Are Oberon and Titania married? Are there priests and marriages in fairyland? Are there fairy babies or only stolen human children? We do know that they are 'spirits of another sort' (III.ii.388) whose alien perceptions condition their interference in human affairs. To Puck, one Athenian looks much like another, and what to Hermia is 'humane modesty' (II.ii.57) to him is a churlish violation of courtesy. But while Puck's unfamiliarity with Athenian social norms creates error, the detachment of Oberon's alien status allows him to intervene effectively as Theseus cannot.

The fairies, of course, are not the only distinct group; Bottom and his friends make up another group, whose scenes broaden the scope of Athenian culture. While *The Comedy of Errors* and *The Taming of the Shrew* focus on family relationships among characters of middling social status and *The Two Gentlemen of Verona* and *Love's Labor's Lost* on the lives and loves of aristocrats, *A Midsummer Night's Dream* represents a diversified social fabric. Admittedly, *Love's Labor's Lost*, with its cast of characters including a king and his courtiers, a curate, a forester, and an agricultural laborer, presents a fuller range of social levels, but it emphasizes the dominant elite culture. In contrast, the artisans of *A Dream* are neither adjuncts nor parallels to the aristocrats; they have their own distinctive interests and activities and their own plot. The play certainly does not give a realistic or detailed version of plebeian culture. The working men are characterized largely by their ignorance – their malapropisms, naïve misconceptions of dramatic illusion, ridiculous solicitude for the sensibilities of gentle ladies, and garbling of a dramatic text. Their lack of upper-class culture is associated with their status as working men. Puck is contemptuous of them as 'rude mechanicals, / That work for bread' (III.ii.9–10), and to Philostrate they are 'Hard-handed men that work in Athens here, / Which never labor'd in their minds till now' (V.i.72–3). These attitudes are demonstrably limited, but it is true that the working men show little interest in the love-in-idleness so irresistible to the leisured class. And it is Bottom's imperviousness to Titania's charms as well as her subsequent loathing of his 'mortal grossness' that make possible the reconciliation of Titania and Oberon and the successful production of *Pyramus and Thisby*. What I am arguing, in short, is that *A Dream* not only creates continuity through change, it creates unity through diversity. While the three plots and three groups of characters are separate, they also intersect, and these junctures of unlikes are necessary for the final harmony. The apparently unreconcilable quarrels among the Athenians and the fairies are settled not by clarification of the issues that produced them but by the interference and distraction of others.

Modern students of the English Renaissance sometimes assume that a monolithic culture, unified through uniformity of beliefs and values, was, if not a reality, at least an almost universal ideal. In fact, emphasis on the desirable heterogeneity of society was commonplace. La Primaudaye's *French Academie*, for example, defines a 'citie or civill company' as 'nothing else but a multitude of men unlike in estates or conditions, which communicate togither in one place their artes, occupations, workes and exercises, that they may live the better ... Of such a dissimilitude an harmonicall agreement ariseth by due proportion of one towards another in their divers orders & estates, even as the harmonie in musicke consisteth of unequall voyces or sounds agreeing equally togither.'[10] In *A Midsummer Night's Dream*, distinct groups pursuing their own objectives, influenced by distinct values, largely unaware of each other's existence, yet operating within the same sphere of time and place and interacting occasionally and crucially, enact such an agreement arising out of dissimilitude. Social harmony is achieved not by the triumph of passionate youth over oppressive age nor by the vindication of established hierarchy and the exorcism of disobedience but by unequal voices agreeing together. The social hierarchy disrupted in the first scene is reasserted in the denouement: Theseus assumes control and the young lovers defer to him. But it is the fact that Demetrius has been brought to see differently that has turned hatred and jealousy into 'gentle concord' (IV.i.143). Oberon's machinations and Theseus' blessing contribute, but the existence of diversity rather than the benevolence of authority makes possible the consensual marriages that constitute the happy ending.

In addition, while Theseus' authoritative voice is necessary to legitimize these marriages, his overruling of Egeus implicitly acknowledges that his power rests ultimately on the cooperation of those he governs.[11] When Hermia and Lysander are pitted against Egeus and Demetrius, Theseus cannot resolve the conflict and defers to the law, but when the lovers have reached a mutually satisfying arrangement, he casually dismisses Egeus' demand for the law. His authoritative voice is a recognition of a *fait accompli*, an articulation of the lovers' desires. The emergence of harmony from discord thus requires mutuality as well as diversity. As La Primaudaye makes the point 'every common-wealth well appointed and ordred ... consisting of many and sundry subjects, is maintained by their unity, being brought to be of one consent and wil, and to communicate their works, artes and exercises together for common benefit and profit.'[12] On the one hand, social harmony depends not on establishing truth but on differing perceptions: what matters is not the objective merits of Hermia and Helena but that Lysander and Demetrius love different women. On the other hand, a sense of community requires a shared perception of reality. As Theseus observes, love, like lunacy and poetry, results from the unverifiable perceptions of individual imagination, but, as Hippolyta reminds him, because the lovers all give the same account of their experience, their testimony represents more than the perception of an individual imagination: their story 'grows to something of great constancy' (v.i.26). Hippolyta's reference to constancy, often cited as an intuitive faith in the lovers' fidelity, taken literally, demonstrates faith in numbers.[13] Bottom's story, which cannot be corroborated, remains untold and inaccessible to the community at large, but the coincidence of the lovers' perceptions increases the probability of truth, or at least of a socially usable version of reality. The resolution of the courtship plot, then, does not endorse established authority: Theseus merely ratifies the arrangement the lovers have made. Nor does it constitute a triumph of individual subjectivity: his ratification is contingent on 'all their minds [being] transfigur'd so together' (v.i.24).

The performance of *The most lamentable comedy and most cruel death of Pyramus and Thisby* demonstrates the dynamics of a unified society in which 'sundry subjects ... communicate their works, artes and exercises together for common benefit.' As Stephen Orgel and others have taught us, such courtly interludes celebrate the established power structure,[14] and indeed, throughout the play the activities of Peter Quince and his fellows are directed towards the noble wedding. Unlike the amateur theatrical in *Love's Labor's Lost*, Peter Quince's production is a success because Duke Theseus magnanimously accepts it as an offering of 'simpleness and duty' (v.i.83) and because the audience's wit at the actors' expense consists of *sotte voce* jokes to each other rather than jibes intended to humiliate the actors. But although the characters gathered to celebrate the multiple weddings are animated by mutual goodwill and a common purpose, the barriers between groups remain. The actors of Pyramus' 'tedious brief scene' (v.i.56) retain their composure while those in the Pageant of the Worthies lose theirs, not simply because their audience is kinder but because they are protected by their incomprehension of sophisticated discourse. Bottom interprets literally and responds condescendingly to the ironic remarks he hears. The aristocratic audience is similarly limited. They show no grasp of the relevance to their own lives of the drama of tragic love. Theseus is incapable of imagining that Bottom, the workingman whom he patronizes so graciously, also has been loved by the Fairy Queen. Nor does he understand that the motives of love and duty he attributes to the tradesmen are actually subordinate to financial ambition. By honoring the Duke they hope to prosper, and by trying to prosper they honor the Duke. The wall that divides Pyramus and Thisby and courteously produces a chink for them to talk through is thus an apt image for the cultural differences between Athenians.

The barrier that separates also joins and can allow limited communication.

The performance in the last scene epitomizes the strategy used throughout the play. Just as the spectators who critically watch the play-within-the-play constitute a spectacle that the theater audience watches critically, so the text continually invites critical scrutiny of the social hierarchy and cultural traditions that its comic structure endorses. Finally, the audience, who have been in the position of privileged spectators aware of all the secret workings of fairy magic beyond the characters' comprehension, is reminded by Puck's epilogue both that their experience has been totally dependent on the efforts of the figures on stage and that as audience they have the power to judge. That is, the theatrical experience, like other social experiences, consists of sundry subjects communicating together.

CHAPTER SEVEN

Deserving and Diversity in *The Merchant of Venice*

'the best deserving a fair lady' (I.ii.118)

Like *A Midsummer Night's Dream*, *The Merchant of Venice* blends the foreign with the familiar in two distinct settings that at once invite and resist thematic oppositions between reason and imagination, law and love. Both plays include a diverse assortment of characters — a stage-struck weaver and a Jewish usurer as well as marriageable aristocrats with their families and servants. In both, changes in personal and social relationships cause and resolve conflict. But the two plays present radically different versions of social change. In *A Dream* the characters' happiness and the audience's satisfaction come from the achievement of stability despite subjective differences and inconstancy, while in *The Merchant* the happy ending depends on the accomplishment of change despite the conservative resistance of old loyalties and the rigidities of law. Here the heterogeneity of society is an intractable problem rather than a means of resolution, and desired change is unavoidably painful.

As the title suggests, *The Merchant of Venice* has a contemporary setting. While classical myth and English folklore distance *A Midsummer Night's Dream* in time and space, Antonio and Shylock live in an immediately recognizable sixteenth-century European city. Venice was a favorite stop for English travelers on the continent in the late sixteenth century and figured prominently in contemporary political and historical discussions as a powerful republic and a wealthy center of trade. Merchants, money-lenders, rich heiresses, and impecunious gentlemen were noticeable figures in London life as well as stock types in drama. The casket test is a stylized representation of the actual constraints on the marriage choices of economically privileged women in sixteenth-century Europe. This is not to deny the exotic glamour of Venice or the fairy-tale quality of Belmont. *The Merchant of Venice* is no more naturalistic and probably less topical than other Shakespearean comedies. But while the elemental, legendary setting and characters of *A Dream* suggest enduring patterns in human experience, the marriage of Portia and Bassanio and the financial arrangements among Shylock, Antonio, and Bassanio seem contingent on conditions in a particular time and place. *The Merchant* directs attention to problems arising from the shifting diversity of social customs and values rather than to constants in human history.

The opening scene sounds the play's key note of warm affection and happy excitement tinged with sadness. Friends meet, respond attentively to each other, and plan to meet again. Antonio's ready willingness to help Bassanio, Bassanio's gratitude, the efforts of Antonio's friends to cure his melancholy, and even the jokes about Gratiano's empty-headed nattering portray Venetian society as genial and generous. Images of Antonio's spice-laden argosies braving perilous seas and of the rich and beautiful Portia drawing suitors from the four corners of the world create an atmosphere of opulence and adventure. Bassanio's eagerness to begin his quest for Portia's golden fleece and Antonio's confidence that the trust and friendship he commands in Venice will enable him to help his friend point optimistically to the future. Yet a tone of apprehension runs through this present happiness and future expectations. In addition to Antonio's inexplicable sadness, the anxieties as well as the wealth of overseas trade are evoked by Salerio's and Solanio's fantasies about Antonio's fleet. Even Bassanio's confidence is not unqualified: he admits the possibility that his venture will fail and that he will return to Venice still encumbered with debt. Unlike *The Two Gentlemen of Verona* and *Love's Labor's Lost*, which also begin with young men confidently planning their futures, the first scene of *The Merchant* dramatizes no conflicts of interest or point of view, but it does portray awareness that actions once initiated might bring unpredictable and uncontrollable consequences.

The first Belmont scene displays a similar blend of optimism and apprehension. The dominant note is happy anticipation. Portia wishes and expects to marry and welcomes the news of Bassanio's imminent arrival. But a muted dissonance is produced not only by her complaints about the harshness of her father's will but also by the repugnance she feels for her suitors. Although Bassanio referred to her 'Renowned suitors' blown in 'from every coast' (I.i.168-9) as evidence of her worth, the object of their suits fears and loathes them. The announcement of their departure, Nerissa's faith that the casket lottery can insure that Portia will marry a man she loves, and Portia's agreement with the description of Bassanio as 'deserving a fair lady' (I.ii.118-19) all point towards a happy union of hero and heroine. Still, the scene ends not with Bassanio's arrival but with that of yet another suitor, the Prince of Morocco, and with Portia's troubled response: 'If he have the condition of a saint, and the complexion of a devil, I had rather he should shrive me than wive me' (129-31).

Portia's disdain for her suitors marks another feature common to Venice and Belmont. Both are scenes of busy activity and change, and in both there is conscious emphasis on human diversity. Shakespeare exploits the comic possibilities of sameness in the plights of the Dromio and Antipholus twins, in the deception of old Vincentio, and in the embarrassment of Puck and of the would-be lovers in Navarre. Such mistakes and substitutions are unimaginable in *The Merchant*. Portia and Nerissa can disguise themselves as Balthasar and his clerk but could not conceivably be mistaken for each other. Nor can we imagine Bassanio and Antonio or Bassanio and Lorenzo as rivals for the same woman. The characters are distinctive to the audience and to each other; in addition, they are fascinated by human diversity and show a marked propensity to analyze and evaluate manners and temperaments. In Venice, for example, Solanio observes that 'Nature hath fram'd strange fellows in her time' and marvels at:

> Some that will evermore peep through their eyes,
> And laugh like parrots at a bagpiper;
> And other of such vinegar aspect
> That they'll not show their teeth in way of smile
> Though Nestor swear the jest be laughable. (I.i.51-6)

Similarly, Gratiano contrasts his own happy, hedonistic self with 'a sort of men whose visages / Do cream and mantle like a standing pond, / And do a willful stillness entertain' (88-90). Portia's portrait of the Count Palentine – 'He hears merry tales and smiles not. I fear he will prove the weeping philosopher when he grows old, being so full of unmannerly sadness in his youth' (I.ii.47-50) – recalls Solanio's account of men of 'vinegar aspect' and Gratiano's rhetorical query: 'Why should a man, whose blood is warm within, / Sit like his grandsire cut in alablaster?' (I.i.83–4). Although Portia is similarly disdainful, her extended flight of wit is less reductive than the Venetians' antithesis of gravity and cheerfulness. She is as repelled by the mercurial changeableness of the Frenchman as by the 'unmannerly sadness' of the Palentine and by the Neapolitan's obsession with horses as well as by the German's drunkenness. Her devastating description of the Frenchman acutely diagnoses the lack of personal integrity in a man of relentless sociability: 'why, he hath a horse better than the Neapolitan's, a better bad habit of frowning than the Count Palentine; he is every man in no man. If a throstle sing, he falls straight a-cap'ring. He will fence with his own shadow. If I should marry him, I should marry twenty husbands' (I.ii.58–63).

Portia also suggests a more thoughtful explanation for such vagaries of human behavior. To Solanio they are totally arbitrary and inexplicable:

> let us say you are sad
> Because you are not merry; and 'twere as easy
> For you to laugh and leap, and say you are merry
> Because you are not sad. (I.i.47–50)

Gratiano claims to 'play the fool' (I.i.79) deliberately. He interprets solemnity as a strategy adopted consciously 'With purpose to be dress'd in an opinion / Of wisdom, gravity, profound conceit,' and he assumes a tone of moral outrage towards those who angle for 'this fool gudgeon, this opinion' (I.i.91–2, 102). In contrast, Portia associates the shortcomings of her unsuitable suitors with differences in nationality. The suitors are introduced by such geographical labels as 'the Neapolitan prince' (I.ii.39), 'the French lord' (I.ii.54), and 'the young German' (I.ii.84). Her portrait of the Scottish lord is a resumé of political-military relations among Scotland, England, and France. Her sketches of the shallow, capricious Frenchman, the affected English traveler, and the drunken German are drawn from the stock of national stereotypes. Compare, for example, the 'Men of France, changeable Camelions' and 'spungie hydroptique Dutch' in John Donne's elegy 'On his Mistres.' In spite of her shrewd common sense and moral insight, Portia's mockery betrays xenophobic hostility to foreigners.

Portia herself is aware of something less than admirable in her attitudes, apologizing 'I know it is a sin to be a mocker, but ...' (I.ii.57–8). Still, her expression of sexual revulsion from the

Moroccan prince does not prejudge his moral and spiritual qualities. In fact, her antipathy towards strangers relates primarily to the value she places on verbal exchange. She contemptuously dismisses the Neapolitan 'for he doth nothing but talk of his horse' (I.ii.40–1), the Count Palentine who 'doth nothing but frown' (I.ii.46), and the Englishman, who speaks 'neither Latin, French, nor Italian' (I.ii.69–70) while she lacks English: 'He is a proper man's picture, but alas, who can converse with a dumb show?' (I.ii.72–3). Portia's attitude recalls Montaigne's endorsement of an old saw: '*We are better in the company of a knowne dogge, than in a mans societie, whose speach is unknowne to us ... A stranger to a stranger is not like a man.*'[1] Portia values communication and understands the significance of a common culture and of the habits of thought encoded in language. Her rejection of her unwanted suitors combines appreciation of the complexity of communication with racism and with reluctance to be kind to people whom she does not recognize as her kind of people.

In short, the exposition of *The Merchant of Venice* introduces a busy, exciting world of variety and change where people look forward eagerly to a future of yet greater wealth and pleasure. At the same time, it insists that this generally enviable world is not perfect. Decisive action risks loss and failure. Great wealth does not produce personal freedom but comes attached with strings of gratitude and duty. A richly diverse cosmopolitan community contains tensions and antipathies. The most admirable people find it easier 'to know what were good to do' (I.ii.12–13) than to do it.

All the lines of action in *The Merchant* grow from the characters' desires to establish new social identities. Launcelot Gobbo wants to become Bassanio's servant rather than Shylock's. Bassanio does not leave Venice impelled by passion like the lovers who flee Athens nor in search of adventure like the young gentlemen from Verona who go to Milan or the young gentlemen from Verona and Florence who arrive in Padua. Bassanio goes to Belmont with the clear objective of transforming himself from a debt-ridden prodigal into a rich married man. Portia and Jessica also want to marry, and while they certainly marry for love, they and the play as a whole put considerable emphasis on marriage as a transformation of their positions in the social order. Jessica will become a Christian wife in a Christian commonwealth instead of the daughter of an alien Jew. Portia's rights and responsibilities will be defined by her position as her husband's wife rather than her father's daughter. For her, the crucial question is which husband she will have, not how she feels towards Bassanio.

In general, external obstacles to the changes desired are overcome quite easily; the problems attracting the interest of characters and audience are internal and moral. Launcelot Gobbo illustrates this focus most explicitly. He treats his desire to change masters as a case of conscience: 'To be rul'd by my conscience, I should stay with the Jew my master, who (God bless the mark) is a kind of devil; and to run away from the Jew, I should be rul'd by the fiend, who, saving your reverence, is the devil himself ... my conscience is but a kind of hard conscience, to offer to counsel me to stay with the Jew. The fiend gives the more friendly counsel: I will run ... (II.ii.22–31). Launcelot Gobbo's decision highlights decisions elsewhere in the play by both likeness and difference. His decision to run away from Shylock proves unnecessary because it turns out that Shylock has already recommended him to Bassanio. Similarly, the external obstacles anticipated by Portia and Bassanio are easily overcome. Bassanio's aspirations are frustrated by lack of money, a problem Antonio gladly solves for him. Portia chafes at the restrictions of her father's will, but, as it turns out, those procedures select the very suitor she herself has chosen. More troublesome for Portia and Bassanio, as for Launcelot, are the moral implications of their actions. While the lovers in *A Dream* think of the crosses true love has to bear as accidents of fate (differences in rank or age, coercion of guardians, loss due to war or sickness), Portia and Bassanio struggle with internal doubts. In this respect, Launcelot stands as a contrast. While he decides to act against his conscience, Portia decides to do what she thinks right. Admittedly, Portia's pledge of fidelity to her father's will comes as a reprimand of an unfavored suitor's hope of winning her some easier way: 'If I live to be as old as Sibylla, I will die as chaste as Diana, unless I be obtain'd by the manner of my father's will' (I.ii.106–8). In fact, remaining unmarried is not a likely option under the terms of her father's will, and Portia pointedly does not resoundingly proclaim how readily she will marry whomever the lottery selects. Still, she *does* administer the lottery and promise to marry Arragon or Morocco if either should choose correctly. And she resists the temptation to teach Bassanio how 'to choose right' (III.ii.11).

Bassanio too makes morally significant choices. First, he has decided to borrow once again from Antonio, and then, when Antonio is driven to borrow from Shylock, he decides to rely on his friend in these new circumstances. Portia and Bassanio do not represent their mental processes as medieval moralities with the devil on one side and conscience on the other as Launcelot Gobbo does, but their decisions have obviously involved internal debate. Portia confesses that she 'can easier teach twenty what were good to be done, than to be one of the twenty to follow mine own teaching' (I.ii.15–17). In his first interview with Antonio, Bassanio is so insistent on acknowledging his indebtedness and on justifying the 'pure innocence' (I.i.145) of his new scheme for recouping his financial losses that he tries Antonio's patience and allows us to infer that deciding to ask his friend for help yet once more has cost him some struggle. After Shylock proposes the bond of flesh, Bassanio's misgivings become explicit: 'You shall not seal to such a bond for me, / I'll rather dwell in my necessity' (I.iii.154–5).

Such misgivings and their impact on existing relationships problematize the proposed changes in allegiance. Bassanio is open to the charge of financial exploitation for his mercenary motives in marrying Portia and for asking Antonio to finance a project that eventually will cost him first place in Bassanio's affections. Even Antonio has been scrutinized as a middle-aged and middle-class merchant buying the friendship of a young aristocrat. For example, while acknowledging that lending money to friends without interest was accepted practice in early seventeenth-century England as well as in the Venice of the play, Ralph Berry comments, 'That is one way of putting it. Another is to say that by lending out money gratis, one makes the recipient one's friend.'[2] And finally, of course, the most disturbing change is Jessica's decision to leave her Jewish father in order to marry her Christian lover, an action that has provoked considerable critical outrage, from Sir Arthur Quiller-Couch's opinion that she is 'bad and disloyal, unfilial, a thief; frivolous, greedy, without any more conscience than a cat and without even a cat's redeeming love of home'[3] to Sigurd Burckhardt's more temperate but essentially similar judgment that Jessica and Lorenzo are 'lawless,' 'spendthrift,' 'thoughtless' and 'aimless.'[4]

In spite of the moral indignation of modern critics, I want to argue that the changes proposed and pursued in these early scenes are presented as desirable as well as desired, welcomed by the community and promising personal happiness for the characters involved. Bassanio's and Portia's mutual interest and the sympathy and support with which their friends respond to their hopes lead us to look forward to their eventual union. Launcelot Gobbo's change of masters seems happy enough. He is motivated by crassly materialistic concerns (better food, more luxurious livery) and succumbs to what he interprets as satanic temptation, but in the event, the change satisfies everyone. Shylock is apparently as glad to be rid of his servant as Gobbo is to be gone. Jessica's flight from Shylock's joyless house draws on classical and Elizabethan comic conventions that pit rebellious children against miserly fathers and on romance traditions that elicit approval for daughters who disobey repressive fathers for love.[5] Her romantic elopement with Lorenzo, their association with images of light and music, and their participation in the harmonies of Belmont are signals for audience acceptance and approval.[6]

Nevertheless, Jessica's elopement is explicitly problematized. Like Launcelot Gobbo, she decides to desert Shylock despite feelings of guilt:

> Alack, what heinous sin is it in me
> To be ashamed to be my father's child!
> But though I am a daughter to his blood,
> I am not to his manners. O Lorenzo,
> If thou keep promise, I shall end this strife,
> Become a Christian and thy loving wife. (II.iii.16–21)

But while Launcelot Gobbo simplistically reduces his moral dilemma to the temptation of change versus the moral imperative of the *status quo* ('"Bouge," says the fiend. "Bouge not," says my conscience' [II.ii.19–20]), Jessica examines and then rejects the moral claims of inherited loyalty. Launcelot's decision to follow the devil instead of his conscience shows him as morally irresponsible, a characterization borne out by his subsequent behavior in Belmont, where he is accused of having to answer to the commonwealth for getting a woman pregnant. The gratuitous cruelty of his deception of his old, blind father followed immediately by an almost instinctual demand for his father's blessing epitomizes his combination of theoretical adherence to traditional morality and behavioral self-indulgence. In contrast, Jessica embraces a morality of manners rather than of blood. While Launcelot earns the condemnation of the commonwealth, Jessica's rejection of her father's cruelty eventually wins her society's protection.

Launcelot Gobbo's unreflective adherence to old mental habits is expressed as superstition and makes him an appropriate antagonist for Jessica, who opts for change. His reaction to getting what he wants from Bassanio, for example, is an exultant exercise in palmistry: 'Go to, here's a simple line of life! Here's small trifle of wives! Alas, fifteen wives is nothing! Aleven widows and nine maids is a simple coming-in for one man. And then to scape drowning thrice, and to be in peril of my life with the edge of a feather-bed, here are simple scapes' (II.ii.160–5). Shylock's fortune-telling – 'There is some ill a-brewing towards my rest, / For I did dream of money-bags tonight' (II.v.17–18) – elicits more dream analysis from Launcelot: 'I will not say you shall see a masque, but if you do, then it was not for nothing that my nose fell a-bleeding on Black Monday last at six a' clock i' th' morning' (II.v.22–6). The clown's parody suggests both his cynicism and his association with Shylock's way of thinking. Similarly, when Launcelot tells Jessica that she is damned because 'the sins of the father are to be laid upon the children' (III.v.1–2), his taunts both echo and parody Shylock's claim that she is his 'flesh and blood' and 'damn'd' (III.i.34, 31) for rebelling against him. Against the clown's and her father's deterministic insistence on biology's unalterable power, Jessica asserts the power of love: 'I shall be sav'd by my husband, he hath made me a Christian!' (III.v.19–20). This is not to argue that Jessica's elopement allegorizes the transition from the Old Dispensation of Judaism to the New Dispensation of Christianity. She has had no Pauline spiritual awakening on the road to the Rialto and leaves her father to follow Lorenzo not Christ. In choosing Lorenzo and Christianity she chooses community rather than isolation.

In Shakespeare's version of mercantile Venice, no one's motives are purely spiritual or altruistic. Typically they mix generosity with self-interest. We need not see Antonio as a sycophantic social climber to recognize that he wants and expects love and gratitude in return for his love and generosity. More forthrightly, Portia freely gives all she has to Bassanio and demands love and fidelity in return. 'There is no such thing as an interest free loan,' as Ralph Berry observes,[7] but that observation should not issue in contempt or cynicism. Transactions of giving and receiving, including financial ones, are the glue holding Venetian society together.[8] Jessica is distinguished from the other inhabitants of Venice and Belmont not because she is more selfish or irresponsible than they, but because she is more sensitive to the pain and loss even longed-for changes bring. Portia suffers anxiously while Bassanio deliberates over the three caskets, but she has no sympathy for the unfortunate Princes of Morocco and Arragon. Bassanio is oblivious to the possibility that his plans could cause Antonio grief. Launcelot Gobbo gives no thought to what effect his departure would have on Shylock or on Jessica. From his callous treatment of his father we can safely infer that he would not care if such thoughts did occur to him. Jessica, on the other hand, is acutely aware that her decision will cost her and her father pain and irrevocable loss. Her only scene with Shylock ends poignantly: 'Farewell, and if my fortune be not cross'd, / I have a father, you a daughter, lost' (II.v.56–7).[9]

A primary function of the Jessica plot is to demonstrate the loss inherent even in positive change. The other characters face less difficult moral dilemmas than Jessica's, but they all have to pay a price for the changes they initiate. In order to court Portia, Bassanio must overcome his misgivings about borrowing from Antonio. Antonio must 'break a custom' (I.iii.64) and become indebted to Shylock in order to finance Bassanio. Portia must sacrifice her independence in order to marry. 'But now,' she reminds Bassanio,

> I was the lord
> Of this fair mansion, master of my servants,
> Queen o'er myself; and even now, but now,
> This house, these servants, and this same myself
> Are yours – my lord's! (III.ii.167–71)

Portia gives up her independence happily, and happily gives all she has to Bassanio, but she is fully conscious that he is 'dear bought' (III.ii.313).

Bassanio proves that he is worth the price she pays by choosing the right casket. As critical commentary has amply shown, the richly ambiguous casket riddle demonstrates Bassanio's moral and emotional insight: his distrust of 'outward shows' (III.ii.73) and his understanding of the generosity and courage love demands. Primarily, I think, it shows his clear-sighted understanding of the world he lives in. For all his excited talk to his friends about being Jason in quest of the golden fleece, Bassanio knows that he does not live in a golden age of heroism but in an age of lead. Silver reminds him of money, the 'common drudge / 'Tween man and man' (III.ii.103–4) in Venetian commerce, and gold symbolizes all the subterfuges, deceptions, and sophistries used in these 'cunning times' (III.ii.100) to mask corruption, ignorance, vice, and ugliness. Meditating on what he knows about his own world rather than on the enigmatic messages on the caskets, Bassanio avoids the naïveté of the Prince of

Morocco, who reasons that gold is the only appropriate setting for a jewel as highly and as generally valued as Portia. Nor does Bassanio practice the kind of denial which the more knowing Prince of Arragon slips into. Arragon deplores the fact that 'estates, degrees, and offices' are 'deriv'd corruptly' and not 'purchas'd by the merit of the wearer' and scorns the 'fool multitude' for trusting outward 'show'; nevertheless, he believes that he will win Portia because he deserves her (II.ix.19–52). Morocco and Arragon are not characterized as evil men. In a universe of perfect justice or in a play exhibiting strict poetic justice, they would not fare as badly as they do in Belmont, where their expectations of perfect conjunction between worth and reward doom them to sterile isolation. When Nerissa and Portia agree that of all possible mates Bassanio is 'the best deserving a fair lady' (I.ii.118–19), the audience accepts their judgment because Portia favors him and also because Bassanio understands that his desert is relative and contingent on Portia's preference. He does not expect a utopian world where things are as they seem to be or where reward exactly corresponds with merit. Nor does he react to his far-from-perfect situation with whatever resignation, cynicism, or cowardice causes Portia's first group of suitors to withdraw from the contest. In full awareness of the dangers and treacheries of the 'cunning times' he lives in, he chooses the lead casket which threatens rather than promises and so accepts the challenge to 'give and hazard all he hath' (II.vii.9) in hope of something better.

Every change exacts its price in Belmont as well as in Venice, then, but *The Merchant* opts for change in spite of anxiety and loss. It implies that it is preferable to be Jessica, who risks everything in abandoning her security as a rich man's daughter while knowing that her happiness depends on her lover's keeping faith, than it is to be Shylock, who determinedly avoids risk and contingency and stubbornly proclaims, 'There is no power in the tongue of man / To alter me' (IV.i.241–2). Thus when Portia inventories her total worth for Bassanio, she rates most highly her capacity and willingness to change:

> But the full sum of me
> Is sum of something; which, to term in gross,
> Is an unlesson'd girl, unschool'd, unpractic'd,
> Happy in this, she is not yet so old
> But she may learn; happier than this,
> She is not bred so dull but she can learn;

Happiest of all, is that her gentle spirit
Commits itself to yours to be directed. (III.ii.157–64)

The changes undertaken by individual characters have far-reaching effects for better and for worse. Portia's marriage to Bassanio, Nerissa's to Gratiano, and Jessica's to Lorenzo not only extend the network of relationships that constitute their community but also complicate already existing patterns in the web, affecting old loyalties as well as creating new ones. The most obvious example of the interconnections among personal relationships is the marriage of Nerissa and Gratiano, which is contingent on the marriage of Portia and Bassanio. Both Nerissa and Gratiano stipulate that they will marry only if Portia and Bassanio do. But if old loyalties thus control new ones, conversely the new relationship of Portia and Bassanio creates another for their friends. More complicated, of course, is Bassanio's impact on Antonio. Bassanio's desire to court Portia activates his friendship with Antonio, enabling Antonio to show his willingness to help. This desire in turn forges a new link between Antonio and Shylock and even brings into play Shylock's friendship with Tubal, from whom Shylock says he will get the money needed.

These reverberations rippling out from individual acts make up the dramatic action. While *A Midsummer's Night's Dream* comprises distinct groups of characters largely unaware of each other's existence, in *The Merchant* characters continually comment on and react in response to each other's movements. Although it is customary to refer to the casket plot, the bond plot, and the Jessica/Lorenzo subplot as separable units, what is most striking is how tightly these lines of action are woven together. Instead of having independent, parallel development, the plots cross and recross, connecting causally.

In both comedies, multiple plots create a sense of social diversity, but the nature of the character groups and of their interrelationships is very different in the two plays. As we have seen, *A Dream* includes characters of separate modes of existence: fairies, working-class artisans, mythic heroes, and aristocrats. With the exception that Theseus and Hippolyta inhabit the same sphere as the aristocrats, each group is distinct, and movement from one sphere to another produces incongruity and confusion. In *The Merchant*, distinctions are less clear and movement more fluid. The Christian and Jewish communities normally do not eat or drink together, but they talk and do business. Lorenzo and Jessica can fall in love without the inherent absurdity of Bottom and Titania. Shylock's world differs sharply from Portia's, but characters travel easily between them. The contrast between Venice and Belmont is not between a world of love and a world of money: people fall in love in Venice, while Belmont figures as a source of wealth. Nor is the proposed distinction between the capitalism of Venice and the land-based wealth of Belmont helpful, since we don't know how Portia's father made his money.[10] Rather, the economic contrast is between financial risk and inherited wealth, two stages in a continuous process, the acquisition of money and the benefits and anxieties it confers.

This similarity and mobility among character groupings are fundamental to the plot structure. While in *A Midsummer Night's Dream* each group has its own story, crossing other story lines only at crucial, isolated points, in *The Merchant* each plot involves the conjunction of distinct groups. Oberon, for example, acts as a catalyst in scrambling and unscrambling the Athenians' love lives, and Bottom enables the reconciliation of Oberon and Titania. But Bottom and Theseus are detached, unmoved by their participation in what are essentially other characters' stories. *The Merchant*, in contrast, functions through connections and confrontations. Each plot is a negotiation between groups: the casket plot and the ring plot between inhabitants of Venice and of Belmont; the Launcelot Gobbo, the Jessica/Lorenzo, and the bond plots between Christians and Jews.

As this description suggests, the similarities that allow constant interaction between Venice and Belmont and between Christians and Jews are counterpointed against differences that create misunderstanding and conflict. Indeed, similarities that facilitate access can dangerously mask significant differences. A common language, for example, impedes understanding between Shylock and the Christian Venetians. When Shylock, musing about Antonio's financial solvency, observes that 'Antonio is a good man' (I.iii.12), Bassanio is offended by what he interprets as a questioning of his friend's moral probity. Conversely, not only do Shylock and the Christians use the same words for different referents, they also use different words for the same phenomenon. The practice that Shylock praises as 'thrift' Antonio condemns as 'interest' (I.iii.50–1), and the biblical story that Shylock cites to illustrate human thrift, Antonio interprets as 'a venture ... sway'd and fashion'd by the hand of heaven' (I.iii.91–3).[11] The language, occupation, and religious heritage they share, then, provoke misunderstanding and animosity.

The emergence of disruptive differences within sameness is not confined to the conflict between Antonio and Shylock but runs throughout the play. Portia's objection to her unsuccessful suitors is basically their foreignness, while Bassanio's major attraction is the fact that he is Venetian. Not only does Portia like those whom she sees as like herself, she also sees as like herself those whom she likes. For example, when she first hears about Antonio, she assumes the traditional wisdom that *similitudo mater amoris* and concludes that Bassanio and Antonio are alike, and both much like her:

> in companions
> That do converse and waste the time together,
> Whose souls do bear an egall yoke of love,
> There must be needs a like proportion
> Of lineaments, of manners, and of spirit;
> Which makes me think that this Antonio,
> Being the bosom lover of my lord,
> Must needs be like my lord. If it be so,
> How little is the cost I have bestowed
> In purchasing the semblance of my soul,
> From out the state of hellish cruelty. (III.iv.11–21)

But when she comes to Venice, Portia must recognize that her 'soul' (Bassanio) and her soul's 'semblance' (Antonio) do not noticeably resemble her or each other.[12]

While Bassanio proved that he was Portia's most deserving suitor by not presuming his own absolute worth or hers, by demonstrating his shrewd appraisal of the pitfalls of contemporary society, and by nevertheless risking his future for the chance of joy, Antonio shows neither such humility nor such hopefulness during his trial. Undoubtedly dignified and courageous, Antonio is also self-denigrating and hopeless. He rejects Bassanio's rather ebullient offer to die in his place by claiming to be 'a tainted wether of the flock, / Meetest for death' (IV.i.114–15). And he answers Balthasar/Portia's request for his last words with a despairing assessment of life in general, offering Bassanio the consolation that:

> herein Fortune shows herself more kind
> Than is her custom. It is still her use

To let the wretched man outlive his wealth,
To view with hollow eye and wrinkled brow
An age of poverty; from which ling'ring penance
Of such misery doth she cut me off. (IV.i.267-72)

Loving and generous, probably beyond Bassanio's capability, Antonio is also demanding and self-aggrandizing. 'You cannot better be employ'd,' he advises Bassanio, 'Than to live still and write mine epitaph' (IV.i.117-18). He needlessly reminds his friend that 'I am fall'n to this for you' (IV.i.266) and equates his willingness to die with his desire for Bassanio to suffer his loss: 'Repent but you that you shall lose your friend, / And he repents not that he pays your debt' (IV.i.278-9). And most consequentially, of course, he competes with Portia in love for Bassanio:

Tell her the process of Antonio's end,
Say how I lov'd you, speak me fair in death;
And when the tale is told, bid her be judge
Whether Bassanio had not once a love. (IV.i.274-7)

In a world of flux, chance, and contingency, Antonio pursues an absolute of devotion through self-sacrifice.

If Bassanio's old friend turns out not to have quite the lineaments, manners, and spirit Portia expects, Bassanio in Venice also proves less like herself than she supposed in Belmont. Whereas Portia resisted the temptation to cheat in administering her father's will, Bassanio justifies bending the law of the commonwealth to save Antonio, urging Balthasar/Portia to 'do a little wrong' in order to 'do a great right' (IV.i.216). Portia has assumed that marriage to Bassanio constitutes a union of their social, economic, emotional, and spiritual lives. It has converted Portia herself and all she has to Bassanio and simultaneously given her the right to Bassanio's love and the authority to enforce that right. His parting with the ring symbolizing their love will be her 'vantage to exclaim on' him (III.ii.174). Their union, she tells Bassanio, has made her 'half yourself' and entitled her to 'the half of any thing' (III.ii.248-9) significantly concerning him. In the trial scene, when Bassanio announces that nothing is more important to him than Antonio and that he would sacrifice his wife as well as his own life in order to save his friend, his understanding of Portia's position in his life is clearly very different from hers. In addition, by complying with entreaties to give up the ring, he shows that he is not quite the 'constant man' (III.ii.247) Portia has supposed.

Portia is not alone in discovering difference where she expected sameness. The Christians generally are eager to assume the unifying bonds of shared values and manners. If their friendly welcome of Jessica exemplifies the virtue of this attitude, their response to Shylock demonstrates its dangers. Antonio's hatred of Shylock's business practices and his trust of the bizarre terms offered for a loan both stem from incomprehension of Shylock's otherness. Because he cannot understand Shylock's defense of lending money for interest as anything but hypocritical sophistry, he misses completely the genuine indignation and anger in the Jew's protests at the humiliation he endures.[13] Because he cannot understand that Shylock has no desire to be part of the Christian community, he accepts the offer of friendship at face value. Assuming that gentle deeds signify gentile leanings, he speculates that 'The Hebrew will turn Christian, he grows kind' (I.iii.178).

One way in which Shylock *does* resemble the Christians is his failure to respect the otherness of other people. Most notably, of course, he assumes that Jessica shares his disdain for Christian manners and customs, that 'the sound of shallow fopp'ry' (II.v.35) offends his daughter's ears as it does his own. Later, his bewildered cry, 'My own flesh and blood to rebel!' (III.i.34), conflates the anguish of love and trust betrayed with parental refusal to acknowledge a child's separateness. Salerio is right, though not admirable in motive or manner, when he tells Shylock that 'it is the complexion of them all to leave the dam' and that there is 'difference between thy flesh and hers' (III.i.29–30, 39–40). In addition, Shylock's understanding of a strange code of business ethics is probably just as limited as Antonio's. Shylock's references to Antonio's 'low simplicity' (I.iii.43) and 'Christian cur'sy' (III.i.49) should be heard, I think, not as Iago-like contempt for innocent virtue but as ironic acknowledgment of what he interprets as the sanctimonious pose by which Antonio masks his real aim, Shylock's financial ruin.

I disagree, then, with those critics who see *The Merchant* resolving difference into sameness as the Christians are revealed as essentially like the Jews they revile.[14] Admittedly, all the characters share some attributes. Christians and Jews alike will bleed if they are cut; in Venice and Belmont alike emotional bonds are construed in financial terms and financial transactions in emotional terms. But more significant, I think, is the gradual revelation of crucial differences within expected sameness. Misunderstandings born of unsuspected differences in perspective and value complicate transactions not only between Christians and Jews but also between men and women and parents and children. Thus, in rough outline, the multiple plots in *The Merchant* operate as a mirror image of those in *A Midsummer Night's Dream*. While in *A Dream* the crossing of plot lines initially complicates and then resolves conflict, in *The Merchant* the opposite is true. While the bond between Antonio and Shylock makes possible Bassanio's courtship and thus his marriage to Portia, it subsequently forces postponement of the marriage's consummation and precipitates the imbroglio over Portia's ring. Bassanio's success in the casket plot brings Portia to Venice to resolve the bond plot, but that process precipitates unexpected complications in the relationships among Bassanio, Antonio, and Portia. Most telling, perhaps, is the degree of misunderstanding complicating the impact of the Jessica/Lorenzo plot on Shylock. His daughter's rejection of him and of his religion for marriage with a Christian intensifies Shylock's hatred of Antonio, who 'hates our sacred nation' (I.iii.48). Furthermore, the clear implication is that Shylock's hatred is exacerbated by his conviction that Antonio was complicit in Jessica's flight. While the circumstances of the elopement are never made clear, Salerio reports that when Shylock and the Duke arrived too late to search Bassanio's ship, Antonio assured them that the run-aways were not on board. Solanio, who has witnessed Shylock's fury at the loss of his daughter and his ducats, replies to Salerio's account of the search: 'Let good Antonio look he keep his day, / Or he shall pay for this' (II.viii.25–6). Yet when Salerio and Solanio meet Shylock, they smugly gloat about their foreknowledge of Jessica's flight and joke about Shylock's loss, apparently oblivious that they are encouraging him to believe that the Christians who begged his help and put themselves in his power meanwhile have been plotting against him.

In *A Midsummer Night's Dream*, mutual incomprehension produces comic incongruity while yoking together without violence the heterogeneous characters who congregate in Duke Theseus' court in the last act. In *The Merchant of Venice*, misunderstanding produces smug contempt and rancorous animosity. Jokes – like Launcelot Gobbo's trick on his father, Solanio's and Gratiano's jibes at Shylock, and Shylock's 'merry sport' (I.iii.145) – often turn ugly.

Animosities fuelled by cultural differences and changed circumstances bring the dramatic action to a crisis. Bassanio's courtship and marriage, Jessica's elopement, the shipwreck of Antonio's fleet, and the hostility between Antonio and Shylock together result in Antonio's trial. Differences not only have helped to create the threat to Antonio, they also frustrate efforts to save him, for conflicting values within the Christian community make his friends temporarily helpless. In *A Midsummer Night's Dream*, Duke Theseus can overrule Egeus' demand for the strict enforcement of the law because the community is unified. But the Duke of Venice cannot so easily brush aside Shylock's demand for justice because the cosmopolitan diversity of Venice as a center of trade precludes such unanimity. The Christians all want to save Antonio, but Christians like Antonio, the Duke, and Portia also want to uphold the rule of law. In a sense, the solution to the problem also comes from diversity. While the men of Venice can see no alternative to either acquiescing in Shylock's murderous revenge or subverting the law, Portia, a woman bringing a fresh perspective from Belmont, breaks through the impasse. She does so by making distinctions, not by confounding them, and by promoting change, not by preserving stasis.

When the news that Antonio has forfeited his bond reaches Belmont, Jessica warns that 'If law, authority, and power deny not, / It will go hard with poor Antonio' (III.ii.289-90). Her prediction is accurate: since Shylock is inflexible, the case must be settled by the state. Although first Solanio and then Bassanio suggest turning political authority against the law, and even the Duke threatens to use his power to dismiss the court, Shylock, Antonio, and Portia agree that the law, authority, and power of Venice must speak as one. Antonio explains:

> The Duke cannot deny the course of law;
> For the commodity that strangers have
> With us in Venice, if it be denied,
> Will much impeach the justice of the state,
> Since that the trade and profit of the city
> Consisteth of all nations. (III.iii.26-31)

And Portia, acting as judge, confirms Antonio's opinion: 'there is no power in Venice / Can alter a decree established' (IV.i.218-19). Economic power, political authority, and law univocally support Shylock's demand for justice.[15]

Although critics have seen Portia's role in the trial scene variously as an allegorical representation of mercy, of justice, and of a reconciliation of the two, her procedure is more closely analogous to that of the casuist who guides the conscience in applying divine law to particular human actions with precision. After failing to persuade Shylock to be merciful, Portia proceeds in the context of civil rather than divine law, but her method is very close to the intricate logic and fine distinctions of casuistry.[16] In judging the case against Antonio, she does not subordinate law to political authority, nor does she mitigate the harshness of the law in the name of mercy. Instead, she interprets the Venetian law of contracts according to the casuistical maxims that a law binds according to its 'intent and purpose' (IV.i.247) and that circumstances alter cases. In the particular circumstances of Antonio's bond, she rules that Shylock is entitled to the pound of flesh specified in the bond but not to spill a drop of his victim's blood. Thus she forces Shylock to confront the difference between a forfeit of hard cash and one of living flesh. By showing that Shylock is using the law as a means to murder, Portia demonstrates that the laws governing contracts do not exist in a legal or social vacuum. Shylock as well as Antonio is answerable to the law, and Venice has laws protecting the lives of its citizens.

The distaste for Portia's subtle casuistry among many recent critics is, I believe, just that: post-enlightenment separation of moral sentiment from intellect with consequent aversion to intricate moral reasoning. H.D. Kittsteiner argues that behind the modern rejection of casuistry lies a new understanding of conscience which he illustrates by quoting thinkers influential in shaping modern consciousness.[17] According to Rousseau, for example, conscience is a reliable moral guide, and 'it is only when we haggle with conscience that we have recourse to the subtleties of argument.' And to Adam Smith, 'books of casuistry ... are generally as useless as they are commonly tiresome.' The intricacies of casuistry are futile attempts 'to direct by precise rules what it belongs to feeling and sentiment only to judge of.'

In contrast to this dichotomy between the complex processes of the intellect and the immediate judgment of a conscience rooted in moral feeling, the conception of conscience dominant in late sixteenth-century Europe was as a part of the practical intellect, at once moral and intellectual and directed towards the judgment of specific cases, a procedure requiring considerable hermeneutic and logical skill. The power that Portia uses to mediate between the harsh Venetian law and Antonio's individual plight is precisely this ability to apply general laws with acute discrimination to the unique circumstances of a specific case. By distinguishing justice from mercy, flesh from gold, and citizen from alien, she transforms Shylock's vindictive triumph into defeat. As readers and audience, we need similar powers of discrimination. We should notice that the Duke's rescinding of the death penalty exhibits 'the difference of [his] spirit' (IV.i.368) from Gratiano's vindictiveness as well as from Shylock's. When Shylock's threat that Antonio's flesh 'Is dearly bought as mine, and I will have it' (IV.i.100) echoes Portia's 'Since you are dear bought, I will love you dear' (III.ii.313), we should notice not only that both Shylock and Portia use their wealth to get what they want, but also that, while Shylock uses his entitlement to justify revenge, Portia uses hers to motivate love. Similarly, we should distinguish Bassanio's willingness to temporize by doing a little wrong from Portia's timely and beneficent rereading of Venetian law.

After dealing with the immediate crisis, Portia acts next to stabilize her marriage by teaching Bassanio his new obligations: that is, she assures his constancy by changing him. Bassanio's decision to value Antonio's love and the 'deservings' (IV.i.450) of his rescuer over his own vow to Portia shows that he has not yet understood his new role. By setting up a choice between Bassanio's promise to her and his gratitude to his friend, Portia forces Bassanio to compare and to discriminate between friendship and marriage. As she explains to Nerissa:

> The crow doth sing as sweetly as the lark
> When neither is attended; and I think
> The nightingale, if she should sing by day
> When every goose is cackling, would be thought
> No better a musician than the wren. (V.i.102–6)[18]

Bassanio needs to learn to distinguish among the confusing and conflicting claims on his attention.

By means of the ring trick, Portia teaches him to subordinate his old loyalty to his new one. More significantly, she teaches that marriage involves trust and obligation as well as emotional sincerity and generosity. As Nerissa explains, the point is not the value of the rings and not even the love they symbolize, but 'your vehement oaths' (V.i.155). The vows that Nerissa, Gratiano, Portia, and Bassanio have taken are not contingent on their personal feelings, so the pedagogic device that Portia uses is appropriately the threat of her own inconstancy. The passage by Hannah Arendt that W.H.

Auden uses as an epigraph for his discussion of *The Merchant* is the best gloss on the ring episode that I have seen: 'The remedy for unpredictability, for the chaotic uncertainty of the future, is contained in the faculty to make and keep promises.' The necessary complement to Bassanio's renewed promise, of course, is Portia's forgiveness: 'The possible redemption from the predicament of irreversibility – of being unable to undo what one has done – is the faculty of forgiving ... Both faculties depend upon plurality, on the presence and acting of others, for no man can forgive himself and no one can be bound by a promise made only to himself.'[19] Portia's and Nerissa's forgiveness, Bassanio's and Gratiano's new vows, and Antonio's guarantee of Bassanio's vow bind them together in a social group on new terms that acknowledge difference as well as sameness. Directed by Portia, the characters achieve unity through diversity and stability through change.

But discordant notes still sound in the *discordia concors* Portia orchestrates in the last two acts. All three marriages create problems as well as satisfying desires and entail loss as well as gain. If Portia's success in both saving Antonio's life and persuading him to ratify her priority in Bassanio's life demonstrates the human capacity to adjust to changing circumstances, Shylock's resistance just as conclusively demonstrates human intractability, both Shylock's and the Christians'. The history of readers, directors, actors, and audiences who have emphasized the pathos of Shylock's condition at the play's end indicates that the action does not resolve in a satisfying image of justice. This sense of unease results partly from the fact that Shylock's villainy is reactive: evil does not originate in him as it does in villains like Don John and Duke Frederick. He does not initiate a plot against Antonio but reacts to the request for a loan, his earlier treatment by Antonio, Jessica's desertion, and the shipwreck of Antonio's fleet. He chooses to persecute Antonio and refuses to be merciful, but he has been driven, tempted, set up. And Shylock's fate is not an anomaly. Throughout the play, the interconnections among the characters and the contingency of events produce undeserved suffering as unpredictably as undeserved benefits.

More disturbing to recent audiences than a sense that the harshness of Shylock's punishment is incommensurate with his crime are the motives behind it and the form it takes – Christian vindictiveness and Shylock's forced conversion. The charge of vindictiveness is inaccurate, I think. Although Gratiano's cruel gloating at Shylock's ruin is certainly ugly, the Christians who impose sentence on Shylock use their power with restraint and clearly want and expect him to feel relief at the mercy they extend to him. Portia's insistence on what the law requires and Gratiano's sadistic delight in Shylock's suffering throw into relief the mercy actually and voluntarily given. The Duke spares Shylock's life before he is asked and proposes reducing the confiscation of half Shylock's estate to a fine. Antonio transforms the compensation Shylock owes him into a trust for his daughter. That is, the Christians essentially force Shylock to do what he ought to do voluntarily: provide for his daughter.[20]

The most distasteful and puzzling part of Antonio's proposal is the stipulation that Shylock become a Christian. It doesn't do to explain away this coercion on the grounds of cultural relativism, arguing that Shylock is being given a chance to save his immortal soul. Forcible conversion is unlikely to have struck Elizabethan audiences as a probable path to salvation. Sixty years later Englishmen hoped to hasten the millennium by inviting Jews to return to England and then converting them, but even then they did not expect to accomplish the conversion of the Jews through legislative or judicial fiat.[21] The best that can be said for this part of Shylock's sentence is that it assumes that Shylock the Jew is assimilable. Although the play perpetuates traditional stereotypes by portraying a usurious, vengeful Jew,[22] it presents Shylock's avarice and malice as socially constructed not as racially determined, a matter of manners not of blood. As Richard Marienstras explains, indiscriminately lumping together as excluded Others such widely different groups as madmen, women, and Jews oversimplifies Elizabethan conceptions of social hierarchy: 'just as important as the social or symbolic placing was the period of time for which one was assigned to it ... The levels of hope and despair in each case varied according to whether they were determined by time or by place.'[23] For example, temporality is essential to Edward Coke's classification of foreigners as friendly foreigners, temporary enemies, enemies with safe-conducts, or perpetual enemies. The exclusions of the first three groups were relative and limited in time. The category of perpetual enemy, which comprised Jews, Turks, heretics, and pagans, was based on nature not on status. Like Launcelot Gobbo, who rejects Jessica's conversion and sees Shylock as 'the devil himself' (II.ii.26-7), Coke 'presumes not that they will be converted ... for between them, as with the devils, whose subjects they be, and the Christian, there is perpetual hostility.'[24] Portia's position is closer to that taken by William Salkeld at the end of the seventeenth century: 'Turks and infidels are not *perpetui inimici*, nor is there a particular enmity between them and us ... for though there be a difference between our religion and theirs ... they are the creatures of God and of the same kind that we are.'[25] Portia's demand for Shylock's conversion assumes a kind of Erastian identification of church and state that demands outward conformity but permits a wide variety of religious beliefs. It integrates Shylock into Venetian society so that he no longer will be vulnerable as an unassimilated alien but leaves his inward beliefs unexamined. This attempt to secure social and political unity through religious uniformity is not far from Elizabeth I's religious policy,[26] and the play as a whole prefers Portia's attitude to the virulent anti-Semitism of such characters as Launcelot Gobbo and Gratiano. Nevertheless, the violence inherent in forcing people's consciences was becoming increasingly evident in the 1590s, and Shylock's enforced conversion foregrounds rather than submerges the hypocrisy and coercion implicit in compulsory conformity. At the least, Portia's demand defines the limits of the Venetians' acceptance of diversity. Some members of the play's first audiences probably would have accepted it as prudent for both Shylock and the state. Others probably would have found it repugnant.

The conclusion of *The Merchant of Venice* roughly conforms in spirit and form to the traditional requirements of comic closure. Young lovers are united and their marriages ratified by society. The danger of physical violence is averted, and economic resources are transferred from the older to the younger generation. The rigidities of law and convention have been made to accommodate the forces of change and vitality. But the fit to comic convention is not exact. Portia's lady-in-waiting marries Gratiano not Antonio, who, though he does not *quite* lose his friend or his life or his fortune, gains nothing. Jessica and Shylock are not reconciled. The happiness and stability achieved, moreover, have been reached by means of threats and coercion. These factors do not ironize the happy ending by implying that to a discerning audience it is not *really* happy. The play does not postpone love and contentment to a metadramatic future possibility as *Love's Labor's Lost* does, and it does not frame happiness as an achievement of art and fantasy as *The Taming of the Shrew* does. But the happy ending is not so much a transcendent union of justice and mercy and of love and law as a precarious balance that is neither perfect justice nor perfect love. Still, it is enough to content the imperfect characters in their quotidian lives. They have intimations of celestial harmony, but as Lorenzo tells Jessica, 'Such harmony is in immortal souls, / But whilst this muddy vesture of decay / Doth grossly close it in, we cannot hear it' (v.i.63–5). In a society of genuinely shared values, the play suggests, there would be marriages of true minds and universal charity with no need for vows, contracts, and laws enforced by the power of the state. In Venice and Belmont, mercy sometimes seasons justice, but the price for diversity and change is conflict and coercion.

Part Four

Court and Country

CHAPTER EIGHT

Pastoral and Parody in *The Merry Wives of Windsor*

'melodious birds sing madrigals' (III.i.18)

In *The Merry Wives of Windsor* and *Much Ado About Nothing* the sources of conflict are not so much the misunderstandings and antagonisms inevitably produced by changing circumstances within diversified communities as attempts by outsiders to exert control over local communities. Falstaff and his men Bardolph, Pistol, and Nym not only try to help themselves to the women and the wealth of Windsor but also provoke and complicate pre-existing familial and amatory tensions. Don Pedro and his entourage similarly disturb the equilibrium of Messina, setting off events that culminate in Hero's disgrace in the church on her wedding-day. As Sherman Hawkins has demonstrated, single settings and plots turning on the intrusion of outsiders link these two plays with *The Comedy of Errors*, *The Taming of the Shrew*, *Love's Labor's Lost*, and *Twelfth Night* and separate them from what Northrop Frye calls the green world comedies, in which the protagonists move from one place to another.[1] But while the strangers who appear in Ephesus and Illyria arrive as shipwreck victims needing protection from human society, Falstaff and Don Pedro arrive in Windsor and Messina respectively with claims for recognition and deference. The visitors in *The Taming of the Shrew* and *Love's Labor's Lost* likewise have abundant resources but do not claim the privileges within the local communities that Falstaff expects as due to his social rank and that Don Pedro assumes as due to his political position. Also, in the earlier plays, the visitors' impacts are benign. Petruchio brings to Padua a refreshing breath of irreverence that rescues the natives from the frustrating restrictions of their own culture. The Princess is a voice of sanity in Navarre; she and the ladies of France free the King of Navarre and his courtiers from the narrow constraints of their own preciosity. In comparison, Falstaff and Don Pedro are troublemakers. Eventually, of course, the events they set in motion end well – Master Ford repents of his jealousy and both Beatrice and Hero find appropriate mates. But these happy endings result not from the introduction of more sane or wholesome values but from the cohesion of the local community and its resistance to external pressures exerted by outsiders claiming superiority.

Although *The Merry Wives of Windsor* is often seen as generically different from the other comedies, an anomalous excursion into satiric city comedy, I am arguing that it gives local habitation and names to material dealt with throughout Shakespearean comedy. Certainly, the middle-class milieu, the several intrigue plots, and Nym's penchant for the word 'humor' show the influence of Jonsonian satire. But none of the comedies is generically pure; all weave intrigue and satire with strands of romance and lyricism. Possibly the dismissal of this play stems partly from critics' inability to accept middle-aged, middle-class women as heroines in a plot of sexual intrigue. Both critics who are delighted and those who are offended by Portia's machinations often see Mistress Ford and Mistress Page as inherently ridiculous. At any rate, both *The Comedy of Errors* and *The Taming of the Shrew* portray marital dissension in middle-class milieus, and *The Merchant of Venice* places similar emphasis on defeating the disrupter of social harmony. Like the other comedies, *The Merry Wives* explores social interaction within a specific human community. Its setting is rural rather than urban. Windsor is a small country town, and its inhabitants include a parson, a doctor, and an inn-keeper, but no artisans like Dekker's Simon Eyre or professional rogues and schemers like Jonson's Face and Subtle. In the final scene the characters plan to celebrate the restoration of social harmony by laughing together around 'a country fire' (V.v.242).

The play's thematic opposition between courtly sophistication and country honesty has been widely recognized,[2] but we should notice also that the threat to Windsor's social harmony is not so much the enticements of courtly splendor per se as the more insidious temptation to doubt the worth of the local and familiar. The citizens of Windsor need not simply to close ranks against an outsider but to renew their faith in themselves and their own. While the restoration of Master Ford's belief in his wife's fidelity is the most elaborately worked out instance, the quarrel between Parson Evans and Doctor Caius provides a clear paradigm of this pattern.

Sir Hugh Evans, the Welsh parson, tries to arrange Master Slender's marriage to Anne Page and in the process offends another of Anne's suitors, Doctor Caius, the French physician, who challenges him to a duel. Act III finds Parson Evans waiting, with considerable trepidation, to answer the challenge: 'Jeshu pless my soul! how full of chollors I am and trempling of mind! I shall be glad if he have deceiv'd me. How melancholies I am! I will knog his urinals about his knave's costard when I have good opportunities for the ork. Pless my soul!' (III.i.11–16). Suddenly, in the course of expressing his malevolence and apprehension, he breaks into song:

'To shallow rivers, to whose falls
Melodious birds sings madrigals;
There will we make our peds of roses,
And a thousand fragrant posies.
To shallow – ' (III.i.17–21)

The delivery of a familiar text in Evans' comic Welsh accent compounds the incongruities inherent in the situation of a clergyman preparing to fight a duel of honor over his role as go-between in a romantic intrigue. Moreover, as Ronald Huebert has pointed out, the Marlowe quotation not only reminds us of Evans' incongruous position but also parodies the conventions of the pastoral love song that were becoming literary clichés by the late 1590s.[3] In the robustly middle-class world of Shakespeare's Windsor, the delicate beauty of Marlowe's poem seems absurdly out of place.

Nevertheless, while the singer and his song may appear ridiculous, Evans' choice of musical texts is less incongruous than critics have allowed. Indeed, the lines he quotes are apt and illuminating both for his immediate situation and for the comic world he inhabits. In a time of anxiety and anticipated danger Evans recalls Marlowe's pastoral lyric not because his thoughts have turned to love but because he longs for the world of peace and safety Marlowe evokes. To Evans, this pastoral ideal of human and natural harmony seems poignantly inaccessible, and he breaks off, exclaiming that he feels as much like crying as singing. When he resumes his song, he interpolates a more melancholy line of pastoral poetry:

> Mercy on me! I have a great dispositions to cry.
> 'Melodious birds sing madrigals –
> When as I sat in Pabylon –
> And a thousand vagram posies.
> To shallow, etc.' (III.i.22–6)

He interjects into Marlowe's love poem a line from Psalm 137, which in a similar metrical version begins:

> When as we sate in Babilon,
>   the rivers round about,
> and in remembraunce of Sion,
>   the tears for griefe burst out:
> We hangd our harpes and instruments,
>   the willow trees upon:
> for in that place men for their use,
>   had planted many one.[4]

Clearly, Psalm 137 intrudes into Evans' memory because it combines the pastoral imagery of river, trees, and music with the direct expression of grief and with elegiac longing for an idealized harmonious community.[5] Like most people, he turns to pastoralism when the stress and complexity of the world are too much for him and he yearns for the peace and innocence of a better world. Parson Evans might even hear in the words of the psalm a warning against contamination by worldly manners and mores.[6]

The most delightful irony implicit in Evans' evocation of the pastoral tradition is the fact that he is in the midst of that harmonious world without knowing it. Specifically, he is in no danger from Doctor Caius' sword. The genial host of the Garter, who has no intention of losing either his doctor or his priest, has misdirected the would-be adversaries to opposite sides of town in order to avoid bloodshed. More generally, the Windsor of Shakespeare's comedy is a community of human and natural harmony where rural virtue triumphs over courtly sophistication. Sir Hugh's quotations signal that the pastoral, along with Plautine comedy, medieval farce, Italian novelle, and English city comedy, is among the generic antecedents of the play's comic form.

The Windsor of *The Merry Wives* is admittedly an unlikely *locus amoenus*. Sir John Falstaff attempts to seduce Mistress Page and Mistress Ford in a busy village, not the fields of Arcady or the forest of Arden. The disreputable knight and those respectable matrons and their families, not lovesick shepherds and innocent nymphs, are at the center of the dramatic action. Still, while Windsor does not provide a wholly natural contrast to urban artificiality, the green world is all around and easily accessible. The basic staples of pastoral landscape are ready to hand: fields with birds, woods with deer, a flowing river, and even an ancient oak all play notable parts in the action and serve the traditional function of bringing sophistication, ambition, and greed to terms with natural simplicity.

For all of Falstaff's natural exuberance, his designs on the deer and the women of Windsor constitute an attack by the civilized vices of greed and pride on bucolic contentment. In Act I, when he is accused by Shallow of beating his men and killing his deer, Falstaff arrogantly admits the charges, brags that he has also kissed the keeper's daughter and broken Slender's head, and taunts Shallow that he would make a laughingstock of himself by his threatened complaint to the Council. Falstaff's attempt to seduce Mistress Page and Mistress Ford originates in greed and is nurtured by vanity, but his greed and arrogance are treated less as individual sins than as the vices of aristocratic culture. The fat knight's social rank is his primary weapon of seduction and makes him confident of success. He woos Ford's wife by flattering her that nature intended her for a more exalted social sphere: 'Thou wouldst make an absolute courtier, and the firm fixture of thy foot would give an excellent motion to thy gait in a semicircled farthingale' (III.iii.62–4), and he has no doubts that he can 'predominate over the peasant,' her husband (II.ii.282). Mistress Ford understands Falstaff's proposals as a temptation to ambition, confiding to her friend that 'if it were not for one trifling respect, I could come to such honor! ... If I would but go to hell for an eternal moment or so, I could be knighted' (II.i.44–5, 49–50).

While Sir John and his followers clearly exhibit the vices of civilization, the denizens of Windsor may seem too concerned with economic advantage and social status and too busy with schemes of matchmaking and revenge to illustrate the contrasting pastoral virtues of humility and contentment. For example, the play opens with Shallow's indignant assertions of the dignity of his social rank and family lineage. Economic considerations, moreover, determine both Master and Mistress Page's choice of husband for their daughter, Mistress Page supporting Doctor Caius, who has money and powerful friends at court, and Master Page favoring Slender, who has land and three hundred pounds a year. Even Fenton, Anne's own choice, admits that he was first attracted to her by her father's wealth. In addition, Falstaff's aggression against the gamekeeper is echoed in Shallow's repeated boasting of the combative prowess of his youth, in Doctor Caius' challenge to Evans, and in the beating Ford administers to the supposed old woman of Brainford. The citizens of Windsor have even been accused of sharing Falstaff's gluttony, exhibiting inordinate appetites for food and drink.

In short, the inhabitants of Windsor share with Falstaff and his followers the capacity for acquisitiveness, pride, and aggression. And that similarity, I think, is just the point. Desires for food, drink, sex, money, and prestige are as basic to life in Windsor as to life in the most worldly and self-indulgent urban or courtly society, but in the simple rural community they are held in check. The citizens of Windsor are conscious of distinctions of social rank but are fundamentally unimpressed by them. The merry wives are immune to the temptation of a knightly lover. Justice Shallow is asserting his right to respect in spite of Falstaff's superior rank when he blusters, 'If he were twenty Sir John Falstaffs, he shall not abuse Robert Shallow, esquire' (I.i.2–4). Although Anne's parents prudently want to ensure their daughter's social and economic position through her marriage, they are not socially ambitious and do not want an aristocratic son-in-law who would marry her 'but as a property' (III.iv.10) to repair his own depleted fortune. Essentially, economic and social status function in Windsor as means of establishing membership within the community, not as means of asserting individual superiority.[7]

The sense of community, moreover, controls the appetitive and aggressive impulses of the citizens. It is true, as Barbara Freedman comments, that 'eating seems to be the major preoccupation of Windsor society; everyone is always coming from or going to dinner,'[8] but it is equally notable that no one eats alone: the references to dining are almost always in the form of invitations offered and accepted. While Falstaff poaches another man's deer, Shallow gives deer to Page, who invites everyone to share his venison pasty and wine. By the same token, the men of Windsor pride themselves on the combativeness that they see as a natural attribute of masculinity. Shallow boasts: 'Bodykins, Master Page, though I now be old and of the peace, if I see a sword out, my finger itches to make one. Though we are justices and doctors and churchmen, Master Page, we have some salt of our youth in us, we are the sons of women, Master Page' (II.iii.44–9). But for all their irascibility and nostalgia for youthful exploits, they accept transformation into pillars of the community. Shallow remembers that he is a sworn justice of the peace come to pacify Caius not to 'make one', that is, join in his quarrel. Reminded of their responsible roles in the community as 'a curer of souls' and 'a curer of bodies' (II.iii.39, cf. III.i.98) and told how they have been tricked by the Host, Evans and Caius drop their quarrel rather than be 'laughing-stocks to other men's humors' (III.i.86).

Life in Windsor is not uneventful, but on the whole people live together there peacefully, controlling potentially explosive situations through various forms of social pressure. Act I, scene i, sometimes criticized as superfluous, demonstrates the social group functioning smoothly, reconciling the differences between Justice Shallow and Falstaff through good will and hospitality. Settling the quarrel between Evans and Caius requires more complicated maneuvers and recourse to the harsher weapons of trickery and ridicule, but again friends intervene to avert disaster. Approaching the play from a psychological perspective, Peter Erickson finds offensive the methods used to control conflict in Windsor.[9] Instead of effecting a 'wholesome purging of aggression' (Erickson, 121), the Windsorites typically redirect it into new plots and projects. Thus Shallow drops his plan to submit his case against Falstaff to the Star Chamber when Evans suggests that he direct his energies to arranging his nephew's marriage to Anne Page. And when Evans and Caius learn how the Host has duped them, they forget their quarrel and immediately make common cause to be revenged on the Host. Although Erickson may be right that avoiding conflict rather than fully resolving basic issues is less than exemplary psychologically and morally, turning to fresh tasks effectively prevents violence from escalating, and Windsor is not unique in finding violence socially useful. Modern sociologists too have recognized that limited aggression can have a cohesive rather than a divisive social effect.[10]

At any rate, *The Merry Wives* emphasizes not the potential for renewed trouble but the containment and resolution of conflict locally. Changing relations between the central government and local communities was a major development and source of tension during the 1590s. Penry Williams observes that 'the consciousness and power of the community is perhaps the most difficult aspect of early modern England for the twentieth-century historian to grasp'[11] and that the 'change in balance between the centre and the regions was probably the most important element in the formation of Tudor policy.'[12] Furthermore, Keith Wrightson argues that social change during the late sixteenth and early seventeenth centuries produced two crucial developments: the integration of local communities into a national culture and an intensification of social stratification.[13] *The Merry Wives* implicitly opposes these controversial developments by presenting a community beset by quarrels of passion and property and yet maintaining order successfully through the cooperation of members of various ranks and without recourse to the machinery of the central government. When Shallow threatens to make a 'Star Chamber matter' (I.i.2) of his complaint against Falstaff, Sir Hugh advises, 'It is not meet the Council hear a riot' (I.i.36). When Shallow longs for personal revenge ('if I were young again, the sword should end it' [I.i.40–1]), Sir Hugh responds, 'It is petter that friends is the sword, and end it' (42–3). Sir Hugh's advice prevails. This reconciliation leads to increased competition for Anne Page and eventually to the prospective duel between Evans and Caius which is settled in its turn. That social harmony is temporary is less significant than that in each case friends intervene to end the quarrel without violence and without interference from outside the community.

Linda Anderson explains the frequency of revenge as a motive for action in Shakespearean comedy by the widespread approval of revenge in Elizabethan England.[14] Citing Fredson Bowers' observation that the private feud was 'finally broken up not so much by Christianity as by the growth of a central power which made attempts to concern itself in what had always been considered private wrongs' and Francis Bacon's reference to 'those wrongs which there is no law to remedy,' she concludes that 'underlying Shakespeare's comedies is a conception of justifiable, public revenge for "wrongs there is no law to remedy."'[15] In applying Anderson's thesis to *The Merry Wives* I want to modify it in order to argue that the repeated revenge plots – that of Shallow against Falstaff, Caius against Evans, Caius and Evans against the Host, Pistol and Nym against Falstaff, Ford against his wife and Falstaff, and Mistress Ford and Mistress Page against Falstaff – suggest not that revenge is permissible in cases where legal redress is impossible but that settling disputes and curbing anti-social behavior informally are preferable to going to law.[16]

In both the deer-stealing controversy and the threatened duel, the peace-makers act as a group: Evans, Page, and the Host are the self-appointed umpires in the first case, and Shallow, Slender, Page, and the Host cooperate to reconcile Caius and Evans. While they are effective as representatives of the community, not as individuals, they transmit the group judgment personally and informally rather than through impersonal institutions. Their power is accepted rather than imposed. With the notable exception of Falstaff and his followers, the residents of Windsor have a sense of themselves as part of a group and are willing to bend to social pressure in order to retain the reassurances of community.

The citizens of Windsor, then, act as Bottom assumes that neighbors should when he laments that 'some honest neighbors' have not reconciled love and reason (*MND*, III.i.145). Although no one in Windsor challenges its hierarchical social structure, they work together in their various schemes regardless of social rank. Such neighborliness, as Wrightson suggests, 'was essentially a horizontal relationship, one which implied a degree of equality and mutuality between partners to the relationship, irrespective of distinctions of wealth or social standing' (Wrightson, 51). Voluntary identification and participation with the community is more important in establishing standing in Windsor society than birth as a determinant of class or nationality. For an English village, Windsor has a remarkably heterogeneous population, including a Welsh parson and a French doctor as well as the Fords, Pages, and Justice Shallow with his three-hundred-year-old coat of arms. Although there are jokes about Evans and Caius, they are mocked affectionately as members of the group. Being a visitor or an alien is no bar to participation in society. Even Shallow and Slender, like Falstaff, are guests at the inn. Falstaff, Bardolph, Pistol, and Nym are outsiders in Windsor not because they are visitors but because they refuse to identify with the group and are impervious to public opinion. The foreign accents of Evans and Caius are mocked as personal idiosyncrasies, as Mistress Quickly's malapropisms are, and cause no real problems in communication. In contrast, Nym's affected language earns Master Page's distrust and defeats his attempt to make Page jealous. And Falstaff, whose command of English surpasses all other characters', utterly misunderstands Mistress Quickly and Mistress Ford. He boasts that he 'can construe the action of [Mistress Ford's] familiar style, and the hardest voice of her behavior (to be English'd rightly) is, "I am Sir John Falstaff's" ' (I.iii.46–8). As Pistol says, he has 'translated her will, out of honesty into English' (49–50), and he suffers for his mistranslation. Windsor society is held together, then, not so much by a shared language as by intelligibly shared values – especially by agreement about permissible sexual activity. The scene where Mistress Quickly hears indecencies in young William's recital of his Latin lesson comically demonstrates that, as society transmits its culture to the young, it passes on not merely grammar and vocabulary but attitudes and assumptions and that the two are distinguishable: proficiency in one does not necessarily imply understanding of the other. Mistress Quickly's presence during the lesson guarantees that William will learn the conventions governing sexual discourse in his community as well as some Latin.

While the heterogeneity of Windsor's population suggests that enjoying the bucolic peace and innocence traditionally symbolized by a pastoral setting depends not on place of nativity or social rank but on values and attitudes, the physical presence of the court itself at Windsor suggests that the courtly vices of ambition and sexual intrigue are temptations for country men and women as well as for courtiers. Mistress Quickly assures Falstaff that he is not the first courtly suitor to address Mistress Ford: 'there has been knights, and lords, and gentlemen, with their coaches; I warrant you, coach after coach, letter after letter, gift after gift ... that would have won any woman's heart ... and yet there has been earls, nay (which is more) pensioners, but I warrant you all is one with her' (II.ii.63–78). Although this flight of fancy is not to be believed literally, it reminds us of the immanence of the court and establishes that it is a matter of conscious choice that the court has no effective reality in the lives of the characters.[17] Just as harmonious social life is possible for a French doctor, a Welsh clergyman, and a down-at-heels aristocrat as well as for the Fords and Pages, so the civilized decadence and individual ambition associated with the courtly ambience are possibilities within ordinary life. Caius, who boasts of his practice among earls, knights, lords, and gentlemen, and Fenton, who is reputed to have 'kept company with the wild Prince and Poins' (III.ii.72–3), as well as Falstaff, have connections with the court, but their preference for integration with the humbler Windsor community is expressed by their desire to marry Anne Page.

The Windsor community that accepts considerable diversity and tolerates a good deal of aggressive, anti-social behavior severely punishes Falstaff. His attack on the Fords' and the Pages' marriages repudiates the friendliness and hospitality that are the means both of creating and of expressing communal solidarity. His adulterous proposals are attacks on Master Ford and Master Page, cuckoldry being largely something one man does to another.[18] His attempts at seduction also obviously insult the women and threaten their sense of their own identity, which depends on their public status as virtuous wives. Falstaff's boasts that Mistress Ford 'gives the leer of invitation' (I.iii.45–6) and that Mistress Page 'gave me good eyes too, examin'd my parts with most judicious iliads; sometimes the beam of her view gilded my foot, sometimes my portly belly' (I.iii.59–62) are evidence not simply of his vanity but also of the strict code regulating female behavior. Thus Mistress Ford's reaction on receiving Falstaff's letter is to reflect uneasily on her own behavior: 'What an unweigh'd behavior hath this Flemish drunkard pick'd ... out of my conversation, that he dares in this manner assay me? ... I was then frugal of my mirth. Heaven forgive me!' (II.i.22–8). Mistress Page expresses even more explicitly the disorientation they both feel at this threat to their sense of themselves: '**Mrs. Ford.** What doth he think of us? **Mrs. Page.** Nay, I know not; it makes me almost ready to wrangle with mine own honesty. I'll entertain myself like one that I am not acquainted withal; for sure unless he know some strain in me that I know not myself, he would never have boarded me in this fury' (II.i.83–9). Because their sense of themselves depends on their place in the community, they can't simply refuse Falstaff's proposal but must prove how wrong he is to themselves, to him, and to the community at large. Thus their revenge is an act of self-definition as well as of self-defense and as much educative as retributive. They don't denounce Falstaff and send him packing; instead they teach him a lesson by humbling his aggressive individualism to the values and authority of their rural community, putting him through a series of experiences that forces him to bow to social pressure and prepares him to understand and accept his place within society. Simultaneously they demonstrate their own virtue to themselves and to the community. Appropriately, they achieve this poetic justice by subjecting their would-be seducer to punishments usually inflicted on adulterous women and cuckolded men. Falstaff's ducking in the Thames recalls the ceremonial ducking of adulterous women, and his disguises as an old woman and as Herne the Hunter allude to the use of female symbols and of horns to ridicule cuckolds in Elizabethan villages.[19]

The staging of Falstaff's humiliation also utilizes burlesque versions of pastoral motifs. In the first episode, the ubiquitous flowing brook of the pastoral landscape has been transformed to the muddy banks of the Thames into which Falstaff is thrown. The traditional symbolism of purity is rendered comically in the domestic details of laundering, and Falstaff's urgent need for purification is reified in the dirty, smelly linen that he shares the buck basket with. The man who woos with talk of jewels and courtly finery is unceremoniously 'Ramm'd ... in with foul shirts and smocks, socks, foul stockings, greasy napkins, that ... there was the rankest compound of villainous smell that ever offended nostril' (III.v.89–93).

As the merry wives anticipate, this first treatment does not cure Falstaff's 'dissolute disease' (III.iii.191–2). Like Duke Senior, who finds that natural adversities 'feelingly persuade me what I am' (AYL, II.i.11), Falstaff is reminded by his rude immersion in the Thames of what kind of man he is – a man with 'a kind of alacrity in sinking,' 'a man ... that am as subject to heat as butter; a man of continual dissolution and thaw' (III.v.12–13, 114–16). But while he is made conscious of his physical grossness and vulnerability, he remains unrepentant and unashamed. He recounts the experience with indignation at the discomfort he has suffered and with undiminished arrogance and contempt for Master Ford, whom he again plans to cuckold, and for Mistress Ford, whom he plans to pass on afterwards to 'Master Brook.'

In his next encounter with the Windsor wives, Falstaff is disguised as a woman. Although a shepherd's costume is a more usual pastoral disguise, Falstaff's female clothing is not unprecedented. Pyrocles in Sidney's *Arcadia* also puts on women's clothing to disguise his pursuit of forbidden love. But while Pyrocles disguises himself as a splendidly beautiful and warlike amazon, Falstaff appears as an outcast old woman. Again, the details of the punishment appropriately travesty the fat knight's pretensions. His favorite persona as suitor has been that of a blunt, virile soldier. For example, his initial love letters concluded:

> Let it suffice thee ... if the love of a soldier can suffice –
> that I love thee. I will not say, pity me – 'tis not a soldier-
> like phrase – but I say, love me. By me,
>
> > Thine own true knight,
> > By day or night,
> > Or any kind of light,
> > With all his might
> > For thee to fight,
> >
> > John Falstaff. (II.i.10–19)

And at his first assignation with Mistress Ford he disdainfully contrasts his own manly courting with that of those effeminate 'lisping hawthorn buds, that come like women in men's apparel' (III.iii.71-2). At their next meeting, when he hears that her husband is coming, this mighty knight begs the woman to devise a disguise for him – 'any extremity rather than a mischief' (IV.ii.73-4). Pyrocles, disguised as the amazon Zelmane, feels only momentary shame at being discovered in his female disguise and justifies his adopted motto, *Never More Valiant*, by fighting bravely and victoriously. But the merry wives have mischievously dressed Falstaff as 'the fat woman of Brainford' (IV.ii.75-6), whom Master Ford believes to be a witch and has threatened to beat, so that, in addition to betraying his cowardice, Falstaff receives a thorough drubbing from the 'peasant' Ford.

This experience shakes Falstaff's self-confidence even if it does not damage his self-esteem. He defensively boasts to 'Master Brook' that, although he has been beaten 'in the shape of a woman[,] ... in the shape of man ... I fear not Goliah with a weaver's beam' (v.i.20-2). In soliloquy he admits that he has been 'cozen'd and beaten too' (IV.v.94), but he boasts to Mistress Quickly of the 'admirable dexterity of wit' (IV.v.117-18) with which he avoided the further humiliation of being exhibited as a witch in the common stocks. He fears public humiliation, but the authority and judgment he respects are the court's: 'If it should come to the ear of the court, how I have been transform'd, and how my transformation hath been wash'd and cudgell'd, they would melt me out of my fat drop by drop, and liquor fishermen's boots with me. I warrant they would whip me with their fine wits till I were as crestfall'n as a dried pear' (IV.v.94-100). Abashed but unrepentant, he wants revenge on, rather than forgiveness from, Windsor society.

His desire to be revenged on Ford incites him to meet Mistress Ford once more and so to fall into the last trap set for him. Mistress Ford and Mistress Page understand that Falstaff has been sufficiently frightened by the last fiasco not to renew his solicitations but that his punishment will not be complete until his shame is made public. Falstaff suffered his dunking in the Thames privately and his beating anonymously; his final humiliation takes place before the entire community. It also penetrates most deeply to the core of his pride. When Ford, disguised as Master Brook, flatters Falstaff that he is renowned for his 'many war-like, court-like, and learned' (II.ii.228) endowments, he shrewdly articulates Falstaff's image of himself. Although his soldierly swaggering and his courtly wooing are perhaps largely tongue-in-cheek, pride in his 'admirable dexterity of wit' is wholly genuine. For example, it provides his enjoyment in mocking country obtuseness and superstition when Slender sends Simple to consult the fortune-telling woman of Brainford (IV.v.30–56). And, of course, a sense of intellectual superiority underlies his whole conycatching scheme. Just as being treated as a piece of dirty laundry has tarnished his pretensions to courtly grandeur and receiving a beating as a weak old woman has undermined his warlike boasting, the last plot is designed to attack his intellectual pride.

For the last, much elaborated punishment, Mistress Ford arranges a midnight rendezvous in Windsor Forest by an old oak tree reputed to be haunted by the spirit of Herne the Hunter. Falstaff, wearing stag antlers in disguise as Herne the Hunter, is caught up in the fabulous, numinous atmosphere: 'The Windsor bell hath strook twelve; the minute draws on. Now the hot-bloodied gods assist me! Remember, Jove, thou wast a bull for thy Europa, love set on thy horns' (v.v.1–4). Although he had planned to manipulate the women sexually for his own financial purposes, they now arouse *him* to an erotic frenzy: 'My doe with the black scut? Let the sky rain potatoes; let it thunder to the tune of "Green-sleeves," hail kissing-comfits, and snow eringoes; let there come a tempest of provocation, I will shelter me here' (v.v.18–21). Suddenly, his sexual fantasy-cometrue is interrupted by Evans, Quickly, and the Windsor children disguised as fairies. The women flee as he hides his eyes in terror: 'They are fairies, he that speaks to them shall die' (v.v.47). The 'fairies' discover and torment him until the Pages and Fords arrive to complete his disgrace by mocking him. Falstaff, who had mocked Simple's credulity so wittily, is totally duped.

The scene at Herne's oak is a burlesque version of the supernatural center of the pastoral landscape. Speaking of the multiple setting of Renaissance pastoral romances, Walter R. Davis suggests thinking of 'a center with two concentric circles surrounding it.' The pattern, he says, implies 'a kind of purification of life proceeding inward: from the ... naturalistic outer circle, to the refined pastoral inner circle and then to the pure center of the world. The center is always supernatural, usually either a shrine ... or the dwelling of a magician. It may be the actual dwelling place of the god, who may reveal himself ... there.'[20]

The spectacle of a fat old man with deer antlers tied to his head being pinched by a motley assortment of villagers got up as fairies obviously is a long way from Calidore's vision of the Graces dancing on Mount Alcidale in Spenser's Legend of Courtesy, yet, for all its absurdity, the scene at Herne's oak functions much as the visit to a supernatural center does in more orthodox pastorals. Calidore, who withdraws from his heroic quest into a pastoral world and then happens upon the Graces dancing to Colin Clout's piping, gains momentary access to the poet's vision of perfect order that embraces the natural and human worlds while transcending them. Falstaff witnesses a humbler artistic production, but even Mistress Quickly is unexpectedly dignified in her role as fairy queen and evokes quite eloquently an image of natural and social order:

> And nightly, meadow-fairies, look you sing,
> Like to the Garter's compass, in a ring.
> Th' expressure that it bears, green let it be,
> More fertile-fresh than all the field to see;
> And 'Honi soit qui mal y pense' write
> In em'rald tuffs, flow'rs purple, blue, and white,
> Like sapphire, pearl, and rich embroidery,
> Buckled below fair knighthood's bending knee:
> Fairies use flow'rs for their charactery. (V.v.65–73)

Although this masquelike pageant can be seen as a reconciliation of country and courtly values, it also can be interpreted as a challenging alternative to the ceremonies held at nearby Windsor castle. The villagers present themselves not as beneficiaries and dependents of their social betters but as fairy benefactors, conferring wholesomeness on the aristocracy. If the ceremonies of the Order of the Garter provide a spectacle of 'sapphire, pearl, and rich embroidery,' the fairies, closer to nature, 'use flow'rs for their charactery.'

The basic action of the pastoral romance, according to Davis, consists of the hero's journey from the heroic world of the outer circle to the peaceful pastoral world, and then to the supernatural center, where the hero resolves his internal conflict and is prepared for his return to the outer world.[21] Sometimes the resolution is simply the supernatural gift of a god, but sometimes the illumination is gained more painfully. In Sidney's *Arcadia*, for example, the center is not a shrine but a cave, which serves as a focus for events that are 'degrading and even shameful as well as instructive and humiliating.'[22] For Falstaff, the process is painful and increasingly humiliating. First, the 'fairies' taunt and torture him for the sinful fantasies of his corrupted heart. After the fairy vision vanishes, the mockery of the assembled company forces him to realize that the only metamorphosis to occur at Herne's oak is, as he ruefully admits, that 'I am made an ass' (v.v.119). What most astonishes him is his own gullibility – that he, witty Jack Falstaff, 'in despite of the teeth of all rhyme and reason' took the villagers for fairies: 'See now how wit may be made a Jack-a-Lent, when 'tis upon ill employment!' (v.v.125–8). The Fords and the Pages taunt and insult him, but it is Parson Evans' voice that Falstaff reacts to most strongly: 'Have I liv'd to stand at the taunt of one that makes fritters of English? This is enough to be the decay of lust and late-walking through the realm' (v.v.142–5). The chorus of ridicule culminates with Evans' denunciation, which elicits Falstaff's surrender: 'Well, I am your theme. You have the start of me, I am dejected. I am not able to answer the Welsh flannel; ignorance itself is a plummet o'er me. Use me as you will' (v.v.161–4).

When Falstaff's wit is humbled to Evans' ignorance, the pastoral values of simplicity and humility have triumphed over wit and worldliness, communality has triumphed over selfish individualism, and Falstaff's punishment is over. He has been exposed, humiliated, and hence controlled. The goal has not been ostracism or even conversion but rather integration, and the Pages begin the process by extending yet one more hospitable invitation, including 'Sir John and all' (v.v.243). Once the threat of adultery has been defeated, the group turns its attention to celebrating marriage – sexuality in its socially controlled form. Anne Page's elopement is discovered and forgiven, and the play ends with a joking reference to middle-aged, married sexuality:

> **Ford.**   Sir John,
> To Master Brook you yet shall hold your word,
> For he to-night shall lie with Mistress Ford.
>
> (v.v.243–5)

In this way, Windsor combines two traditions: the pastoral world as a place of innocence and chastity and the pastoral world as a place of full sensual gratification.

While *The Merry Wives* ends happily with plans for everyone to return to town and 'laugh this sport o'er by a country fire' (v.v.242), mockery, the weapon that brings Falstaff's greed and lust under social control, also can be socially divisive. Suffering scorn and ridicule creates the desire to mock others in revenge. Thus when the Host ridicules Caius and Evans, they abandon their duel rather than be laughingstocks only to ally themselves in a plot to have revenge on him. Poor Master Ford's double fear – of being revealed to public scorn as a cuckold and of being ridiculed by Page as a jealous fool for unwarranted suspicion – drives him to the absurd position of wanting to prove his wife guilty of adultery so that he can be 'reveng'd on Falstaff, and laugh at Page' (II.ii.311). This potentially destructive process of mockery begetting mockery does not develop into an uncontrolled cycle of revenge largely because of its communal nature. No one pursues a goal of private vengeance; instead, each person who feels aggrieved enlists friends and neighbors in his scheme, whose end is always public ridicule. No one rejects the group judgment or perpetuates his grudge beyond the public acknowledgment of guilt. For example, Ford explicitly submits himself to the judgment of the group each time he sets out to prove Falstaff's adultery (III.iii.149–51; IV.ii.160–5), and admits his fault and asks for forgiveness when his suspicions prove wrong (III.iii.218, 224–7; IV.iv.6–9). Although Parson Evans occasionally reminds him of his weakness, Mistress Ford asks no additional penance. And Master Page, rather than gloating, exemplifies characteristic Windsor moderation by warning Ford against being 'as extreme in submission as in offence' (IV.iv.11).

The pattern works out most clearly, indeed almost schematically, in the three plots against Falstaff. The first involves only the women – Mistress Ford, Mistress Page, and Mistress Quickly. In the second, the men cooperate unwittingly: Ford beats Falstaff without knowing it. Significantly, as the group opposing Falstaff widens, Falstaff's sub-group disintegrates, and the men's involvement results directly from his followers' revenge against him for turning them away. Finally, the men, women, and children of Windsor all participate in the last plot. As the group widens, the revenge becomes less private. In the first episode, the women Falstaff has most directly misjudged and insulted punish him. In the second, the agent of persecution is Master Ford, the man he has consciously tried to injure. In the third, that role is taken by Parson Evans, a disinterested representative of the community. Once Falstaff has submitted, he is invited to participate in the favorite communal activities of feasting and shared laughter.

On the whole, then, social solidarity and cooperation operate beneficently in the Windsor of Shakespeare's imagination, defeating anti-social aggression and controlling the use of the powerfully coercive weapons of social pressure. But the play also acknowledges the danger to individuality inherent in the power of social coercion. Abraham Slender, who is perfectly willing to marry anyone Justice Shallow tells him to but cannot comprehend the idea that his own feelings could be at all relevant to the matter, is a potent warning of how individual mind and will can be stunted in a tightly-knit society. Still, Slender is the only happy and hopeless victim of this power that we see in Windsor. If the threat of divisive individualism is defeated by social cohesion, the possible tyranny of this cohesion is prevented by its fluidity and informality. Anne Page can disobey her parents and marry the man she wants because her mother and father disagree. They close ranks to defeat a common enemy but pursue their goals for Anne singly and secretly. This division enables Anne to act independently and justifies her doing so. Just as the citizens of Windsor defend the integrity of their community without repudiating their connections with the national culture associated with the court, the women of Windsor act independently without attacking the established gender hierarchy. Mistress Page's attempt to outwit her husband and Anne's success in outwitting both her parents do not constitute a direct assault on ideas of patriarchal, hierarchical authority, but they suggest, even more subversively, that such orthodoxies are irrelevant abstractions with little relation to the actual functioning of a harmonious society. Peter Erickson points out that for all the play's affirmation of female power, it confines women to a 'chaste / unchaste paradigm,'[23] but we should also notice that the wives' plot against Falstaff is explicitly designed to establish their freedom of action as well as their chastity:

> We'll leave a proof, by that which we will do,
> Wives may be merry, and yet honest too. (IV.ii.104–5)

Henceforth anyone finding 'the leer of invitation' in their spirited friendliness is warned to heed the Garter motto, *Honi soit qui mal y pense*. Still, in Windsor the extent of a wife's, or a husband's, or a parent's power is left conveniently vague. When Anne and Fenton return and defer obediently to Anne's parents, the group rallies to reconcile the Pages to the marriage, and the rebellious marriage becomes part of the 'sport' that 'Sir John and all' will laugh over by their country fire.

The narrative patterns of *The Merry Wives* draw heavily on the conventions of the pastoral tradition and dramatize its assumption that outside the pressures and rigidities of sophisticated society people can achieve harmony with their environment. In one line of action, a man embroiled in conflict retires to a natural setting, where, after a period of contemplation, he puts away his sword, makes peace with his enemy, and re-enters society as a peacemaker and moral instructor. In another plot line, a young aristocrat, who is good at heart but corrupted by worldly society (indicated by his mercenary motives and reputation for profligacy), falls in love with a village lass. Purified by the experience, he overcomes obstacles and wins her hand in marriage. In the main plot, a knightly exile from court enters a rural society where, although evil exists, moral issues are simplified and clarified and where his pride is humbled. Impelled by disappointment in love, he moves further from man-made institutions into the natural world until he reaches a sacred place where the human and divine meet. Here he experiences humiliation and a revelation about the natural sources of social harmony and then re-enters society a sadder but wiser man.

While the play's plot structure and symbolic motifs derive from the highly artificial, conventionalized traditions of pastoral literature, the tone and texture of the dramatic events are realistic, farcical, and unromanticized. The action on stage is often rowdy and boisterously physical. The setting is rural England, not a remote and glamorous Arcadia. The cast of characters includes popular comic fictional characters and ordinary bourgeois English men and women rather than lovelorn shepherds. The prose dialogue contains a good deal of 'hack[ing] our English' (III.i.77-8) and very little of the rhetorical elegance of Sidnean or Spenserian pastoral. This incongruous combination is doubly satirical, pointing at once to the pastoral conventions' distance from reality and to ordinary life's banality and pettiness in comparison with the idylls of the poetic imagination. But the parodic tension between pastoral framework and low-comedy rendering does not destroy the connection between them. After all, poetry typically works by disjunctions, disrupting familiar associations and established connections and forging new ones. The pastoralism of *The Merry Wives* doesn't provide solid evidence either for William Empson's argument for its leveling tendencies or for Louis Montrose's for its affirmation of aristocratic power.[24] But it does function socially to endorse local loyalties and to urge the possibility of an achievable balance of self-fulfillment and social solidarity in spite of human imperfections. It offers an interpretation of the pastoral ideal of harmony compatible with ordinary life. The harmony in this imaginative model may derive from nothing more exalted than human sociability – the desire to belong that is the other side of the fear of mockery and isolation – but it should not be despised. In Shakespeare's Windsor the pastoral values of simplicity, humility, and fidelity are elusive and transitory but always accessible; dramatic action grows out of the struggle by the inhabitants to maintain this equilibrium.

CHAPTER NINE

The Unauthorized Language of *Much Ado About Nothing*

'and two men ride of a horse, one must ride behind' (III.v.36–7)

In the first scene of *Much Ado About Nothing*, when Claudio and Don Pedro make fun of Benedick's use of a conventional verbal formula, Benedick retorts: 'Nay, mock not, mock not. The body of your discourse is sometime guarded with fragments, and the guards are but slightly basted on neither. Ere you flout old ends any further, examine your conscience' (I.i.285–9). When Benedick accuses his friends of guarding their discourse with fragments that are 'but slightly basted on,' his attack is both rhetorical and moral. Assuming the value of elegant language, he claims that Don Pedro and Claudio also resort to 'old ends' of conventional verbal formulas and, moreover, fail to integrate them gracefully into their own language. At the same time, he implies that these 'fragments' that 'guard,' that is, decorate and/or protect, are inauthentic embellishments on the true body of their discourse. The pun registers Benedick's awareness that the rhetorical authority invoked by proverbs, classical allusions, and traditional tropes and figures is a means both of self-display and of self-protection. More significant is the ambivalence towards language implicit in his metaphor. 'Guards' suggests that words are extrinsic to truth, but 'the body of your discourse' acknowledges that words also constitute the meaning that is decorated or hidden. Benedick understands language as the material of the social self, the means by which people present themselves to others, and prides himself on his witty, elegant language. At the same time, he is deeply suspicious of the capacity of language to obscure truth.

Benedick's interest in language and his ambivalent attitude

towards it are not individualizing traits but typical of the characters in *Much Ado About Nothing*. In the opening scene that introduces Shakespeare's Messina, almost all the characters speak with self-conscious artfulness, ranging from the Messenger's rhetorical flourishes to Beatrice and Benedick's exchanges of wit. That the Prince's messenger should speak with elegant formality and the young aristocrats with spirited wit is, of course, entirely decorous; what is striking is the frequency with which characters talk about the problematics of language. The Messenger protests, in a standard rhetorical figure, that he is unable to do justice to Claudio's merits: 'He hath borne himself beyond the promise of his age, doing in the figure of a lamb the feats of a lion. He hath indeed better bett'red expectation than you must expect of me to tell you how' (I.i.13–17). Benedick calls Beatrice 'a rare parrot-teacher' (I.i.138), implying that she speaks meaningless chatter, learned by rote. Beatrice's response – 'A bird of my tongue is better than a beast of yours' (I.i.139) – implies that Benedick is sub-human, incapable of rational speech.

These gibes at falling short of a human standard of discourse are based on a conception of language as the distinguishing human trait and as the basis of civilization. These, of course, are Renaissance commonplaces. According to Ben Jonson, for example, '*Speech* is the only benefit man hath to express his excellencie of mind above other creatures. It is the Instrument of *Society*.'[1] But if the characters in *Much Ado* assume that language is the basis of harmonious social relations, they also know that it can be the source of misunderstanding and conflict. They are acutely aware of a potentially dangerous disjunction between the literal sense of words and the meaning of a discourse. Don Pedro, for example, assumes a general skepticism about the identity of tongue and heart when he reports Leonato's invitation to hospitality with the assurance 'I dare swear he is no hypocrite, but prays from his heart' (I.i.150–2). And Benedick assumes a gap between truth and ordinary social discourse when he asks Claudio: 'Do you question me ... for my simple true judgment? or would you have me speak after my custom ... ?' (I.i.166–9). Conscious of the misunderstandings arising from such ambiguities of tone, Leonato anxiously apologizes for Beatrice's barbed references to Benedick: 'You must not, sir, mistake my niece. There is a kind of merry war betwixt Signior Benedick and her' (I.i.61–3). Claudio, too, as he confides his love for Hero to his friends, is careful to avoid misunderstanding, replying to Benedick: 'Thou thinkest I am in sport. I pray thee tell me truly how thou lik'st her' (I.i.177–8) and tentatively accusing Don Pedro: 'You speak this to fetch me in, my lord' (I.i.223). Similarly Benedick asks Claudio: 'But speak you this with a sad brow? or do you play the flouting Jack ... ? Come, in what key shall a man take you to go in the song?' (I.i.182–6).

The characters, then, both distrust and delight in the multivalency of the language they use to engage and to struggle with each other. In addition, as Leonato's concern that the Messenger not misunderstand Beatrice and as Claudio's suspicion that Don Pedro's speech is intended to 'fetch [him] in' indicate, they are also aware that language is inextricably implicated in relationships of power. For example, Leonato's concern with the nuances of social discourse is nicely illustrated in his short exchange with the Messenger. Leonato's first speeches are straightforward and stylistically plain: 'I learn in this letter that Don Pedro of Arragon comes this night to Messina' (I.i.1–2); 'How many gentlemen have you lost in this action?' (I.i.5–6). In contrast, the Messenger speaks with elaborate artifice, reporting, for example, of Claudio's uncle: 'I have already deliver'd him letters, and there appears much joy in him, even so much that joy could not show itself modest enough without a badge of bitterness' (I.i.20–3). In response, Leonato first anxiously checks whether he has interpreted the metaphor correctly: 'Did he break out into tears?' (I.i.24). Then he replies in the same euphuistic style: 'A kind overflow of kindness. There are no faces truer than those that are so wash'd. How much better is it to weep at joy than to joy at weeping!' (I.i.26–9).[2] Leonato's eagerness to understand and to speak the language of the court shows not only his use of language to create social bonds, but also his awareness of the ambiguity of language and of its involvement in hierarchies of power.

I have examined what Kier Elam calls metadiscourse[3] in the first scene of *Much Ado* in order to suggest that the play is centrally concerned with the social nature of language – with the power of language and with language as an articulation of power. The witty repartee, elaborate rhetoric, compliments, accusations, and apologies function as means of social cohesion, establishing relations between people, and simultaneously as expressions of relative power. The Messenger, reporting on the casualties in the recent battle, equates language and power, explaining that Don Pedro's forces lost 'But few of any sort, and none of name' (I.i.7). To have a name in Messina is to be recognized as a participant in its power structure; to be powerless is to be nameless.

While all the characters are aware of language as an expression of social and political hierarchy, it is Don John who illustrates most clearly the Renaissance association of speech and sociability. In his popular commentary on Aristotle's *Politics*, for example, Louis LeRoy explains that men are 'naturally Civill and publicke, that is to say, by their naturall disposition, enclining to live in societie: as it appeareth by Speech, which was in vaine bestowed upon them if they should live solitarily without companie and conversation. And if by chance there be any such monster extant, which by a particular inclination should shun and avoid Civill societie, hee ought to be reputed as most wicked, a lover and stirrer up of warres and seditions ...'[4] In the first scene Don John signals his anti-social nature by announcing his laconic style: 'I am not of many words' (I.i.157). When he next appears, in private conversation with his companion Conrade, he identifies himself as 'a plain-dealing villain,' who, on hearing of an intended marriage, immediately wonders whether it will 'serve for any model to build mischief on' (I.iii.32, 46-7). And he explains his rejection of social discourse as an expression of his anti-social nature: 'I cannot hide what I am: I must be sad when I have cause, and smile at no man's jests; eat when I have stomach, and wait for no man's leisure; sleep when I am drowsy, and tend on no man's business; laugh when I am merry, and claw no man in his humor' (I.iii.13-18). For Don John, adapting to other people is a painful infringement of freedom: 'I am trusted with a muzzle, and enfranchis'd with a clog, therefore I have decreed not to sing in my cage' (I.iii.32-4). While Don John's determination 'not to sing in [his] cage' is the converse of Benedick's desire to figure out what key Claudio is in so that he can 'go in the song,' they are talking about the same thing: the discourse that enables social relationships also controls individual expression.

Beatrice and Benedick, whose verbal battles are clearly power struggles, understand the power of language. Hence Beatrice describes Benedick as 'too like my lady's eldest son, evermore tattling' (II.i.9-10), and he calls her 'my Lady Tongue' (II.i.275). When Benedick addresses Beatrice as 'my Lady Tongue' or 'Lady Disdain' (I.i.118) and when Beatrice renames Benedick 'Signior Mountanto' (I.i.30), they are utilizing the connection between naming and power deeply embedded in Western culture. Adam's ability to name the creatures was interpreted as demonstrating his knowledge of their natures and thus as evidence of his right to dominion over them.[5] According to most Elizabethan language theorists, Adam's descendants inherited this power collectively: custom, not individual genius, is the basis of language.[6] Thus, the logician Ralph Lever warns, 'no man is of power to change or to make a language when he will.'[7] Beatrice and Benedick, then, by exercising the power to create names, not only try to claim dominion over each other but pretend to an Adam-like independence from social control.

Their name-calling and reciprocal accusations of talking too much are significant indications of their understanding of themselves and of each other in relation to society. Beatrice recognizes that, while language is an expression of power, it can also function to create the illusion of power. She suspects Benedick of words without substance. He talks a good war, but she is skeptical about his prowess as a soldier. He is like a child, 'evermore tattling,' not a man of action. He is the 'Prince's fool' (II.i.204), whose verbal wit amuses but does not command respect. He is gregarious and likable, but shallow and fickle: 'he hath every month a new sworn brother' (I.i.72-3). If Don John's taciturnity indicates a monstrous incivility, Beatrice fears that Benedick is too socially compliant. He is 'the Prince's jester,' who becomes 'melancholy' if his jokes are not laughed at (II.i.137, 148).

Even though Beatrice interprets Benedick's loquacity as evidence of unmanly weakness and dependence on social approval, she uses her own verbal dexterity to gain independence in a male dominated society. When Leonato warns her that her shrewish tongue will prevent her from getting a husband, she protests that spinsterhood is a blessing. She does not want a husband, she tells her uncle, 'till God make men of some other mettle than earth. Would it not grieve a woman to be overmaster'd with a piece of valiant dust? to make an account of her life to a clod of wayward marl? No, uncle, I'll none. Adam's sons are my brethren, and truly I hold it a sin to match in my kinred' (II.i.59-65). Beatrice's witty speech defines a genuine dilemma: her society urges her to marry but structures marriage so that she must submit to a master whose superiority she does not admit. Men are not made of a different clay, but of the same stuff as she. More specifically, she complains, a man such as Don John 'says nothing' (II.i.8), while Benedick talks too much. Beatrice, then, must either subordinate herself to an equal, or, as she jokingly suggests to Don Pedro, marry her social, though not her sexual, superior. And *that* alternative she rejects on the grounds that 'Your Grace is too costly to wear every day' (II.i.328-9). Beatrice, then, is aware of the coercive power of the hierarchical society, but instead of responding with Don John's sullen resentment, she exploits the gap between literal and actual meaning to mock masculine pretensions without offending the victims of her wit: 'But I beseech your Grace pardon me,' she apologizes gracefully, 'I was born to speak all mirth and no matter' (II.i.329–30).

Like Beatrice, Benedick warns his listeners against interpreting his wit literally, and in his customary role as 'a profess'd tyrant to their sex' (I.i.168–9) condemns women in general and Beatrice in particular. While Beatrice interprets Benedick's talkativeness as an unmanly substitution of words for deeds, Benedick condemns hers for its intimidating power: 'She speaks poniards, and every word stabs ... I would not marry her, though she were endow'd with all that Adam had left him before he transgress'd. She would have made Hercules have turn'd spit, yea, and have cleft his club to make the fire too' (II.i.247–54). By characterizing Beatrice's discourse as emasculating aggression, Benedick accuses her of inverting the hierarchy of the sexes. His antipathy is not limited to 'my Lady Tongue' but includes all women, basically because a woman's word cannot be trusted. 'Because I will not do them the wrong to mistrust any,' he declares, 'I will do myself the right to trust none' (I.i.242–4). Benedick, of course, is voicing traditional attitudes. If the talkative woman is a rebel against the orthodox sexual hierarchy, she is also a recognizable cultural stereotype – the shrew. Similarly, the association of women with duplicity is inscribed clearly in Western culture at least since the story of Eve's tempting Adam to eat the apple. In this misogynistic tradition, the charge of female duplicity usually is associated with sexual promiscuity.[8] Certainly Benedick's mistrust of women is essentially skepticism about their sexual fidelity. He invariably associates marriage with cuckoldry. 'Cuckoo' is a word that strikes terror into the heart of the bachelor Benedick, not so much because he fears personal betrayal, as because he imagines vividly the public shame of being labeled a cuckold. If he should ever submit to marriage, he tells his friends, they are entitled to: 'pluck off the bull's horns, and set them in my forehead, and let me be vildly painted, and in such great letters as they write, "Here is good horse to hire," let them signify under my sign, "Here you may see Benedick the married man"' (I.i.263–8).

Beatrice and Benedick, then, epitomize the ambivalence towards language endemic to their society. Like the other inhabitants of Messina, they use language to create engaging social presences with which to establish relations with other people and also to protect and distance themselves from others. They delight in wordplay and admire people, as Benedick says of the ideal woman, 'of good discourse' (II.iii.33–4); at the same time they are skeptical of the veridical force of language and fear its powers of deception and coercion. And they associate these dangers with gender and with sexual relationships. Benedick's cuckoldry jokes echo Leonato's. In the first scene, when Don Pedro politely remarks, 'I think this is your daughter,' Leonato responds, 'Her mother hath many times told me so' (I.i.104–5). And Beatrice's accusation 'He wears his faith but as the fashion of his hat' (I.i.75–6) applies to Benedick the generalized sentiments of Balthasar's song: 'Men were deceivers ever ... To one thing constant never' (II.iii.63–5).

By the fashion in which they guard their own and criticize the other's discourse, Benedick and Beatrice make evident the contradictions inherent in their culture's definition of marriage. It is the expected norm of social behavior, encouraged by figures of authority like Leonato and Don Pedro. But it requires women to subordinate themselves to fallen Adam's sons, prone to deception and inconstancy, and requires men to entrust their honor to untrustworthy women. These contradictions are brought to a crisis by Don John's plot to disrupt the marriage of Claudio and Hero by accusing Hero of infidelity.

The deception responsible for Hero's disgrace is a verbal construct. As Borachio confesses, it was done 'partly by [Don John's] oaths ... but chiefly by my villainy, which did confirm any slander that Don John had made' (III.iii.156–9). The slander consists of and is nourished by the attitudes encoded in the cultural discourse. The association of female speech with sexual promiscuity underlies the charge against Hero – that she did 'Talk with a ruffian at her chamber-window' (IV.i.91). And the stereotype of female duplicity makes the charge credible and prevents her from defending herself. Everything she says is used against her literally. Her denial – 'I talk'd with no man at that hour, my lord' – convicts her: 'Why then you are no maiden' (IV.i.86–7). By denying that Hero's speech has any relation to truth, the male authorities – her betrothed husband, her father, and her ruler – try to destroy her. Claudio tells her that the purpose of his accusations is 'To make you answer truly to your name' and insists that her name itself is proof of her guilt: 'Hero itself can blot out Hero's virtue' (IV.i.79, 82). Dehumanized by being deprived of language, Hero to her father's eyes becomes not a speaking subject but the objectified printed text of the story Claudio has told: 'the story that is printed in her blood' (IV.i.122). And so Leonato mourns that:

> she is fall'n
> Into a pit of ink, that the wide sea
> Hath drops too few to wash her clean again. (IV.i.139–41)

Hero's helplessness under this bewildering attack is total because not only is she effectively silenced but no one speaks to defend her. Beatrice never doubts her cousin's innocence, but she remains silent. Her distrust of glibness has become disdain for language as a tool of feminine weakness. She is contemptuous of men who substitute words for physical force: 'men are only turn'd into tongue ... He is now as valiant as Hercules that only tells a lie, and swears it' (IV.i.320–2). Her strongest wish is to be a man who could avenge her wronged cousin's honor, and her only strategy for fighting the injustice is to persuade Benedick to kill Claudio. Beatrice, who earlier claimed to be the equal of any man, shows that she is controlled by the patriarchal values of her society when she despairs: 'I cannot be a man with wishing, therefore I will die a woman with grieving' (IV.i.322–3).

If Beatrice has been co-opted by the collective prejudices of her culture, Hero's other potential defenders, her father and her lover, have also been colonized quite literally. Although most critics who comment at all on the setting of *Much Ado* perfunctorily characterize it as a sophisticated, courtly world, the most significant fact about Messina is that it is an Italian city-state ruled by Spain.[9] Leonato, the Governor of Messina, is subject to the authority of Don Pedro, Prince of Arragon. In Shakespeare's source for the Hero and Claudio story, Bandello's *Novella 22*, the relations between the natives of Messina and their Spanish rulers provide a framework for the plot. Bandello begins by describing the political context of his story:

> During the year of Grace MCCLXXXIII the Sicilians, no longer able to endure French domination, rose one day of the hour of Vespers and with unheard of savagery murdered all the French in Sicily – for so it was treacherously concerted throughout the island. Nor did they massacre only the men and women of the French nation, but on that day slew all Sicilian women who could be suspected of being

pregnant by Frenchmen ... whence arose the melancholy fame of the 'Sicilian Vespers.' King Piero of Arragon hearing of this came quickly thither with his army, and made himself lord of the Island.[10]

In the happy ending, after the calumniated heroine has been exonerated, Bandello emphasizes the integration of the Sicilian and the Spanish nobility. King Piero provides the heroine's dowry as if she were his own daughter and gives her father an honorable office in Messina. In the final paragraph, Bandello links the story to contemporary political circumstances by praising the political and military deeds of descendants of Sir Timbreo of Cardona, who 'was the first who in Sicily founded the noble race of the lords of the House of Cardona, of which there live today both in Sicily and in the Kingdom of Naples many men of no little esteem. In Spain also flourishes the noble breed of Cardona, producing men who do no shame to their ancestors both in arms and in the senate' (2:134). In Bandello's narrative, Messina welcomes King Piero's victory, but there are tensions between the citizens of Messina and their Spanish rulers.[11] Sir Timbreo (the Claudio figure) first tries to seduce Fenecia (the Hero figure), the daughter of a poor Messinese nobleman. Only when Fenecia virtuously rejects him does Timbreo decide to marry her, 'although he thought that he was demeaning himself by so doing' (2:113). When Timbreo is duped into believing that Fenecia is unchaste, her father assumes that his accusations are an excuse not to marry a woman who is his inferior in wealth and rank.

In Shakespeare's version, the historical details are vague (we do not know the year or the enemy in the recent battle), but the setting and political structure are insistently clear. The repetition of the name 'Messina' four times in the first few minutes of dialogue (I.i.2, 18, 39, 114) alerts us that the action takes place in a remote provincial city ruled by Spanish overlords.[12] The epithets 'Don,' for the Prince of Arragon and his brother, and 'Signior,' applied consistently to the Italians, are frequent reminders of the political situation. As in Bandello, the relations between the Spanish and the Messinese are cordial. Indeed, in *Much Ado*, although the Sicilian setting is a reminder of the infamous Sicilian Vespers and the potential for violence in the colonial enterprise, the emphasis is on the Italians' eager acquiescence to Spanish domination. While Sir Timbreo is Spanish, Claudio and Benedick are Italian followers of the Spanish Prince. Leonato, a native of Messina, is delighted when he hears the rumor that the foreign ruler intends to court his daughter and apparently just as pleased to accept the son-in-law that Don Pedro actually proposes to him. Equally as significant as the Italians' deference to Don Pedro is the ruling Spaniards' control of Messinese society. In Bandello, a Messinese nobleman approaches Leonato on Sir Timbreo's behalf, and King Piero figures only as the authority who rewards the virtuous at the end of the story. The plot to discredit Fenecia originates in sexual jealousy: a Messinese nobleman in love with Fenecia deceives Sir Timbreo in hopes of winning her after Timbreo renounces her. In *Much Ado*, of course, Don Pedro himself is the matchmaker, and Don John is responsible for the slander.[13] Hero is not the primary object of the plot but an expendable casualty in the murky hostility between the two Spanish princes.

The control of society by a colonial authority is dramatized in the first scene by Don Pedro's appropriation of Claudio's discourse. As soon as they are alone, Claudio begins to tell Don Pedro of his love for Hero. Don Pedro cuts him short, mocking his bookish wordiness:

> Thou wilt be like a lover presently,
> And tire the hearer with a book of words.
> If thou dost love fair Hero, cherish it,
> And I will break with her, and with her father,
> And thou shalt have her. Was't not to this end
> That thou began'st to twist so fine a story? (I.i.306–11)

Overriding Claudio's protest that his love requires 'a longer treatise' (I.i.315), Don Pedro plans to disguise himself as Claudio and to woo Hero in his stead, promising to

> take her hearing prisoner with the force
> And strong encounter of my amorous tale. (I.i.324–5)

Don Pedro insists on being the author of Claudio's story and has no doubts about the effectiveness of the tale he will tell.

Don Pedro's control of social discourse results from the deference paid to his political power and serves as a means of exercising and maintaining that power. Controlling language is an effective way of controlling the people who use it. After arranging Claudio's marriage with his consent, Don Pedro decides to make a match between Beatrice and Benedick without their knowledge. This time, instead of speaking for someone else, he directs the speech of others, teaching Hero, Leonato, and Claudio what to say. Although Don Pedro uses his power altruistically, the misunderstanding when Benedick and Claudio think that Don Pedro has courted Hero for himself warns of the dangers inherent in being appropriated into someone else's discourse.

These dangers are realized in Don John's plot. As Borachio outlines the plan, its object is to convince Don Pedro that 'he hath wrong'd his honor' (II.ii.23) by arranging Claudio's marriage to Hero. When Claudio was told that Don Pedro had betrayed him, he suffered passively and privately, and the mistake was easily corrected. When he is told that Hero is unchaste, he reacts to the dishonor to his Prince as well as to himself and immediately plans Hero's public disgrace. Instead of coming to nothing as had the previous deceptions and misunderstandings, the slander of Hero has serious consequences, partly, as I have already argued, because of the presuppositions about Hero as a woman, and partly because of political relationships. Claudio feels his first loyalty to Don Pedro, not to Hero and not to Leonato. In this situation, Don Pedro can assert his power and vindicate his honor without needing to speak or even to direct Claudio how to speak; he can rely on Claudio, who identifies his own interests with those of his Prince, to speak for him.

Even Leonato, who in Bandello's story defends his daughter, in *Much Ado* makes common cause with Hero's accusers. At the beginning of the wedding scene, he is a proud father whose only child is marrying a nobleman in an alliance arranged and blessed by the Prince himself. His sense of patriarchal authority is expressed in his assumption of control over language. He opens the scene peremptorily: 'Come, Friar Francis, be brief – only to the plain form of marriage ...' (IV.i.1–2). When Claudio answers 'No' to the friar's first question – 'You come hither, my lord, to marry this lady' – Leonato presumes to interpret Claudio by criticizing the friar's diction: 'To be married to her. Friar, you come to marry her' (I.i.4–8). And when the friar asks Claudio whether he knows of any impediment to the marriage, Leonato interrupts: 'I dare make his answer, none' (IV.i.18). But when Claudio savagely denounces Hero, Leonato's expansive confidence collapses, and he appeals to Don Pedro: 'Sweet Prince, why speak not you?' (IV.i.63). And when Don Pedro pronounces Hero guilty, Leonato accepts his word. Denying that 'the two princes' (IV.i.152) and Claudio would lie, he laments the outrage to his honor and wishes for his daughter's death.

Hero's disgrace, then, exposes problems already present in Messinese society. The conventional rhetoric of Claudio's denunciation associates Hero's supposed wantonness with the stereotype of female duplicity and sensuality:

> You seem to me as Dian in her orb,
> As chaste as is the bud ere it be blown;
> But you are more intemperate in your blood
> Than Venus, or those pamp'red animals
> That rage in savage sensuality. (IV.i.57-61)

And the cruelty of Don Pedro and Claudio justifies Beatrice's disdain and fear of established authority. 'Princes and counties!' she exclaims with sarcastic contempt. 'Surely a princely testimony, a goodly count, Count Comfect, a sweet gallant surely!' (IV.i.315-17). At the same time, the characters' distrust of language intensifies. Claudio's outrage is directed as much at Hero's deceitfulness as at her sexual misconduct, and Beatrice is overwhelmed by the power of the 'public accusation' and 'uncover'd slander' (IV.i.305) that have dishonored her cousin.

If events in the church seem to confirm the characters' worst fears, to the audience aware of their source in lies and deception the scene is an even more devastating critique of social discourse. Language, which according to Renaissance theory should bind people together in a civilized community, is portrayed as an unreliable guide to truth and a powerful instrument of coercion. The citizens of Messina, by speaking with the collective voice of their patriarchal culture and by articulating the desires of their foreign ruler, have lost the authority to order their own lives. Just how deeply encoded in language are the relationships of dominance and submission becomes clear when Leonato, finally persuaded of Hero's innocence, accosts Claudio and Don Pedro. Although Leonato shows contempt for Claudio by calling him 'boy' and using the familiar 'thou' form of the pronoun (V.i.79), he calls Don Pedro 'my lord' and continues to observe the pronominal convention by addressing him respectfully as 'you' (V.i.48). During this encounter, Don Pedro condescends to Leonato as an 'old man' (V.i.49-50, 73) and brushes him aside: 'I will not hear you' (V.i.107). As soon as Leonato and his brother withdraw, Don Pedro joins Claudio in laughing at their impotent rage.

This dramatic representation of sovereign political authority as a callow young man mocking the ineffectual anguish of a subject obviously provokes a critical attitude toward the uses of power. Just as obviously, as I have tried to trace Shakespeare's portrayal of the role of language in the dynamics of power, my own rhetoric has become misleading. Talk about the dangers of colonialist verbal appropriation comes out of twentieth-century, not sixteenth-century, discourse.[14] Shakespeare's contemporaries recognized the threat of foreign domination, and Shakespeare was aware, as was Francis Bacon when he analyzed the idols of the market place, that language is implicated in dangerous confusions of thought. But Shakespeare's Messina is not an Orwellian image of thought-control, and *Much Ado About Nothing* is not propaganda for a Sicilian liberation movement. Like the other comedies, *Much Ado* celebrates human community and the cohesive power of language even as it exposes dangers inherent in both. The pathos of Hero's disgrace and Leonato's grief is contained by knowledge that Dogberry and his friends are on the way to deliver Borachio's sworn statement that will reveal the truth.

Language, which creates the crisis, also resolves it. The collective nature of social discourse, which makes it a powerful coercive force to frighten Benedick with the name of cuckold and to drive the disgraced Hero from society, also limits authoritative control. In Mikhail Bakhtin's terms, language is a *heteroglossia*, an unsystematic collection of the voices of diverse social groups that guarantees the dispersion of creative authorship and authority throughout society.[15] In addition, the inherent imprecision and fluidity of language create spaces where unknown and unofficial truths can emerge. The diversity of social discourse and the polysemic fluidity of language, its capacity for irony and resonant ambiguity as well as misunderstanding and deception, prevent total control of the community by any univocal authority.

I have already noted one form of this verbal creativity in Beatrice's parodies of hierarchical power: when, for example, she tells Don Pedro that he is 'too costly to wear every day' (II.i.328–9), or when she instructs Hero how to deal with patriarchal authority in selecting a husband: 'it is my cousin's duty to make cur'sy and say, "Father, as it please you." But yet for all that, cousin, let him be a handsome fellow, or else make another cur'sy and say, "Father, as it please me"' (II.i.52–6). The plot to trick Beatrice and Benedick into love enacts more fully the benign results of the multivalency of social discourse. Not only are the staged conversations fictions created to deceive their unwitting audiences, they are cooperative efforts that depend for their success on their listeners' susceptibility to other voices. Beatrice and Benedick are able to fall in love because they trust their friends' praise of the other's merits, because they believe their friends' report that they are loved by the other, and because they accept their friends' accusations that their own speech misrepresents the truth.[16] The possibility of verbal ambiguity, moreover, allows their love to flourish – a potential exploited most delightfully perhaps in Benedick's imaginative deconstruction of Beatrice's invitation to dinner: 'Ha! "Against my will I am sent to bid you come in to dinner" – there's a double meaning in that. "I took no more pains for those thanks than you took pains to thank me" – that's as much as to say "Any pains that I take for you is as easy as thanks"' (II.iii.257–62).

Just as Benedick's discovery of double meanings in Beatrice's words allows him to requite the love he finds there, misunderstandings and ambiguities contribute to Hero's vindication. Midway through the scene of the interrupted wedding, Friar Francis announces his belief in Hero's innocence. 'By noting of the lady,' he explains, he has 'mark'd' (IV.i.158), as evidence of her innocence, the blushes that Claudio had interpreted as a sign of 'guiltiness, not modesty' (IV.i.42). The friar presents his 'noting' and 'marking' as at once a reading of ambiguous signs and as a writing, with himself as an author of more credible authority than Claudio:

> Trust not my *reading*, nor my *observations*,
> Which with experimental seal doth warrant
> The tenure of my *book*; trust not my age,
> My reverence, calling, nor divinity,
> If this sweet lady lie not guiltless here
> Under some biting error. (IV.i.165–70; italics added)

He then counsels Leonato to hide Hero away and 'publish it that she is dead indeed' (IV.i.204).

The friar's book, of course, is only partly accurate. When the news of Hero's death is published, Claudio does not feel remorse or regret for his lost love as predicted. But the fiction is also intended for the community as a whole, and in that object the plan succeeds. When the watchmen tell the sexton about the plot to slander Hero, he believes them because their account fits the facts as he knows them: 'Hero was in this manner accus'd, in this very manner refus'd, and upon the grief of this suddenly died' (IV.ii.61–3). The line from Borachio's confession of his part in the plot to the full revelation of the truth is hilariously circuitous. In his drunken ramblings, Borachio deplores men's subservience to social conventions and fads, exclaiming on 'what a deformed thief this fashion is' (III.iii.124). The watch who overhear him are more concerned to arrest the notorious thief named Deformed than to reveal Don John's treachery. Master Constable Dogberry, hearing the accusation against Don John, is indignant: 'Why, this is flat perjury, to call a prince's brother villain' (IV.ii.41-2). But eventually, through the attempt to apprehend the thief Deformed and to record the full extent of the 'perjury' against Don John, Borachio's story is told. By repudiating Hero publicly, Claudio and Don Pedro involve the whole community that includes the friar, Dogberry and the watch, Borachio, and the sexton. Social discourse, then, in addition to courtly formality and sophisticated wit, includes the friar's fiction, Borachio's drunken ramblings, Dogberry's malapropisms and homely aphorisms, and the sexton's conscientious recording of the testimony of the watch. Out of this strange mixture, truth emerges. Significantly, the society that in the beginning of the play counted only those 'of name' is saved by its most despised members, most effectively by the efforts of a nameless sexton.

The power of Don Pedro's authoritative discourse, then, is limited, as Dogberry understands in his own muddled way. Instructing the watchmen in their duties, he tells them: 'This is your charge: ... you are to bid any man stand, in the Prince's name' (III.iii.24-6), but, he continues, if the culprit will not stand: 'Why then take no note of him, but let him go ... and thank God you are rid of a knave' (III.iii.28-30). They should, for example, 'call at all the alehouses, and bid those that are drunk get them to bed' (III.iii.42-3), but if the drunks decline to obey, Dogberry's advice is to 'let them alone till they are sober' (III.iii.45-6). What Dogberry recognizes is the futility of attempting to impose control over those who do not accept your authority. Or, as he explains, as representatives of 'the Prince's own person' (III.iii.75), the watch are empowered to detain any man at all, even the Prince himself, but in practice they can stop the Prince only if 'the Prince be willing, for indeed the watch ought to offend no man, and it is an offense to stay a man against his will' (80-2). Although originally it seemed that Don Pedro and the collective values of society constituted authority in Messina and that Don Pedro would compose the 'amorous tale' of Claudio and Hero, it has emerged that Don John, rejecting that authority, has told another story. As Ursula tells Beatrice, 'Don John is the author of all' (V.ii.98-9). With the attribution of authorship comes responsibility. Don John is held accountable, and Hero is vindicated.

Hero's vindication is also a vindication of language. While her name is blackened, words seem useless. Leonato rejects Antonio's consolatory advice as hollow:

> brother, men
> Can counsel and speak comfort to that grief
> Which they themselves not feel, but tasting it,
> Their counsel turns to passion, which before
> Would ...
> Charm ache with air, and agony with words. (v.i.20–6)

If speech is only air to Leonato in his grief, the written word is equally powerless:

> For there was never yet philosopher
> That could endure the toothache patiently,
> However they have writ the style of gods. (v.i.35–7)

Yet before the scene is over, Borachio's confession testifies to the power of words: 'My villainy they have upon record, which I had rather seal with my death than repeat over to my shame' (239–41). And Don Pedro and Claudio understand that power: '**D. Pedro.** Runs not this speech like iron through your blood? **Claud.** I have drunk poison whiles he utter'd it' (v.i.244–6).

Appropriately, the reparation that Don Pedro and Claudio must make for the damage their words have done is verbal. 'I cannot bid you bid my daughter live – / That were impossible,' Leonato says,

> but I pray you both,
> Possess the people in Messina here
> How innocent she died, and if your love
> Can labor aught in sad invention,
> Hang her an epitaph upon her tomb,
> And sing it to her bones, sing it to-night. (v.i.279–85)

Human language is not omnipotent – it cannot resurrect the dead – but it is, in Jonson's phrase, 'the instrument of *Society*' that can restore Hero's good name in the community, her life in society.[17] To object, as critics have done, that Claudio's observances at Hero's tomb seem too formal and conventional to express love and remorse convincingly is, I think, to miss the point. Events have demonstrated the radical uncertainty of individual perceptions, which are inextricably involved in cultural codes and conventions and susceptible to ignorance and error. This treacherous instability can be controlled at least partially by the openness and permanence of communal and written forms of discourse.[18] By writing an epitaph and participating in a communal ritual, Claudio gives formal shape to his obligations to Hero, demonstrating not intense romantic feeling but commitment and responsibility. The necessary complement to Claudio's epitaph is the song that Balthasar, as representative of the social group, sings, asking forgiveness for Hero's detractors.

Much Ado About Nothing achieves its happy ending not by resolving conflicts and coming to rest on a harmonious major chord but by dramatizing a dynamic tension between impulses towards freedom and towards responsibility and order. While social discourse constitutes an unavoidable, arbitrary authority, its diversity and multivalency also limit its power to enforce conformity. If the slipperiness of language exerts a centrifugal force that threatens social cohesion, the written word and the collective nature of language provide a measure of stability. When Benedick and Beatrice would disclaim their love, they are protected from their own skittishness through the efforts of their friends and the stabilizing power of the written word. Their friends produce sonnets each has written as evidence of their mutual love. Beatrice and Benedick fall in love in the terms available in their culture, but they continue to resist the rigidifying, coercive force of linguistic formulas and cultural norms. Benedick, the dedicated bachelor, decides to accept the yoke of marriage, but he speaks of his decision as defying rather than conforming to social expectations and conceives of marriage in terms of change rather than permanence: 'since I do purpose to marry, I will think nothing to any purpose that the world can say against it, and therefore never flout at me for what I have said against it; for man is a giddy thing, and this is my conclusion' (v.iv.105-9). He acknowledges authorship of his 'halting sonnet' (v.iv.87) as evidence of his love for Beatrice, but he knows that the conventional love sonnet is not his style. As he tells Beatrice, they are 'too wise to woo peaceably' (v.ii.72), and the linguistic forms appropriate to them are the destabilizing ones of parody, ambiguity, irony, and paradox. They first declare their love in language that is a triumph of ambiguity: '**Bene**. I do love nothing in the world so well as you – is not that strange? **Beat**. As strange as the thing I know not. It were as possible for me to say I lov'd nothing so well as you, but believe me not; and yet I lie not: I confess nothing, nor I deny nothing' (IV.i.267–72). In the last scene, they reaffirm their love in language that denies it: '**Bene**. Come, I will have thee, but by this light, I take thee for pity. **Beat**. I would not deny you, but by this good day, I yield upon great persuasion, and partly to save your life, for I was told you were in a consumption' (V.iv.92–7). And Benedick's last word on marriage is a mock encomium of cuckoldry: 'Prince, ... get thee a wife. There is no staff more reverent than one tipp'd with horn' (V.iv.122–4). Benedick's paradoxical valuing of the cuckold's horn over the staff of office does not constitute a rejection of political authority or of male dominance, but his playful, ironic language acknowledges the contingency of both authorities.

Claudio and Hero do not speak with the ironic wit of Beatrice and Benedick, but their marriage too embodies a tension between acceptance and defiance of social hierarchy. Claudio's acceptance of an unknown and unseen bride from Leonato revises the form of the earlier betrothal by asserting Leonato's authority at the expense of Don Pedro's. This modification of the way the political hierarchy functions is not, of course, a repudiation of Spanish hegemony any more than Benedick's encomium of cuckoldry is a repudiation of male dominance. But both gestures imply limits to hierarchical power.

Much Ado About Nothing is not an attack on the principle of hierarchy, but it does reveal hierarchical structures as often arbitrary, contradictory, dangerous, and irrelevant. In one of the 'old ends' with which he guards his discourse, Dogberry suggests that hierarchy is unavoidable: 'and two men ride of a horse, one must ride behind' (III.v.36–7). But Dogberry has also suggested the theory that political authority governs by the consent of the governed: 'it is an offense to stay a man against his will' (III.iii.81–2). The ordering, centralizing language of official hierarchy is only one of the competing voices heard in Messina. No one defies Don Pedro's authority at the end of the play, but no one listens to him much either. Whereas Bandello's story of the slandered bride moves from an account of the violent overthrow of a political authority to a description of the integration of the rulers with the ruled, Shakespeare's moves from a dramatization of excessive deference to political authority to a kind of marginalization of that authority. At the end of the play Don Pedro is addressed respectfully as Prince, but his voice is only one among many and a relatively minor one at that. After discovering that he has been repeating slanders authored by Don John, Don Pedro is noticeably chastened and silent, but his experience is only an especially humiliating version of the common one. Even Don John is not in fact 'the author of all' as alleged: Borachio invents the story he tells. In one sense, all the characters in *Much Ado* are 'parrot-teachers.' Their speech is made up of old ends of common linguistic usages, rhetorical conventions, and social customs that compose an authorless discourse which they have only the illusion of creating and controlling. But there is another sense in which they are all authors, who, out of the ambiguous, polysemic fluidity of social discourse, create the texts of themselves and, through their dialogues with each other, authorize their society.

Part Five

Renewal and Reciprocity

CHAPTER TEN

Changing Places in Arden: *As You Like It*

'one man in his time plays many parts' (II.vii.142)

While in *The Merry Wives of Windsor* and *Much Ado About Nothing* the tranquility of provincial communities is disrupted by visitors from outside, in *As You Like It* and *Twelfth Night* trouble is native born. Rather than having to resist seduction and domination by socially and politically superior outsiders, the protagonists must confront conflicts generated within their own social groups. In both plays, erosion of social cohesion is well under way when the dramatic action begins. Reminders of death in the early scenes introduce societies that have suffered crucial losses and have been unable to contain the centrifugal forces that weaken social bonds. While the plots of *The Merry Wives* and *Much Ado* develop intrigues that threaten or protect social stability, the dramatic action of *As You Like It* and of *Twelfth Night* primarily consists of the process of rebuilding a society that has disintegrated.

In *As You Like It*, the tyrannies of Oliver and Duke Frederick are the direct causes of the first movement of the action, the breakup of society that disperses the major characters into the forest of Arden. The double villainy of Frederick and Oliver suggests that some flaw in society itself has allowed or even facilitated their greed and malice. From the perspective of sixteenth-century England, the social structure portrayed is archaic. Duke Frederick is sovereign within his domain. No central government restrains his usurpation of his brother's place or forces Oliver to provide his brother with the legacy and education stipulated in their father's will. The illegality of these actions, however, receives little emphasis in the dialogue.

And Frederick's ability to manipulate the law in order to seize Oliver's property certainly does not suggest that an undeveloped government bureaucracy is the core of the problem. Instead, the dramatic focus is on the death of Sir Rowland de Boys and the exile of Duke Senior as the crucial events that have destabilized conditions in the two initial locales, the country estate and the court. Both losses are old news, events that occurred in some unspecified past, presumably more recent than the unremembered deaths of Orlando's and Rosalind's mothers, but long enough ago that, as the play opens, the children are not feeling acute personal grief so much as a sense of loss and displacement.

For Orlando, his father's death means primarily loss of social rank. His older brother Oliver has deprived him of the manners and means to qualify as a gentleman. Orlando does not covet his brother's wealth and power. Although he is not greatly impressed by the 'poor a thousand crowns' (I.i.2–3) left him in his father's will, his complaint is not the inadequacy of his inheritance but being denied what he sees as his birthright, his status as a gentleman.[1] Orlando believes that gentility is his by nature: 'the gentle condition of blood' (I.i.44–5) is his biological inheritance. But although he feels within himself 'the spirit of [his] father' (I.i.22, 70), even direct descent from Sir Rowland de Boys is not enough to make him a gentleman. What bothers Orlando most is that his brother 'mines [his] gentility with [his] education' (I.i.21), denying him 'gentleman-like qualities' and training him instead 'like a peasant' (I.i.68–70). Birth is the basis of his claim, but natural gentility must be developed through education. And it must be acknowledged. In addition to appropriate manners and accomplishments, Orlando needs confirmation of his status by others. What 'nature gave me,' he complains, Oliver's 'countenance seems to take from me' (I.i.18–19).

The brothers' quarrel in the opening scene is about Orlando's place in the social hierarchy. Oliver's peremptory challenges to Orlando – 'Know you where you are, sir? ... Know you before whom, sir?' (I.i.40–2) – insist on his superior position. Orlando professes willingness to defer to his older brother but demands for himself acceptance as a gentleman, 'the place of a brother' (I.i.19–20) which must be conferred by Oliver. If Orlando feels out of place among the peasants on his brother's estate, he feels equally disoriented in Oliver's presence. In a hierarchical society where political and economic status as well as personal allegiances are based on kinship, Orlando has no recognized place.

Rosalind has suffered less severe loss than Orlando. Her father is alive and well, living in the forest of Arden. She has been brought up with Duke's Frederick's daughter and has received an education appropriate to her birth. Still, she too is conscious of her poverty and sad, thinking about 'the condition of [her] estate' (I.ii.15). But Rosalind responds differently to the loss of social rank. While Orlando vents his frustration and anger at Oliver, Rosalind more diplomatically and more generally attributes life's inequities to Fortune, whose 'benefits are mightily misplac'd' (I.ii.34–5). Orlando looks to the past; Rosalind's thoughts tend towards the future. When Celia urges her to be merry, love is the topic Rosalind proposes for discussion. When Celia suggests mocking 'the good huswife Fortune from her wheel, that her gifts may henceforth be bestow'd equally,' Rosalind wryly notes that 'the bountiful blind woman doth most mistake in her gifts to women' (I.ii.31–3, 35–6). The direction of her thoughts suggests that what distresses Rosalind most about the condition of her estate is the uncertain marriage prospect of a young woman in her anomalous position. And, finally, while Orlando assumes that kinship should determine one's place in the social order, Rosalind insists that individual merit supersedes blood ties. When Duke Frederick banishes her because she is her 'father's daughter' (I.iii.58), she replies sharply, 'Treason is not inherited, my lord' (I.iii.61). Orlando wants above all to be recognized as his father's son; Rosalind demands to be judged independently and thinks less about her father than her 'child's father' (I.iii.11).

Of course, these contrasts are not absolute. Orlando sees his brother's selfishness as an instance of 'the fashion of these times' (II.iii.59), and Rosalind is acutely aware of her usurping uncle's personal responsibility for her plight. Orlando does not rely wholly on pride in being Sir Rowland de Boys' son. He goes to court to win from the Duke, through his own merit, the honor denied him by his brother. Rosalind feels family loyalty. She indignantly defends her father's honor from the implication of treason, and she falls in love with Orlando at least partly because her father loved his father. The differences between Orlando's and Rosalind's responses to their analogous situations, then, do not initiate a clear contest between competing views of human society. The play clouds the issue of social power even while raising it.

By carefully selecting evidence it would be possible to find in the play an attack on the aggressive acquisitiveness of an increasingly individualistic social ethos. The discrepancy between gentle birth and economic impotence suffered by Orlando and Rosalind and Orlando's complaint that in the present 'none will sweat but for promotion' in contrast with the 'constant service of the antique world' (II.iii.60, 57) hint at the transition from a society of inherited rights and loyalties to a system based on wealth. In this reading, Frederick's and Oliver's violations of family bonds would constitute a critique of an emergent pattern of social classes derived from individual ability and ambition.

But seeing Duke Frederick and Oliver as the vanguard of an emergent meritocracy is hardly a promising approach to the play's social dynamics. The social structure dominated by Duke Frederick is essentially feudal, a system of estates in which the individual's place is determined by birth. The system of primogeniture, which makes Oliver his brother's better, is explicitly associated with tradition, not innovation. Frederick's usurping of his brother's place is a family affair, a struggle for power among competing nobles. While he violates traditional rights, he also ignores individual merit and initiative. Not only does he banish Rosalind because she is her father's daughter, he refuses to reward Orlando because he is his father's son. Similarly, Oliver is guilty both of repudiating the bond of blood linking him to Orlando and of denying his brother the means to make his own way in the world.

A more cogent case can be made for reversing the terms of the argument. From this perspective, the French setting allows the play to condemn the injustices of a hierarchy of inherited power without directly attacking contemporary English social order. In contrast with the nascent capitalism of *The Merchant of Venice*, where conflict erupts between economic and political power, in the feudal world of *As You Like It*, social rank defines political and economic power. The villainies of Frederick and Oliver, then, expose not the acquisitiveness of an emergent social order but the abuses invited by a traditional order based on kinship. This approach, however, obviously cannot produce a total reading of the play either. While Oliver's and Frederick's tyrannies certainly demonstrate inherent social injustices, the happiness promised in the last scene relies as heavily on inherited privilege as do the cruelties of the opening scenes.

Undoubtedly theater audiences and readers in various times and places have associated the play's representations of injustice with actual social phenomena and will continue to do so. But the ways in which we make these connections are shaped more by our own presuppositions than by whatever political agendas shaped the texts. Shakespeare's comedies, like most early modern political discourse, assume the necessity of social and political hierarchies, but their explorations of forms and operations of hierarchical power are at least potentially subversive. The ideas about social justice articulated within *As You Like It* do not constitute a case for or against particular institutions or practices, but they uncover inconsistencies and contradictions and suggest that the possible ways of structuring society are varied, susceptible to discussion, and dependent on human choice. By foregrounding the claims of kinship and of individual merit, the play registers the ambivalences of a culture that was imbued with an ideology of inherited privilege yet worked increasingly on the basis of individual behavior.[2] Similarly, the quarrel between Orlando and Oliver points to contemporary anxieties about primogeniture.

While protecting the integrity of family property was generally respected, so too were the desire and obligation to provide for all one's children. Ralph Houlbrooke recounts a fifteenth-century case which demonstrates that Orlando's concern with loss of social rank as well as Oliver's repudiation of their father's wishes was grounded in historical reality: 'Lying on his death bed in 1444, William Paston concluded, somewhat late in the day, that the meagre provision he had made for his younger sons would force them to "hold the plowe be the tayle." He resolved to give them certain manors. He would not, he told his eldest son John, give so much to one that the rest should not have enough to live on. But after his father's death John ruthlessly prevented the implementation of these oral provisions.'[3] The conflicts among the descendants of William Paston and of Sir Rowland de Boys reveal the tensions generated by a system of inheritance that perpetuated the blood tie it regulated and denied the family bond it preserved. Primogeniture was widespread, particularly among the aristocracy, but its use was by no means uniform, inheritance practices varying geographically as well as by class. Indeed, according to Francis Bacon, in 1600 the rules and customs governing the distribution of property were so chaotic that inheritances were tossed upon a sea of legal uncertainty.[4] Thus Orlando's plight comments on unstable social conditions, and his complaints, as Louis Montrose has fully documented, contribute to a body of literature bitterly protesting the inequities and abuses of primogeniture.[5]

Nevertheless, the play does not condemn primogeniture unequivocally. Orlando's resentment is directed at Oliver's abuse of the system rather than at Sir Rowland's decision to leave the bulk of his property to his oldest son. More important than Orlando's articulation of the suffering of the younger son or Duke Senior's claim to the rights of the elder son is the conjunction of their contrasting perspectives. Significant too is the play's demystifying language. While justifications of primogeniture often invoked scripture and nature, in *As You Like It* primogeniture has been established by the 'courtesy of nations' and 'tradition' (I.i.46, 47). Orlando may assume that the link between birth and social entitlement is self-evident, but his language reminds us that, while biological inheritance is undeniable, its social significance is humanly constructed. Furthermore, the setting in feudal France implies that such conventions are geographically and historically contingent. Thus, in spite of the characters' tendency to attribute their troubles to forces beyond human control, their problems obviously result from expectations and pressures exerted by social power. When Rosalind regrets that she is 'out of suits with Fortune' (I.ii.246) or when Amiens refers to the 'stubbornness of fortune' (II.i.19), they express a sense of impotence but do not obscure the human agency responsible for the political and economic circumstances beyond their personal control.

As You Like It presents no blueprint for a perfect society. The play as a whole endorses neither Le Beau's image of a 'better world' where merit is rewarded nor Celia's ideal world where the gifts of fortune are distributed equally. But the play does present society as disintegrating because it fails to satisfy certain needs. Much of the present unease is experienced as an abrupt break with the past. The distress both Rosalind and Orlando feel about their fathers arises primarily from the repudiation of the past by the present. Orlando must struggle to remember the past because Oliver has ignored his father's will and abandoned his father's values. So too Rosalind feels pressure from Celia to forget her banished father in present pleasure. And if the instability of present society is a measure of its lack of continuity with the past, it is also an expression of the lack of any clear expectations about the shape of the future. In most of the comedies, we first meet the young protagonists as they are planning their futures. There are worlds of difference, of course, between Kate's anxiety about dancing barefoot at Bianca's wedding and Portia's about a loveless marriage, between Petruchio's intention to marry wealthily and the King of Navarre's vow of celibacy, and none of these expectations is fulfilled as imagined. Still, the rule is expectation which subsequent action realizes, frustrates, or transforms. The first appearances of Rosalind and Orlando are striking not merely because they are engaged in the process of remembering, but because neither seems able to imagine a future either to dread or to hope for.

A corollary to the repudiation of the past and the absence of future vision is the lack of both security and freedom. All the characters – old Adam, Charles the wrestler, Oliver, and Frederick as well as Orlando and Rosalind – are threatened. They cannot live safely in the situations in which we find them as the play opens, and they all feel constrained by the power of others. Even Duke Frederick, ostensibly the most powerful among them, not only feels threatened by Rosalind and Orlando, but demonstrably is frustrated in every action he initiates.

Finally and most strikingly, the social order fails to provide a workable balance of individual and communal identity. Orlando is the clearest instance. Without recognition by others, he is confused about his own identity. Deprived of participation in established cultural practices, 'such exercises as may become a gentleman' (I.i.72), he feels unable to develop his individual talents. Without a confident sense of himself, he is unable to establish relations with others, standing 'a mere liveless block' (I.ii.251) to Rosalind's overture. Rosalind is less undone by her situation than Orlando, but she too is involved in this vicious circle. Alienated by her father's banishment, she responds to Celia's offer of love and friendship with a pointed reminder of the condition of her own estate and the protest that she can rejoice in Celia's fortune only by forgetting her own.

In terms of plot, then, the most significant consequence of Oliver's replacement of his father and Frederick's of his brother is that Orlando and Rosalind are left without clearly defined social roles. They are dissatisfied with their marginalized positions, and they constitute threats to Oliver and Frederick. This rigidly hierarchical social structure cannot tolerate displaced people. Even before Adam warns Orlando that 'This is no place, this house is but a butchery' (II.iii.27), it has become clear that there is no place for Orlando with his brother and no place for Rosalind at court. But at the same time that this society is marked by destabilizing estrangement and isolation, it also demonstrates the interdependence of its members. A direct consequence of Frederick's theft of his brother's place has been to alter the positions of everyone else. Rosalind and

Celia have also changed places: Celia is now the Duke's daughter and Rosalind his niece. Orlando has become the object of suspicion as the son of the Duke's enemy instead of a potential recipient of patronage as the son of a worthy father. Rosalind's banishment is also Celia's banishment and Touchstone's. The political insecurities that deny Orlando favor at court combine with Oliver's jealousy to drive Orlando into exile. Celia's decision to go with her cousin sends Oliver after Orlando. Thus, the personal and political ties among characters are so intertwined that Duke Frederick's usurpation of his brother's place eventually impels all the major characters to follow Duke Senior into exile.

Because Rosalind is an unusually articulate and enterprising heroine who reflects on the nature of love and engineers an extended albeit fictionalized courtship for herself, life in the forest of Arden usually is discussed as a period of moral and emotional growth.[6] Less attention has focused on the explicitly social and political concerns of the forest scenes. A political action and its consequences transfer the dramatic action to the forest. Once in Arden, the refugees are as much engaged in the re-establishment of a social order as in self-reflection or flirtation.

For these characters who have escaped from oppression and violence, the forest of Arden offers the possibility of a better world, not because it is closer to nature, but simply because it provides an opportunity to start again. Physical nature demands their attention but exerts no moral authority. That Duke Senior can find tongues in trees and sermons in stones is more to his credit than to nature's. And while the description of the wounded deer abandoned by its kind is not an especially horrifying picture of nature red in tooth and claw, it does point to compassion as a human value not inherent in impersonal nature. The allegorical detail of Jaques' reported moralizing of the spectacle, moreover, keeps our attention on the human parallels and on the act of interpretation.

> 'Ay,' quoth Jaques,
> 'Sweep on, you fat and greasy citizens,
> 'Tis just the fashion. Wherefore do you look
> Upon that poor and broken bankrupt there?'
> Thus most invectively he pierceth through
> The body of the country, city, court,
> Yea, and of this our life, swearing that we

Are mere usurpers, tyrants, and what's worse,
To fright the animals and to kill them up
In their assign'd and native dwelling-place. (II.i.54–63)

Jaques extends the play's anatomizing of social ills to include city life as well as the court and country. Even in the process of condemning anthropocentrism, he appropriates nature for his own purposes. Like the Duke's uneasiness about shooting the 'native burghers of this desert city' (II.i.23), Jaques' sentimental moralizing demonstrates the human disposition to anthropomorphize nature. Conversely, Jaques' boast that he can 'suck melancholy out of a song, as a weasel sucks eggs' (II.v.13), Orlando's description of his care of Adam as 'like a doe' nurturing her fawn (II.vii.128), and Rosalind's threat to be more jealous 'than a Barbary cock-pigeon over his hen' (IV.i.150–1) naturalize human conduct. But in spite of the impulse to humanize nature and to naturalize humanity, the recurrent figures linking men and women with animals and plants function as comparisons between unlikes rather than as identifications of the human and the natural. In *A Midsummer Night's Dream* human and non-human nature imperceptibly merge, but in *As You Like It* the natural and the human are always distinct.

Nature in the forest of Arden is first of all a source of physical suffering. The winter wind may be less cutting than the perfidy of flattering courtiers, but it still bites and makes the body shrink with cold. Nature unsoftened by human intervention is painful for all the exiles, but for an old man such as Adam, it is life-threatening. In the form of a 'suck'd and hungry lioness' (IV.iii.126) it would have killed Oliver except for Orlando's intervention. In so far as the forest is a world of nature, then, it establishes human cooperation as necessary for survival. Nature is not wholly dangerous and destructive, of course. A primary function of cooperative human effort is to utilize nature: the deer and sheep of Arden supply food and clothing, a cave offers protection, and trees afford shade and a convenient place to display love poems. But the forest is not an imitable model for human behavior. Nature imposes limitations on human enterprise, but within those limitations it is manipulated for human ends.

As I argued earlier in chapter 8, *The Merry Wives of Windsor* participates in the pastoral tradition by dramatizing a conflict between the values of court and country and by preferring the innocence of rural simplicity to courtly sophistication. Although *As You Like It* is often regarded as a version of pastoral and exemplifies the movement from corrupt society to an innocent rural setting that is typical of pastoral romances,[7] it rejects the pastoral assumption that value resides in the natural world. There is little textual justification for the wide critical consensus that the visitors are regenerated by achieving harmony with nature during their stay in the forest. Those who spend time in the forest give no evidence of needing regeneration, and those who need it, Oliver and Frederick, repent before they can experience the rhythm of forest life. They are converted from their evil ways, moreover, by the exemplary human virtue of Orlando and 'an old religious man' (V.iv.160). In fact, *As You Like It* invokes such pastoral motifs as the oppositions between court and country and between action and contemplation in order to subvert them. The shepherd Corin is 'a true laborer' (III.ii.73) with greasy hands who shows little inclination for piping delightful melodies. It is not the natives but the courtly refugees who seem to 'fleet the time carelessly' (I.i.118) and who idealize their forest sojourn as a life of pastoral *otium*. They actually live, however, not by watching flocks graze but by the anti-pastoral activity of hunting in order to survive.[8] What emerges when Touchstone and Corin debate the relative merits of the country and the court is not only that the question is irresolvable but that the lives of shepherds and courtiers alike are governed by social conventions: 'Those that are good manners at the court are as ridiculous in the country as the behavior of the country is most mockable at the court' (III.ii.45-8). In spite of Touchstone's accusation to Corin, 'thou art raw' (III,ii,72), Corin is obviously no less civilized than Touchstone, but the product of another culture with different norms of behavior, language, and thought.

The exiles who gather in the forest of Arden leave their homes because they are compelled to, not because they are disillusioned with human depravity and long for solitude. Celia and Rosalind set off to find Rosalind's father, and Orlando's announced goal, 'some settled low content' (II.iii.68), indicates that he too is looking for a niche in human society that will give him security and freedom. Although newcomers to the forest call it 'uncouth' and 'wild' (II.vi.6; V.iv.159), the forest of Arden is not the mysterious wilderness that the exiles from Athens wander through in *A Midsummer Night's Dream*. With its areas for hunting and grazing, it is already nature methodized before the exiles arrive. Indeed, as Richard Marienstras has pointed out, 'forest' is as much a legal as a geographical label, designating a valuable property where common law is replaced by special laws that protect the forest and reserve its pleasures for the privileged.⁹ 'Hunting in Forests, Chases, and such like priviledged places of pleasure,' declared John Manwood, 'is only for Kings, Princes, and great worthy personnages, and not for mean men of mean calling or condition.'¹⁰ Much of the important action, moreover, takes place not in the wooded area where the Duke and his worthy followers hunt, but in the cleared land bordering the forest. Here in the purlieus of the forest is the house and the 'sheep-cote fenc'd about with olive-trees' (IV.iii.77) where Aliena and Ganymede become the nexus of a network of relationships that creates a new social order.

The nucleus of the emergent society is a relationship produced by nurture, not nature. In growing up together Celia and Rosalind have formed ties 'dearer than the natural bond of sisters' (I.ii.276). Their artificial sisterhood is stronger than the blood relationship of Celia to her father and stronger than the natural brotherhoods of Orlando and Oliver and of Duke Frederick and Duke Senior. Similarly, bonds of personal love and loyalty unite Touchstone with Celia, Adam with Orlando, and Duke Senior with his men. These relationships function most prominently not by satisfying private emotional needs but by providing a means of achieving social identities.

For example, when Celia offers her cousin support in banishment, Rosalind's replies are brief and listless until Celia proposes assuming a recognizable social position by dressing in 'poor and mean attire'(I.iii.111). Inferior social rank apparently is less paralyzing for Rosalind than no rank at all, and she immediately plans her own role as Ganymede, for the first time taking the initiative in dialogue with Celia. Orlando develops a similar concentration of purpose through interaction with Adam. Like Rosalind, Orlando is initially confused and directionless when told he must flee. 'Why, whither, Adam, wouldst thou have me go?' he asks, complaining that the only alternative to being murdered by his brother is to become a beggar or thief:

> This I must do, or know not what to do;
> Yet this I will not do, do how I can. (II.iii.29, 34–5)¹¹

More important in reviving Orlando's spirits than Adam's offer of his five hundred crowns of savings is his request to 'let me be your servant' (II.iii.46). Adam's proposal to follow allows Orlando to lead.

Celia and Adam give Rosalind and Orlando purpose and direction by enabling them to form recognizable social identities. Significantly, they assume dominant roles as man and master, but equally important, they are not inspired by dreams of regaining their lost social status. Orlando hopes for 'some settled low content,' and Rosalind happily settles into a simple rural life. They continue to think in terms of social hierarchy and are contented with humble rank. What makes action possible for both is a useful function to serve. Orlando becomes Adam's protector, and Rosalind empowers herself by 'comfort[ing] the weaker vessel' (II.iv.6).

Like the other residents of Arden, Rosalind and Orlando are not concerned with getting back to nature but with asserting their humanness in the face of impersonal nature. They solve the basic problem of physical survival by joining forces with others of their kind, Rosalind and Celia by finding a place in the local agricultural economy and Orlando and Adam by joining Duke Senior's band of hunters. Simultaneously with its representation of society as controlling nature for human ends, the play presents civilization as the regulation of natural human appetites for mutual benefit. The exhausted newcomers to the forest are dependent on the compassion and generosity as well as the skill and industry of others. Duke Senior's admonishment to Orlando, 'Your gentleness shall force, / More than your force move us to gentleness' (II.vii.102–3), articulates personally the principles embodied in the ritualized hunt, the control of aggression and the submergence of individual needs in collective ones. And while rituals of hunting and hospitality regulate appetites for food, rituals of courtship and marriage regulate sexual appetites. Just as Duke Senior reprimands Orlando's apparent lack of civility, Jaques counsels Touchstone: 'Get you to church, and have a good priest that can tell you what marriage is' (III.iii.84–6). Indeed, the recurrent metaphoric identification of women with deer and of the horns of the hunter with those of the married man suggest that the two pursuits are closely related, different aspects of aggression.

In the process of creating human order in the forest, the exiles consciously rectify the deficiencies of the society they have left. Although in one sense this endeavor involves breaking with their past, in another sense the forest society is a deliberate extension of civilized tradition. Amiens' song implies that the oppression they have escaped was due to such failures of memory as 'ingratitude,' 'benefits forgot,' and 'friend rememb'red not' (II.vii.174–90).

Orlando's entrance with old Adam on his shoulders recalls Aeneas bearing Anchises from the ruins of old Troy to the founding of new Troy and emblemizes the fidelity of the new community in the forest to the values of the old. Thus Orlando's meeting with Duke Senior involves a ritualistic recital of a common past:

> **Orl.** If ever you have look'd on better days,
> If ever been where bells have knoll'd to church,
> If ever sate at any good man's feast,
> If ever from your eyelids wip'd a tear,
> And know what 'tis to pity, and be pitied,
> Let gentleness my strong enforcement be ...
> **Duke S.** True is it that we have seen better days,
> And have with holy bell been knoll'd to church,
> And sat at good men's feasts, and wip'd our eyes
> Of drops that sacred pity hath engend'red;
> And therefore sit you down in gentleness.
> (II.vii.113–18, 120–4)

In addition to providing a standard of shared values, a remembered past guarantees continuity of personal identity. Duke Senior recognizes 'effigies' of Sir Rowland 'limn'd and living' in Orlando's face and announces, 'I am the Duke / That lov'd your father' (II.vii.193–6).

The society that takes shape in the forest of Arden satisfies and controls human appetites and honors traditions of friendship, religion, hospitality, and compassion. It also perpetuates specific forms of conduct. After finally receiving recognition as his father's son, Orlando sets about acquiring civilized manners. In his first scene, Orlando assaults his brother. In his next appearance on stage, he defeats Charles the wrestler. Soon he blunders into Duke Senior's gracious settlement brandishing a sword. But Orlando is no 'rude despiser of good manners' (II.vii.92) and proves an apt student of civility.[12] What Orlando gains from his sojourn in the forest is not self-understanding or access to nature but a place in a supportive community and the language and manners of a gentleman. While the education of the gentlemen of Verona involves painful lessons in the value and limitations of civilized conventions, Orlando makes no false steps. As soon as distress no longer drives him to violence, he turns to developing the verbal facility he so conspicuously lacked when Rosalind stunned him into silence. The poetry he is soon strewing about the forest shows he has absorbed the values and manners of the sylvan court and become an enthusiastic, if somewhat literal-minded, participant in the enterprise of imposing human civilization on the natural world:

> Why should this a desert be?
> For it is unpeopled? No!
> Tongues I'll hang on every tree,
> That shall civil sayings show. (III.ii.125–8)

The influence of Amiens and Jaques is clearly evident in the 'civil sayings' with which he plans to cover the forest, but while his reflections on man's 'erring pilgrimage' (III.ii.130) and on 'violated vows' between friends (III.ii.133) show Orlando modeling himself on the Duke's philosophical courtiers, the role he adopts primarily is not Monsieur Melancholy but Signior Love, who praises Rosalind's 'many parts' and vows 'to live and die her slave' (III.ii.149, 154). In this too Orlando is shaping his experience to a conventional model. As Jaques points out, a young man is expected to be a lover, 'Sighing like furnace, with a woeful ballad / Made to his mistress' eyebrow' (II.vii.148–9). To Ganymede/Rosalind's scrutinizing eye, Orlando lacks some of the signs of the lover – 'A lean cheek ... a blue eye ... an unquestionable spirit ... then your hose should be ungarter'd, your bonnet unbanded, your sleeve unbutton'd, your shoe untied, and every thing about you demonstrating a careless desolation' (III.ii.373–81). But for all his 'rather point-device' dress (III.ii.382), Orlando's sentiments are conventional enough. Like Claudio in *Much Ado* and indeed like all courtly lovers, Orlando guards his discourse with fragments of traditional love language.

By gaining acceptance as a gentleman, Orlando is able to turn his attention to the codes and conventions of aristocratic culture. By establishing himself as the son of Sir Rowland, he becomes ready to take on the role of lover. Rosalind, in contrast, delays returning to her role as Duke Senior's daughter and continues to play Ganymede. What is she waiting for? One answer to this central critical question is that she enjoys the privileges of masculinity. By assuming 'a swashing and a martial outside' (I.iii.120) and the manners of a 'saucy lackey' (III.ii.296), she enjoys a freedom impossible in her anomalous position in Frederick's court, where she was known for her 'silence' and 'patience' (I.iii.78). Nevertheless, after she finds Orlando, her boy's disguise gives her more discomfort than delight. One frequent answer to the question of what Rosalind is up to – that she uses the liminal experience in the forest as a period of self-discovery – also seems inadequate. Although her disguise lets her find out how Orlando talks about her in her absence and how her love survives his presence, it does not facilitate any deep probing of her psyche.

Another common explanation for Rosalind's prolonged masquerade is that it allows her to teach Orlando about love. More specifically, critical commentary often describes Rosalind as intent on correcting the stereotyped sentimentality of Orlando's derivative Petrarchism. Some male critics seem delighted by Rosalind precisely because they believe that she expresses full womanly devotion herself – 'O coz ... that thou didst know how many fathom deep I am in love! But it cannot be sounded' (IV.i.205-7) – without desiring any silly romanticism from her lover – 'men have died from time to time, and worms have eaten them, but not for love' (IV.i.106-8). What Rosalind does, however, is to devise a strategy for hearing as much as possible of Orlando's conventional love talk. She certainly is aware of his limitations as a prosodist and knows a hyperbole when she hears one; nevertheless, her criticism is designed not to correct Orlando's idealistic ardor but to ascertain that it can withstand such commonsensical scoffing.

When Rosalind overhears Orlando's conversation with Jaques, she obviously appreciates his nimble wit, just as Sylvia in *The Two Gentlemen* is pleased when her lover proves his adroitness as a courtier in 'a fine volley of words ... quickly shot off' (*TGV*, II.iv.33-4). Speaking to Orlando as Ganymede, Rosalind maneuvers the conversation to the topic of love and arranges the scenario in which he courts her as she plays Rosalind. Despite Ganymede's announced intention of curing Orlando's love, Rosalind clearly is giving him a chance to practice wooing and herself a chance to hear him. It is Phebe, not Rosalind, who devastatingly rejects the extravagances of love, taunting Corin:

> Now I do frown on thee with all my heart,
> And if mine eyes can wound, now let them kill thee.
> Now counterfeit to swound; why, now fall down,
> Or if thou canst not, O, for shame, for shame,
> Lie not, to say mine eyes are murtherers! (III.v.15-19)

Phebe's scorn for Petrarchan hyperbole is construed as pride and punished with humiliation and coercion.[13] Rosalind invariably follows ridicule of romantic clichés with requests for more. When Orlando reacts to her revisionist readings of legends of tragic love by declaring, 'I would not have my right Rosalind of this mind, for I protest her frown might kill me' (IV.i.109-10), she relents: 'By this hand, it will not kill a fly. But come, now I will be your Rosalind in a more coming-on disposition; and ask me what you will, I will grant it' (IV.i.111-14).

Rosalind works on the assumption that Orlando does not need to gain detachment from fashionable linguistic codes but to learn them. She urges Orlando to speak as a lover, and she does not make his wooing easy. The 'Rosalind' she presents to him is, as she promises, 'changeable, longing and liking, proud, fantastical, apish, shallow, inconstant, full of tears, full of smiles' (III.ii.411-12). This mercurial persona allows her to accomplish several things. First, she helps to prepare Orlando for the courtly world he aspires to. Jaques' cynicism about love is, after all, as much a part of courtly discourse as is Petrarchan devotion. At the same time, she encourages Orlando to imagine himself as an accepted lover. Silvius' wooing of Phebe and Phebe's infatuation with Ganymede's contemptuous disdain have shown Rosalind the perverse attraction of the unobtainable. By alternating sarcastic skepticism with eager compliance, she prepares Orlando for the move from unrequited to reciprocal love. Orlando has added the role of lover to the role of son. Rosalind directs him to the next step, that of married man, a role conspicuously absent from Jaques' summary of the parts a man plays in his time. Instead of playing disdainful mistress, Ganymede's Rosalind hurries Orlando to the altar and then lectures him on the perils of married life. Her mocking predictions of marital infidelity and jealousy are less apt as explorations of their personal emotions than as strategies for redirecting Orlando's attention from the linguistic conventions of love to the social discourse about marriage.

Like Kate in *The Taming of the Shrew*, Orlando will find a secure place in society through marriage, but the civilizing process he needs is very different. Kate's rebelliousness masks a profound subjection to societal conventions so that she needs to learn the detachment that allows her to control them. Orlando's case is simpler. Although he is eager to claim that he has known 'some nurture' (II.vii.97), he also complains that his breeding has not differed from 'the stalling of an ox' (I.i.10-11). Whereas Kate must learn the exhilaration of imaginatively substituting her own time scheme for the conventional one, Orlando must learn that coming 'within an hour of my promise' (IV.i.42-3) does not satisfy society's demand for punctuality. So too, if he is to become a good husband for

Rosalind, he must be able to articulate his love and also able to cope with the social conventions which, though they glamorize an unrequited lover, demeaningly stereotype wives as jealous, moody, unfaithful, and devious.

Rosalind, then, uses her disguise not so much to explore her own emotions or to shape Orlando's emotional and moral growth as to experiment with social roles. But the clearest indications of what she is waiting for before she returns to being Rosalind publicly are given by Oliver's arrival, the event that precipitates the end of her masquerade. Partly, of course, Rosalind's self-revelation provides the climax to the rhythm of personal emotion. Orlando's injury, his courage and magnanimity in saving his wicked brother's life, and his declaration that he 'can live no longer by thinking' (v.ii.50) move Rosalind to transform her mock marriage into a real one. More important, Oliver's arrival and his conversion make the marriage of Rosalind and Orlando an economic and social possibility. Rosalind shows her consciousness of the economic obstacle to marriage with Orlando when, as Ganymede, she teases that she would as soon marry a snail: 'he carries his house on his head; a better jointure I think than you make a woman' (IV.i.55–6). Whether or not she overhears Oliver's gift to Orlando of all Sir Rowland's estate as she enters in Act V, Oliver's change of heart makes clear that Orlando will no longer be penniless and that return to the old society is possible.

Although I have argued throughout this chapter that the exiles are engaged in rebuilding society during their time in the forest, it is also true that the band of courtly and philosophical hunters is too small and specialized to provide a satisfactory social context. It is understandable that Rosalind should conceal her identity from her father if for no other reason than that a male hunting camp in the forest is no place for young women like Rosalind and Celia. The cottage 'in the skirts of the forest, like fringe upon a petticoat' (III.ii.335–7) is more comfortable for them, even though it requires Rosalind to retain her role as male head of household. From this position, she and Touchstone interact with both the displaced courtiers and the natives of Arden and so forge a rudimentary society consisting of 'divers orders & estates ... agreeing equally togither.'[14] The courtly and native sub-groups are too homogeneous alone and too disparate together either to resolve their problems or to constitute a dramatically credible representation of human society. Silvius, Phebe, William, and even Corin are too absorbed in immediate personal concerns to initiate a communal life. Duke Senior, for all his praise of rural simplicity, remains aristocratically exclusive. His welcome to Orlando is significantly contingent: '*If* that you were the good Sir Rowland's son ... Be truly welcome hither' (II.vii.191–5; italics added).

But Rosalind sees multiple connections between herself and others in various social ranks. She recognizes the familial bond with her father, confides intimately in her childhood friend, commits herself emotionally to Orlando, argues with Jaques, and empathizes with Silvius, intervening actively to help him. In his own way Touchstone also serves a cohesive function both by wooing Audrey and by affirming the universal corporeality which is the ultimate basis for common human experiences. Even Touchstone's insistence on his courtly superiority to the country people is integrative rather than divisive. His contentiousness, like Jaques', produces engagement rather than isolation between people with different experiences and values.

In the comic denouement, the heterogeneous residents of the forest join together at least temporarily to form a community with shared values and purposes. The antiphonal responses to Silvius' definition of 'what 'tis to love' (V.ii.83) enact the common experience linking men and women, courtiers and shepherds. Rosalind achieves a similar effect as she arranges the dramatic anagnorisis: 'I will marry you ... I will satisfy you ... I will content you ... As you love ... meet. As you love ... meet. And as I love ... I'll meet' (V.ii.113–20); and as she stipulates the conditions making social harmony possible: 'Keep you your word, O Duke ... You, yours, Orlando ... Keep your word, Phebe ... Keep your word, Silvius' (V.iv.19–23). Rosalind, Orlando, and Phebe exemplify their unanimity by endorsing Silvius' expression of love. Rosalind's incantatory repetitions encompass Duke Senior as well as the lovers and commit the participants to responsible action. The enactment of community and continuity culminates in Hymen's reuniting of father and daughter and blessing of all four couples in a civil ritual:

> 'Tis Hymen peoples every town,
>   High wedlock then be honored.
> Honor, high honor, and renown
>   To Hymen, god of every town! (V.iv.143–6)

Since the play dramatizes the rebuilding of a fragmented society, not the survival of a threatened one, its festive conclusion forgives penitents rather than exposing and punishing violations of social norms. Although the renewed society is based on newly formed personal relationships, it selectively perpetuates that part of the past fostering social cohesion. Living in the forest has no visible effect on the exiles' sense of social order. Touchstone's assertions of superiority to Corin, Audrey, and William parodically foreground Orlando's desire to establish his rank and Jaques' assumption of the privileges of social superiority in relation to Touchstone and Rosalind's in relation to Phebe and Silvius. The political, social, and familial structures displayed in the opening scenes are endorsed by the eagerness with which characters seek subordinate positions within them. Orlando's pursuit of the role of son, Adam's of servant, and Rosalind's of wife affirm the benignity of traditional hierarchies.

The re-establishment of legitimacy and the reaffirmation of kinship are necessary though not sufficient requirements for social harmony. As Peter Erickson points out, it is the restored Duke Senior who authorizes festive closure.[15] In *Much Ado*, where communal harmony requires the marginalization of political power, authority is contested until the last line. After the confusions in Messina have been brought to a conclusion and the pairs of lovers are united, Benedick decides that the situation calls for dancing: 'Let's have a dance ere we are married, that we may lighten our own hearts and our wives' heels' (*MA*, V.iv.117–19). Leonato tries to exert authority to control festivity: 'We'll have dancing afterward' (V.iv.120). But the irrepressibly irreverent Benedick is defiant: 'First, of my word; therefore play, music' (V.iv.121). And Benedick has the last word: 'Strike up, pipers' (V.iv.128–9). In contrast, Duke Senior is unchallenged as he assumes authority to direct the form of communal celebration:

> Play, music, and you brides and bridegrooms all,
> With measure heap'd in joy, to th'measures fall.
> (V.iv.178–9)

These affirmations of patriarchal hierarchy constitute a politically conservative image of social harmony, as several critics have argued.[16] But the play also questions the social order that the characters endorse. The disequilibrium in the early scenes comes largely from the displacement of Rosalind and Orlando, and the security in the closing scenes rests on the recognition of kinship and the restoration of inherited rank. But the acknowledgment of kinship is necessary primarily in order to validate new relationships. The reconciliation of Oliver and Orlando and the reunion of Rosalind and Duke Senior function most significantly as means for effecting the unions of Celia and Oliver and of Rosalind and Orlando. Although literary pastoral often suggests that social structures are rooted in nature itself, *As You Like It* discovers the grounds of society in cooperative human efforts to control nature and to define roles that validate individuals for socially useful functions. Instead of presenting particular social and political systems as sanctified by nature, it detaches social from natural order. The presiding deity is the civic Hymen rather than bounteous Ceres of *The Tempest*. The closing rituals contain individual desires within communal bounds, but the verbal form that promises stability is so insistently conditional that it simultaneously makes such unanimity contingent on fallible individual perception:

> **Duke S.** If there be truth in sight, you are my daughter.
> **Orl.** If there be truth in sight, you are my Rosalind.
> **Phe.** If sight and shape be true,
> Why then my love adieu!
> **Ros.** I'll have no father, if you be not he;
> I'll have no husband, if you be not he;
> Nor ne'er wed woman, if you be not she.
>
> (v.iv.118–24)

As Touchstone observes, 'much virtue in If' (v.iv.103). *As You Like It* imagines a peaceful and fruitful society unified through codes and structures that are not immutable and irresistible but contingent and flexible.

The ritualistic language of the last act, which subsumes individual voices within the expression of communal solidarity, simultaneously emphasizes individual differences. When Silvius explains what it is to love, he speaks for Phebe, Orlando, and Rosalind as well as himself. And when Phebe responds, 'If this be so, why blame you me to love you?' (v.ii.103), Silvius echoes her puzzled helplessness. But when Orlando asks the same question of no one, as though he were mesmerized by the patterned repetition, the universal language of love suddenly dissolves into unintelligible noise – 'the howling of Irish wolves against the moon' (v.ii.109–10). Rosalind's riddling promises mean different things to different people, and the parallelism of Hymen's and of Jaques' blessings on the four pairs of lovers foregrounds the variety of relationships included within marriage. Throughout the play, rituals of wooing and wedding display diversity while creating unity. Similarly, the traditional discourses of love, pastoralism, and philosophical debate exert a centripetal force by incorporating individual voices within unitary languages – and in doing so work centrifugally by displaying individual accents. The language each character speaks, like Jaques' melancholy, is 'compounded of many simples' (IV.i.16), and each voice is distinctive. The festive conclusion is not so much a harmonic blending as a contrapuntal fugue in which individual voices contribute to the whole by moving separately.

The play achieves closure by providing each character with a socially sanctioned place and role to play. Phebe's manipulated acceptance of Silvius ('Thy faith my fancy to thee doth combine' [V.iv.150]) has aroused little skepticism among critics and audiences because it satisfies the expectations of inclusion generated by the comic form. But if social recognition is necessary, so too is flexibility. Inherited roles may disappear through external events or prove inadequate. Roles are determined by age, circumstances, relations with other people, and individual temperament as well as by kinship. Jaques is surely right when he says that one man 'plays many parts' (II.vii.142). And while in Act II he limits the parts to seven sequential roles, in Act IV he proposes a different group of seven including scholar, musician, courtier, lawyer, and lady as well as lover and soldier. The roles men and women play are multiple and always provisional. All major characters change roles during the course of the action. And if Duke Frederick's past usurpation of his brother's role proves destructive, the characters' adaptability in discovering new roles rebuilds society. Rosalind, of course, is particularly resourceful in experimenting with parts ranging from saucy lackey and shrew to submissive daughter and wife and in coaching others in new, empowering roles.

Critics often are suspicious of a sense of identity based on social role. Lawrence Danson, for example, distinguishes between contingent social selves and stable psychological selves and argues that *As You Like It* achieves closure through Rosalind's 'discovery' of herself, which constitutes both the completion of the plot and the perfection of a stable psychological self.[17] I am arguing instead that the play denies the distinction between social and psychological selves. Against Jacob Burckhardt's description of the Renaissance discovery of the self as the process of distinguishing the individual from social groups, Natalie Davis has argued that in sixteenth-century France 'embeddedness did not preclude self-discovery, but rather prompted it.'[18] Davis describes strategies by which women achieved self-expression and some autonomy through rather than in opposition to the patriarchal family and suggests that 'a thread of female autonomy may have been built precisely around [the] sense of being given away, that women sometimes turned the cultural formulation around and gave themselves away.'[19] *As You Like It*, I think, presents a similar version of social life in which people achieve a sense of self through participation in socially defined groups. By affirming their family bond Oliver and Orlando renegotiate the power relations established by primogeniture and achieve their distinctive desires. Similarly Rosalind reconceptualizes patriarchal marriage by giving herself away. By telling her father and Orlando 'To you I give myself, for I am yours' (V.iv.116–18), she enacts simultaneously her power to achieve her own heart's desires and her place within a community. Her marriage integrates her into a patriarchal society, but the course of the comic action indicates that the quiet part she plays after giving herself to Orlando is as provisional as her other roles. Her parodic rehearsal as Ganymede/Rosalind promises that as wife she will be just as resourceful as Mistress Page and Mistress Ford in finding ways to be merry in a theoretically subordinate position.

The ending is exhilarating and liberating because it redeems the past through repentance and reconciliation and because it promises a future of unknown possibilities. Concomitantly, social cohesion is created through re-establishing recognized structures and through expanding social perimeters. Significantly, neither of Jaques' taxonomies of the parts people play includes the role of contemplative he announces in his last speech. The social unity in the last scene is only temporary and depends as much on tolerating differences as sharing values. William, Corin, Phebe, and Silvius will remain in Arden when the exiles leave. Duke Senior's family is able to return to court because Frederick has adopted a new role as convertite and chosen values other than courtly ones. Jaques will join Frederick at least temporarily. The future plans of Celia and Oliver are unclear. Although Duke Senior and Jaques assume that Oliver will return to his 'land ... and great allies' (V.iv.189), Oliver has told Orlando that he intends to remain in Arden and to 'live and die a shepherd' (V.ii.12). Perhaps the newlyweds will spend six months in each place. At any rate, the group on stage soon will disperse: the festivities are as much a farewell as a reunion.

As You Like It

Thus unlike *Much Ado* and *Merry Wives*, where solidarity within a local community is the source of strength, *As You Like It* finds stability through diversity and diffusion. While *Much Ado* and *Merry Wives* develop through intrigue plots which expose wrongdoers, *As You Like It* develops through dispersal and inconclusive discussion. Debates about the relative merits of court and country, action and contemplation, and marriage and celibacy, and conflicts between idealization and satiric deflation, are unresolved and unresolvable, existing not to recommend an ideal balance but to indicate areas of continuing tension. Most Shakespearean comedies implicitly suggest that what is good for one is good for all – marriage, say, for Kate as well as Bianca or wealth for Bassanio as well as Antonio. *As You Like It* suggests that a peaceful society is possible because some people like to dance and others are for 'other than dancing measures.' It portrays a comic commonwealth like the spiritual community Milton describes as the only kind possible 'in this world': 'it cannot be united into a continuity, it can but be contiguous ... neither can every piece of the building be of one form; nay rather the perfection consists in this, that out of many moderate varieties and brotherly dissimilitudes ... arises the goodly and graceful symmetry that commends the whole pile and structure.'[20]

CHAPTER ELEVEN

The Principle of Recompense in *Twelfth Night*

'pleasure will be paid, one time or another' (II.iv.70)

Twelfth Night begins with remarkably little conflict. The opening scenes introduce no villain bent on dissension and destruction, nor do they reveal disruptive antagonism between parents and children or between love and law. In contrast to the passion and anger of the first scene of *A Midsummer Night's Dream*, the restless melancholy that pervades the beginning of *The Merchant of Venice*, or the brutality and tyranny that precipitate the action in *As You Like It*, the dominant note of Orsino's court and of Olivia's household is static self-containment. A sense of grief and loss permeates the opening scenes as it does in *As You Like It*, but, as many critics have noted, a strain of complacent self-absorption dilutes the poignancy of Orsino's frustrated love and of Olivia's grief for her dead brother. Orsino's concentration on his own emotions cuts him off from real personal relationships as effectively as does Olivia's withdrawal or Sir Toby's careless hedonism. People in Illyria, as in most of Shakespeare's comic commonwealths, assume that living as a part of a human society is natural and necessary, but they show little conscious pleasure in its benefits. They participate in remarkably few communal activities. Olivia's mourning and Orsino's melancholy preclude the feasts and masques and even the appeals to authority that draw characters together in many of the comedies. The shipwreck that causes Viola and Sebastian to seek refuge in Illyria implies a need for protection from physical nature, but nature's harshness is not emphasized. In *The Comedy of Errors* Egeon remembers the long-past wreck vividly and bitterly, and *As*

You Like It dramatizes the desperate need for food and for protection from icy winds and wild beasts. But in *Twelfth Night* the harshness of physical nature is filtered through human hope. A witness describes Sebastian, a possible drowning victim, as 'like Arion on the dolphin's back ... hold[ing] acquaintance with the waves' (I.ii.15–16). Soon Viola describes tempests as 'kind' and the sea as 'fresh in love' (III.iv.384), and eventually Orsino refers to the shipwreck as 'this most happy wrack' (V.i.266). In general, characters are less disturbed by their physical vulnerability to nature's power than they are apprehensive of and annoyed by other people. Viola has been saved from drowning only by chance, but she spends little time contemplating her narrow escape. Her concerns on arriving in Illyria are to learn about the country's political and social condition and to plan how she can best enter Illyrian society. And in spite of being assured of the nobility and virtue of its most powerful figures, she decides to assume a protective disguise rather than to reveal immediately her condition as an unprotected woman in a strange country. Viola's involuntary exile and the self-absorption of the native Illyrians present a spectacle of isolation rather than confrontation, not so much a society in disorder as a series of discrete individuals without the interconnections that constitute a society.

While *As You Like It* moves from violent conflict to harmonious stability, *Twelfth Night* transforms isolation and fragmentation into mutuality and cohesion. Both plays trace the renewal of societies that have been unable to contain the centrifugal forces generated by societal tensions. *As You Like It* locates the source of conflict largely in competitive desires for wealth and power that deprive some members of recognized places in society. It achieves comic closure through the reaffirmation of traditional values and loyalties and through the acceptance of diversity and diffusion. Illyria is plagued with stagnation rather than violence. Instead of being deprived of inherited social roles, its citizens suffer from rigid adherence to roles they have chosen. It achieves social harmony not through recognizing kinship and restoring inherited rank but by relinquishing old habits and relationships and creating new ones with a stranger of unknown parentage and rank. It ends, not with a communal ritual that foregrounds diversity and preludes dispersal, but with frenzied activity that promises unity.

While the beginning of *Twelfth Night* is unusually static, the conclusion is strikingly active. Far from tying up a few loose ends, the last scene contains major events in both the double main plot and the sub-plot. Both pairs of lovers meet with full awareness for the first time. Viola finally wins Orsino's love, Orsino and Olivia, in different ways, discover who it is they love, and Malvolio is released from imprisonment. Beginning calmly and purposefully enough with Orsino's first attempt to woo Olivia in person, the scene gathers intensity through a series of increasingly bitter confrontations. Orsino's banter with Feste is interrupted when Antonio appears, ominously under armed guard. Recognition as the duke's old enemy, however, is less galling to him than the apparent ingratitude of Sebastian (Cesario/Viola). At Olivia's entrance the tone darkens further with Orsino's jealous spite and threat to murder his presumed rival, to 'sacrifice the lamb that I do love' (v.i.130). On the priest's confirming Cesario's marriage to Olivia, Orsino's rage is replaced by even more bitter contempt at such betrayal. In quick succession Cesario/Viola has provoked condemnation as an 'ingrateful boy' (v.i.77) from Antonio, sorrow at the faithless cowardice of her new husband from Olivia, and, from the man she loves, a threat of death and disgusted rejection as a 'dissembling cub' (v.i.164). The crescendo of pain and anger climax in the bloody spectacle of Sir Andrew's and Sir Toby's broken heads and Toby's vicious attack on his friend: 'Will you help? – an ass-head and a coxcomb and a knave, a thin-fac'd knave, a gull!' (v.i.206–7).

At the midpoint of the scene, as Sir Toby and Sir Andrew exit to find help for their bleeding heads, Sebastian enters and the scene reverses direction. In the first half, relationships disintegrate in the whirling confusions of mistaken identities emanating from Viola's disguise. In the second half, new relationships form from the revelation and identification of the twins, Sebastian and Viola. The scene performs the conventional function of uniting lovers and reuniting family, but the emphasis is less on restoration and reconciliation than on the discovery of unexpected relationships and acceptance of new obligations. Sebastian's reunions with Antonio and Viola reveal that Olivia is betrothed not to a cowardly, faithless boy but to a strong, loyal man. By identifying Viola, Sebastian's appearance transforms Orsino from Cesario's master and Olivia's unsuccessful suitor into Viola's future husband and Olivia's prospective brother-in-law. Viola suddenly hears herself being hailed as Olivia's sister and Orsino's mistress. Through marriages prospective and already performed, Maria, Toby, Olivia, Sebastian, Viola, and Orsino become one extended family, in households that include Malvolio, Fabian, and Feste.

In *Twelfth Night*, then, the comic movement from disorder to harmony is more particularly the creation of links among people. The personal and societal problems at the beginning of the play result not from envy, aggression, or malice, but from a no less insidious and equally common ambition for self-sufficiency. As the social anthropologist Claude Lévi-Strauss points out, 'mankind has always dreamed of seizing and fixing that fleeting moment when it was permissible to believe that the law of exchange could be evaded, that one could gain without losing, enjoy without sharing. At either end of the earth and at both extremes of time, the Sumerian myth of the golden age and the Andaman myth of the future life correspond ... removing to an equally unattainable past or future the joys, eternally denied to social man, of a world in which one might *keep to oneself*.'[1] Orsino's vision of self-surfeiting desires, Olivia's projected isolation, Toby's life of unconfined pleasure, and Malvolio's 'practicing behavior to his own shadow' (II.v.17) are all versions of this dream of inviolable autonomy. Their various attempts to create these solipsistic paradises in Illyria produce an atmosphere of sterility, a society without cohesion. While a current of self-indulgence runs through Orsino's and Olivia's pain, the real dangers of isolation from the protection of human society threaten the more cheerful characters. Viola and Sebastian are separated and shipwrecked in a strange country, Sir Toby and Feste are threatened with dismissal from Olivia's household, and Antonio is banned from Orsino's territory on pain of death. By the end of the play this sense of incipient disintegration has disappeared from the enlarged, cohesive group, and the communal joy and affection are achieved largely in terms of what Lévi-Strauss, in the passage quoted above, calls the law of exchange.

Instead of celebrating personal and social harmony with the dancing and wedding festivities that end most of the comedies, the final scene of *Twelfth Night* demonstrates the mutual obligations imposed by the complicated, new relationships. Public recognition of Viola's female identity depends on recovering her 'maid's garments' (V.i.275) from the sea captain who befriended her. The captain, in prison under some legal obligation to Malvolio, cannot be released until Malvolio is satisfied. The need for Malvolio reminds Olivia of her responsibility to him and Feste of the letter in his charge. The letter brings Malvolio's release, which in turn precipitates Fabian's confession of responsibility. Meanwhile Olivia's and Sebastian's wedding festivities wait on Orsino's and

Viola's, and Viola remains Cesario until Malvolio is pacified. This cycle of mutual dependence gives an open-ended quality to the ending of the play. Our confident expectation that 'golden time' (v.i.382) will bring happiness to the lovers is complemented by our sense of continuing obligations. Reciprocal love, the design of *Twelfth Night* implies, naturally culminates not in a private dreamworld of complete fulfillment, but in the give-and-take of human society.

This happy, albeit imperfect, ending is possible only when the major characters have come to terms with the inescapable mutuality of communal life through a series of exchanges, often financial transactions. We usually think of the *The Merchant of Venice* as Shakespeare's treatment of the relationship of wealth to love, but as Porter Williams, Jr., has pointed out, 'Seldom in a play does money flow so freely' as in *Twelfth Night*.[2] Viola gives gold to the sea captain, Antonio gives his purse to Sebastian, Orsino sends jewels to Olivia, Olivia showers gifts on Cesario, Viola offers to divide her wealth with Antonio, and they all repeatedly give money to Feste. Economic advantage is not a prime motive for any of the characters, but hardly a scene goes by when they are not engaged in giving or receiving money or jewels. The lovers in the forest of Arden may rely on Hymen to arrange their nuptials, but in Illyria Olivia knows that someone must pay for the double wedding that is to replace the differences and frustrations of the past with a joyous alliance:

> My lord, so please you, these things further
>   thought on,
> To think me as well a sister as a wife,
> One day shall crown th'alliance on't, so please you,
> Here at my house and at my proper cost. (v.i.316–19)

Illyria definitely is not Gonzalo's imaginary commonwealth without trade, service, or riches.

This emphasis on giving and receiving serves, as Porter Williams says, to contrast the generous and loving nature of Viola, Orsino, and Olivia with the selfishness of Malvolio and Sir Toby, but he oversimplifies, I think, when he suggests that the money and gifts that change hands so freely 'symbolize generous love and friendship' and that 'such giving and receiving must be done without counting the cost or measuring the risk.'[3] Orsino's financial generosity is patently not identified with generous love. Admittedly, he does not count the cost in his courtship of Olivia. His motives are not mercenary and his emissaries bear jewels; nevertheless, his love is self-regarding. In the first scene, for example, when he makes the expected pun on Curio's suggestion to hunt the hart, he first seems to be directing his thoughts beyond himself, thinking of the noble Olivia:

> **Cur.** Will you go hunt, my lord?
> **Duke.** What, Curio?
> **Cur.** The hart.
> **Duke.** Why, so I do, the noblest that I have. (I.i.16–17)

But immediately we discover that the noble heart Orsino pursues is his own:

> O, when mine eyes did see Olivia first,
> Methought she purg'd the air of pestilence!
> That instant was I turn'd into a hart,
> And my desires, like fell and cruel hounds,
> E'er since pursue me. (I.i.18–22)

His love for Olivia does not give rise to thoughts of serving her or sharing with her but of reigning supreme in her:

> when liver, brain, and heart,
> These sovereign thrones, are all supplied and fill'd
> Her sweet perfections with one self king! (I.i.36–8)

And when he speaks of Olivia paying a 'debt of love' (I.i.33) to her brother or when he advises Cesario against loving a woman 'not worth thee' (II.iv.27), he assumes that giving love entitles one to receive love. In the meantime he seeks solitude: 'for I myself am best / When least in company' (I.iv.37–8).

Viola too is generous, but while her love is more selfless than Orsino's, her economic liberality is less purely spontaneous and more thoughtful. When she gives gold to the sea captain, she does so explicitly in gratitude for the comfort he has given her: 'For saying so, there's gold' (I.ii.18). She promises to pay him more in return for the specific help she requests from him.

> I prithee (and I'll pay thee bounteously)
> Conceal me what I am, and be my aid
> For such disguise as haply shall become
> The form of my intent. (I.ii.52–5)

She is fully aware that she takes a risk in trusting him:

> And though that nature with a beauteous wall
> Doth oft close in pollution, yet of thee
> I will believe thou hast a mind that suits
> With this thy fair and outward character. (I.ii.48–51)

And she is not averse to reinforcing his good will with the hope that 'It may be worth thy pains' (I.ii.57). Just as she gladly pays for the help she needs, she expects to earn her way with the duke she proposes to serve, confident that she can prove 'worth his service' (I.ii.59). Like the other characters, Viola is tempted by the attractions of solitude – she would like to join Olivia in her isolated grief and postpone being 'delivered to the world' (I.ii.42), but she readily accepts the necessity of taking part in the commerce of human society.

The idea of reward for service rendered continues in Viola's first scene with Orsino. The short scene opens with Valentine commenting on Viola/Cesario's advancement: 'If the Duke continue these favors towards you, Cesario, you are like to be much advanc'd; he hath known you but three days, and already you are no stranger' (I.iv.1–4). The dialogue between Orsino and Viola ends with the duke's promise:

> Prosper well in this,
> And thou shalt live as freely as thy lord,
> To call his fortunes thine. (I.iv.38–40)

The effect is not to stress Orsino's generosity or to suggest his vulgarity in offering reward but to show that Viola belongs: she has become an active participant in the reciprocal relationships that bind the social group together. Indeed, the play as a whole, I think, illustrates the principle of reciprocity, the unwritten rule, according to Marcel Mauss and Lévi-Strauss, by which the exchange of goods creates mutually satisfying relationships among individuals and groups.

Building on Mauss' seminal study of the gift in primitive societies, social anthropologists point out that exchanges of goods may be complex social events – at once legal, economic, religious, aesthetic, and morphological – rather than solely, or even primarily, economic transactions.[4] Most basically, 'the agreed transfer of a valuable from one individual to another makes these individuals into partners' because it implies that the gift will be reciprocated with a counter-gift, usually of equivalent or greater value.[5] Through

Twelfth Night

the principle of reciprocity, then, the act of exchange binds the giver and the recipient in a relationship. To give is to create an obligation; to take is to imply a willingness to pay that debt. Consequently, to refuse a gift is an insulting rejection of relationship with the giver, and to take without repaying is either humiliating failure or an act of aggression in the eyes of the whole society.

The principle of reciprocity operates most clearly through Feste. His first scene, Act I, scene v, establishes his position as a professional entertainer. After Maria's warning that his absence has threatened his security as Olivia's fool, Feste calls our attention to the difficult and demanding nature of his profession and then successfully fools Olivia out of her bad humor. In return, he receives her support and protection when Malvolio attacks him. In Act II he sings, first for Sir Toby and Sir Andrew, and then for Orsino, demonstrating each time that he who pays the piper calls the tune. There is nothing demeaning in the financial aspect of the transaction, despite A.C. Bradley's worry that Feste is offended and disgusted by Orsino's offer of payment.[6] Feste sings for pleasure, as he tells Orsino, but 'pleasure will be paid, one time or another' (II.iv.70–1), and he pockets as his due the money Toby, Andrew, and Orsino pay for the pleasure he has given them. The scenes where Feste is paid for his foolery follow the same pattern. In Act III, scene i his witty wordplays elicit coins from Viola as well as an appreciative analysis of the fool's art. Similarly, at the beginning of Act V, scene i Orsino pays for Feste's excellent foolery and promises further bounty if he will carry a message. Feste's cleverness in getting his tips doubled, as he tells Orsino, is not 'the sin of covetousness' (V.i.47), but part of his performance, rather like the plea for applause by the epilogue to a Renaissance play. Often, Feste expresses gratitude for these payments in a wittily pertinent blessing: 'Now the melancholy god protect thee' to Orsino, and to Cesario: 'Now Jove, in his next commodity of hair, send thee a beard!' (II.iv.73; III.i.44–5).

The only significant departure from the pattern of a mutually satisfying exchange of talented performance for money comes when Feste tries to deliver to Sebastian a message intended for Cesario. Feste's words, of course, make no sense at all to Sebastian, who in exasperation tips the fool in an effort to get rid of him:

> I prithee, foolish Greek, depart from me.
> There's money for thee. If you tarry longer,
> I shall give worse payment. (IV.i.18–20)

Instead of begging for more or invoking a witty blessing on his benefactor, this time Feste responds with open contempt: 'By my troth, thou hast an open hand. These wise men that give fools money get themselves a good report – after fourteen years' purchase' (IV.i.21–3). When the young man seems to deny his identity and his relationships with people in Illyria, Feste's words – his medium of exchange – lose their value, and the exchange process breaks down. 'No, I do not know you, nor I am not sent to you by my lady, to bid you come speak with her, nor your name is not Master Cesario, nor this is not my nose neither: nothing that is so is so' (IV.i.5–9). Because Sebastian cannot receive Feste's message, his offer of money is not part of a reciprocal exchange but, from his point of view, an insulting dismissal, and from Feste's, a wise man's folly.[7]

Sebastian's refusal to participate results, of course, from Feste's mistake, not from Sebastian's rejection of the principle of reciprocity. His scenes with Antonio stress his dual awareness that taking implies an obligation to give and that gifts of love cannot be reduced to an economic transaction. 'Recompense,' Shakespeare's word for the idea of reciprocity, is the subject of his first speech: 'My stars shine darkly over me. The malignancy of my fate might perhaps distemper yours; therefore I shall crave of you your leave, that I may bear my evils alone. It were a bad recompense for your love, to lay any of them on you' (II.i.3–8). He pursues isolation because he feels unable to enter into a balanced mutual relationship. But when Antonio persists in offering help and protection, Sebastian understands that rejecting such love would be unkind, although gratitude is the only recompense he can give:

> My kind Antonio,
> I can no other answer make but thanks,
> And thanks; and ever oft good turns
> Are shuffled off with such uncurrent pay;
> But were my worth as is my conscience firm,
> You should find better dealing. (III.iii.13–18)

Similarly, Sebastian values the pearl Olivia gives him as a symbol of the wonder of her love and reciprocates by vowing eternal love.

Thus, the transfer of wealth from one person to another in *Twelfth Night* creates and expresses a wide variety of relationships – entertainer with audience, employer with employee, friend with friend, and lover with beloved. Concomitantly, repudiating the principle of reciprocity signals the breakdown of community and the outbreak of hostility. The extreme case is Antonio, who is excluded from Illyria because he refuses to repay what he has taken from Duke Orsino. His offense, he explains to Sebastian,

> might have since been answer'd in repaying
> What we took from them, which for traffic's sake
> Most of our city did. Only myself stood out,
> For which if I be lapsed in this place
> I shall pay dear. (III.iii.33–7)

Antonio knows that because he has refused to repay, he will pay dearly if he is recognized, for the ugly obverse of the reciprocity binding people harmoniously together is the requital of injury with injury in a divisive cycle of revenge. Similarly, when it appears that Sebastian is unwilling to return his purse, Antonio's love turns to hostility. The refusal is a denial of their relationship, and to claim no relationship is to create a hostile one. Antonio has sincerely believed his love to be totally selfless and his generosity to expect no return. But in the crisis produced by Orsino's revenge and by the confusion of brother and sister, he discovers that he has counted on receiving loyalty and gratitude in return for giving Sebastian 'His life' and 'My love' (v.i.80, 81). Without such recompense, love is impossible, and his adulation is transformed to scorn.

Sir Toby's relationship with Andrew Aguecheek clarifies the principle of reciprocity by negative example. Toby coaxes money from the thin-faced knight, who receives nothing in return but deceptive assurances of success in his courtship of Olivia. Because Toby is exploitative and Andrew foolish, we see their companionship as a travesty of friendship. Its disintegration in the last act is no loss and no surprise. Toby's high-spirited gaiety is equalled by his selfish disregard for other people, but even he realizes that 'pleasure will be paid, one time or another,' and he marries Maria 'in recompense' (v.i.364) for her part in the gulling of Malvolio.

Only Malvolio stands outside the lines of exchange that link the characters in increasingly complex patterns of relationship. He is the only major character who pays Feste nothing and neither gives nor receives a gift. He lacks the 'generous' and 'free' temperament that provides a sense of proportion, as Olivia tells him (I.v.91–3). But he is no more greedy than Sir Toby, who calculates that he has cost Sir Andrew 'some two thousand ... or so' (III.ii.54–5), or than Sir Andrew, who expects to repair his fortune by marrying Olivia. The measure of Malvolio's self-love is not his miserliness or covetousness but his presumptuous belief that he lives in a sphere above and beyond ordinary human relationships. His contemptuous dismissal of Toby, Fabian, and Maria – 'Go off, I discard you. Let me enjoy my private' (III.iv.89–90) – epitomizes his attitude towards other people. Maria's attempts to define what is so odious about Malvolio – he is a 'puritan' and a 'time-pleaser' (II.iii.140, 148) – at first sound contradictory, if a puritan is one who self-righteously condemns lapses from a moral ideal and a 'time-pleaser' one who cynically manipulates worldly affairs for self-aggrandizement. But Maria is right both times; the puritan and the politician meet in Malvolio's self-esteem and in his contempt for people and for human relationships as ends in themselves. This total lack of identification with other people both incites and provides the means for Malvolio's gulling. When his insults provoke the conspirators to revenge, they can easily persuade him that Fortune has singled him out for greatness. He is 'opposite with a kinsman' and 'surly with servants' (II.v.149–50) before Maria's letter reinforces his desire to 'wash off gross acquaintance' and his assumption that he condescends to speak to ordinary mortals as 'nightingales answer daws' (II.v.162–3; III.iv.35–6).

In *Twelfth Night* money symbolizes not love so much as a broader engagement with the real, imperfect world; paying, lending, giving, and taking are signs of willingness to have commerce with human society. Because the attitude that controls Malvolio's response to other people is 'I am not of your element' (III.iv.124), he does not take part in the exchanges of wealth that engage the other characters. Even when he is duped into believing that Olivia has given him her love and, by marrying him, will give him wealth and power, he feels no obligation or gratitude. He thanks 'Jove' and 'my stars' (II.v.172), but not Olivia. Malvolio believes, or at least tries to believe, that no human actions, not even his own, are responsible for his good fortune and that no mundane circumstances can prevent his perfect felicity: 'Nothing that can be can come between me and the full prospect of my hopes. Well, Jove, not I, is the doer of this, and he is to be thank'd' (III.iv.81–3). Since Malvolio believes that his social advancement is divinely ordained, he feels no obligation or gratitude. His faith that life can conform totally to his desires, that he can receive without giving and enjoy without sharing, indicates his ignorance of how society works. The lovers in their illusions and self-deceptions are not as out of touch with reality as is Malvolio, who does not understand that pleasure must be paid and that insults give offense.

Malvolio's misunderstanding of how economic exchanges function socially is matched by his ignorance of how language works to bind society together. He has no comprehension of the multivalency of language or of the interactive nature of discourse. When he turns a gift into an insult, contemptuously tossing Olivia's ring to the ground for Cesario to stoop for, he is not intentionally distorting Olivia's message but expressing his own disdain for the young page. Because he lacks sympathy with his fellow humans, he is unable either to hear the longing hidden in Olivia's message or even to report her words accurately. His failure to understand other people causes him to misinterpret Olivia's feelings about himself and to underestimate the offense he has given Maria, Andrew, Fabian, and Feste. The success of their revenge teaches Malvolio the vulnerability he shares with the rest of mankind. In his distress he appeals to Feste for help and promises 'I will live to be thankful to thee for't'; 'It shall advantage thee ... '; 'I'll requite it in the highest degree' (IV.ii.82–3, 111, 118). A demonstration of dependency so humiliating and a promise to reciprocate offered under duress do not promise Malvolio's sudden conversion to brotherly love. But even his departing curse – 'I'll be reveng'd on the whole pack of you' (V.i.378) – in the theater, does not inspire the dread or pathos critics often solemnly attribute to it. Malvolio may never learn with Prospero that the 'rarer action is / In virtue than in vengeance,' but even his comically impotent fury registers his dawning awareness that he is 'One of their kind' (*Tempest*, V.i.27–8, 23). In suffering wrong and experiencing the desire to hurt back, he is at least entering the rough give-and-take of the real world. And Olivia's immediate sympathy and Orsino's command to 'Pursue him, and entreat him to a peace' (V.i.380) suggest the possibility of future reconciliation.

While all the characters take part in the process of exchange, Viola is distinguished by her fuller understanding of the conscious and unconscious operation of the principle of reciprocity. Hating ingratitude more than any other vice,[8] she repays Orsino's trust and favor with loyal service, faithfully wooing Olivia for him despite her own longing to be his wife. The heart of her plea to Olivia is the principle that love deserves recompense; 'My master, not myself, lacks recompense' (I.v.285), she replies tartly when Olivia offers to tip her. However great Olivia's beauty, she argues, Orsino's love could be 'but recompens'd' (I.v.253) by winning her. Indeed, Viola breaks through Olivia's reserve by teaching her that the gifts of nature too bring an obligation to give in return, 'for what is yours to bestow is not yours to reserve' (I.v.188–9). The lesson Olivia learns – 'ourselves we do not owe' (I.v.310) – strikingly resembles the 'basic theme' Marcel Mauss' English editor finds in the anthropologist's analysis of reciprocity – 'one belongs to others not to oneself.'[9]

Viola becomes a cohesive agent in Illyria because she understands the collective and reciprocal nature of social discourse. Malvolio disparages Feste's wit because it is interactive: 'Unless you laugh and minister occasion to him, he is gagg'd' (I.v.86–8). Viola praises it on the same grounds:

> This fellow is wise enough to play the fool,
> And to do that well craves a kind of wit.
> He must observe their mood on whom he jests,
> The quality of persons, and the time;
> And like the haggard, check at every feather
> That comes before his eye. This is a practice
> As full of labor as a wise man's art. (III.i.60–6)

Malvolio interprets all language, written and oral, as a univocal message that he is blessed by fortune; Viola, like Feste, dallies with words, exploiting their ambiguities to communicate with others while simultaneously expressing her secret frustration. While Malvolio assumes that words are trustworthy signs of his destined greatness, Viola understands that, although a witty 'corrupter of words' (III.i.36) like Feste can make words do many things, their relation to reality is circuitous and unreliable. People may construe a name as evidence of guilt, as Hero learns painfully in *Much Ado*,[10] but Feste need not worry that dallying with his sister's name will make her wanton. So too, when Orsino stubbornly insists that his message to Olivia must win her love, Cesario/Viola tries to warn him that there are limits to the power of the most eloquent declaration of love.

Orsino's talk about love reveals not only his self-absorption and exaggerated expectations of the power his verbalized desires can exert over others but also his own subjection to culturally entrenched linguistic patterns which carry ready-made perceptions and attitudes. His stance as unrequited lover adoring Olivia from afar derives from literary Petrarchism. And at the same time that he casts Olivia as the chaste and beautiful 'sovereign cruelty' (II.iv.80) worthy of his devotion, he also assumes female inferiority: 'women are as roses, whose fair flow'r / Being once display'd, doth fall that very hour' (II.iv.38–9); 'their love may be call'd appetite, / No motion of the liver, but the palate' (II.iv.97–8). This inconsistency does not imply conscious hypocrisy. Rather, it demonstrates the combination of awe and contempt for women as Other that marks not only Orsino's personal psychology but his culture. The ambivalences and inconsistencies of European cultural traditions have taught Orsino as a man to dominate and control women and as a noble soul to worship a remote ideal with a love that is, as Andrew Marvell explains, by definition 'begotten by Despair / Upon Impossibility.'[11]

While Orsino unquestioningly accepts both misogynistic and idealizing traditions as reliable descriptions of emotional reality, Viola deliberately exposes the gap between learned linguistic forms and actual situations. Sent as Orsino's emissary to court Olivia, she mocks the language both Orsino and Olivia expect from her: 'Most radiant, exquisite, and unmatchable beauty – I pray you tell me if this be the lady of the house, for I never saw her. I would be loath to cast away my speech; for besides that it is excellently well penn'd, I have taken great pains to con it' (I.v.170–4). Sharing Feste's skill in responding to the occasions others offer, Viola uses vocabulary from the discourses of theater, politics, navigation, diplomacy, religion, and art to expose the inaccuracy of verbal constructs. Through this process, she elicits from Olivia a parody of Petrarchism's objectification of women: 'I will give out divers schedules of my beauty. It shall be inventoried, and every particle and utensil labell'd to my will: as, *item*, two lips, indifferent red; *item*, two grey eyes, with lids to them; *item*, one neck, one chin, and so forth' (I.v.244–9). Finally, Viola provokes Olivia to drop verbal games and to give a straightforward account of her feelings about Orsino. Olivia praises him, distinguishing with careful precision between what she imagines, what she knows certainly, and what she accepts by report, and yet insists that no catalogue of admirable qualities, however accurate, can create love:

> Your lord does know my mind, I cannot love him,
> Yet I suppose him virtuous, know him noble,
> Of great estate, of fresh and stainless youth;
> In voices well divulg'd, free, learn'd, and valiant,
> And in dimension, and the shape of nature,
> A gracious person. But yet I cannot love him. (I.v.257–62)

Still, for all their mockery of ready-made verbal formulas, Viola and Olivia understand that language is necessarily conventional. As Ralph Lever notes in his *Arte of Reason*, 'no man is of power to change or to make a language when he will.' Or in Ben Jonson's version: '*Custome* is the most certaine Misstresse of Language.'[12] In spite of ridiculing Petrarchan clichés, Viola herself characterizes Olivia as the 'cruel fair' of tradition:

> Lady, you are the cruell'st she alive
> If you will lead these graces to the grave. (I.v.241–2)

> I see you what you are, you are too proud;
> But if you were the devil, you are fair. (250–1)

And in spite of recognizing that Olivia's declaration that she cannot love Orsino is irrefutable, Viola employs traditional Petrarchan metaphors to reject Olivia's literal statement as inadequate:

> If I did love you in my master's flame,
> With such a suff'ring, such a deadly life,
> In your denial I would find no sense,
> I would not understand it. (I.v.264–7)

As Cesario, she deftly mocks the 'poetical' (I.v.195) speech she is commissioned to deliver and uses the gaps between tenor and vehicle to expose the absurdity of Olivia's remoteness, but she also knows that metaphoric language is the only language we have. She recognizes too that if language distorts and coerces, silence is death. Whereas Feste's hypothetical sister demonstrated the limits of language, Viola's demonstrates its necessity. The history of her father's daughter is a blank: she 'never told her love, / But let concealment like a worm i' th' bud / Feed on her damask cheek' (II.iv.110–12). Thus Viola identifies her love for Orsino with his for Olivia and expresses it in unashamedly 'poetical' language. If she loved as Orsino does, she tells Olivia, she would

> Make me a willow cabin at your gate,
> And call upon my soul within the house;
> Write loyal cantons of contemned love,
> And sing them loud even in the dead of night;
> Hallow your name to the reverberate hills,
> And make the babbling gossip of the air
> Cry out 'Olivia!' O, you should not rest
> Between the elements of air and earth
> But you should pity me! (I.v.268–76)

Like Touchstone, Viola finds much virtue in 'if.' She discovers in the indirections of art a partial solution to the problem of public forms that deny and distort private truths. By exploiting the ambiguities of language, she relieves her frustration. By parodying fossilized metaphors, she breaks through the barriers Olivia has erected. But to express her own unrequited love, she appropriates and revivifies Petrarchan language.

Thus, just as Viola knows that language is necessarily conventional, she knows that culturally sanctioned forms of thought and feeling are inescapable. For all her criticism of stereotyped roles as unrequited lover or disdainful beauty and her advocacy of the human obligation to love and to give, Viola recognizes that returning love for love sometimes is impossible. She cannot deny that Olivia does not love Orsino or that Orsino loves Olivia, not her. So too it is impossible for her to reciprocate the love Olivia gives to Cesario, a fiction Viola has created. And so, just as she tries to persuade Olivia to reciprocate Duke Orsino's love, she tries to show him the futility of his stubborn refusal to accept rejection. Giving, moreover, may not be as generous as it seems. Although Olivia may be right that 'Love sought is good, but given unsought is better' (III.i.156), giving love where it is not wanted can be selfish, a self-indulgent demand that forces the beloved to reciprocate or to seem cruel and ungrateful. In short, the reciprocal nature of human relationships does not entitle one to expect exact recompense: 'to give a dog and in recompense desire my dog again' (V.i.6–7), as Feste accuses Fabian.[13]

Understanding the principle of reciprocity, then, doesn't provide a panacea for all the problems of life in society. Individual purposes and desires may not converge so that Jack has Jill and all comes out well. Viola can avoid Malvolio's solipsistic belief that talking to other people is like 'nightingales answer[ing] daws' and Orsino's self-defeating modes of thought and feeling. By renewing the poetry of unrequited love, she can even refuse the sterile passivity of smiling at grief 'like Patience on a monument' (II.iv.114). But since telling entails a listener who understands, Viola cannot tell her love. Her indirect expression of feeling creates new frustration, not fulfillment. Like Malvolio, Orsino, and Olivia, she is trapped within the self-protective role she has constructed from the material available in her culture. Of course, choice is possible within these constrictions. Orsino, who does not understand the cultural origins of his self-image or the coercive force of the principle of reciprocity, doesn't recognize the self-glorification in his love for Olivia. When he admonishes his messenger to 'Be clamorous, and leap all civil bounds, / Rather than make unprofited return' (I.iv.21-2), he is trying to force Olivia to return his love. When she refuses, his insistence that he 'cannot be so answer'd' (II.iv.88) reveals his love to be, at least in part, a determination to dominate and an egoist's conviction that reality must conform to his will. In contrast, Viola, who is conscious that giving love involves asking for love, denies herself the joy of offering her love to Orsino. And she begins to regret her male disguise when she realizes the falseness of her position in relation to Olivia. As Cesario, she clearly tells Olivia she can never love her, but even so, she accepts Olivia's gifts, sparing her the pain and humiliation of having these symbols of love rejected.

Recognizing the reciprocal nature of human relationships, then, does not imply a cynical denial of altruism and generosity. Viola can selflessly hide her love for Orsino and act kindly to Olivia because she knows that she cannot give without taking or take without giving. But not even Viola can sort out the tangled relationships that make up the plot of *Twelfth Night*. Happiness is contingent on circumstances produced by time and chance beyond anyone's control. Fortune gives and takes capriciously; time gives and inevitably takes; those we love do not always love us in return. So Viola says, 'O time, thou must untangle this, not I, / It is too hard a knot for me t' untie' (II.ii.40-1). Or as Malvolio puts it: "Tis but fortune, all is fortune' (II.v.23).

The sorting out of couples in the last scene is a gift from fortune and the culmination of the reciprocal exchanges we have been tracing. In the course of the action, all the major characters have been tempted by the dream of self-sufficiency, but have been forced, by circumstances and by their own needs and desires, into relationships where they become aware of their obligations to and dependence on others. Cesario/Viola is the key figure in the process. She triggers Olivia's abandonment of her vows of celibacy and provides her with the humbling experience of finding the real world intractable to her will. In a different fashion but to similar effect, she teaches Orsino that he may want something he cannot have and gives him real human love as an alternative to a self-centered fantasy. When all fantasies of limitless personal power and happiness collapse in the last scene under the pressure of the destructive aspect of reciprocity, Orsino and Olivia are ready to relinquish gladly their dreams of Olivia and Cesario for the real love of Viola and Sebastian. Finally repelled from worshipping at 'uncivil' Olivia's 'ingrate ... altars' (V.i.112, 113), Orsino's first reaction is the angry cruelty that is so often the corollary of sentimentality. But when Viola reveals her identity, he asks for her hand and gives her his in grateful recompense for 'service done him' (V.i.321).

Circumstances of place, time, and fortune can cohere to reveal Viola's identity and make possible the reciprocal love of Orsino and Viola because of Sebastian's opportune arrival. Antonio's startled reaction – 'How have you made division of yourself?' (V.i.222) – points to the plot mechanism that creates this happy ending. The sudden reversal from hostility and disintegrating relationships to love and alliance results from the amazing yet natural division of Cesario into Viola and Sebastian. This separation of brother and sister into two independent people symbolically illustrates Lévi-Strauss' theory in *The Elementary Structures of Kinship* that the principle of reciprocity binds people together in stable societies through the prohibition of incest and its wider social application, the custom of exogamy. He speculates that incest 'in the broadest sense of the word, consists in obtaining by oneself, and for oneself, instead of by another, and for another' (489). Both the incest taboo and the practice of marrying outside the immediate group are essentially rules of reciprocity: 'I will give up my daughter or my sister only on condition that my neighbour does the same ... the fact that I can obtain a wife is, in the final analysis, the consequence of the fact that a brother or father has given her up' (62). The functional value of reciprocal exchange in marriage alliances and of the prohibition of marriage within certain degrees is to maintain 'the group as a group ... avoiding the indefinite fission and segmentation which the practice of consanguineous marriages would bring about' (479). The practice of reciprocal exchange in marriage alliances 'provides the means of binding men together, and of superimposing upon the natural links of kinship ... [those] of alliance governed by rule' (480).

As in *The Comedy of Errors*, an apparent impasse suddenly evaporates when twins finally meet on stage, but this time the comedic solution to confusion and conflict consists not in the reunion of a family but in the subordination of blood ties to exogamous alliances. It is only when Olivia's exclusive allegiance to her brother is relinquished, when Sir Toby's claim to consanguineous control of his niece is repudiated, and when brother and sister are brought together so that they can be publicly divided, that a harmonious and cohesive society becomes possible.[14] The strangers from across the sea rescue the native Illyrians both from the sterility of self-preoccupation and from the divisive violence of their inevitable conflicts. Viola and Sebastian free Orsino and Olivia from illusions of exclusive self-fulfillment and total dominance and give them instead the shared happiness of reciprocal love.

The portrayal of exogamous marriage in *Twelfth Night* differs from Lévi-Strauss' model in one important respect: in Illyria women are agents rather than objects of exchange. According to Lévi-Strauss, marriage exchanges entail the commodification of women: 'The total relationship of exchange which constitutes marriage is not established between a man and a woman ... but between two groups of men, and the woman figures only as one of the objects in the exchange, not as one of the partners between whom the exchange takes place' (115).[15] But in *Twelfth Night*, where fathers are notably absent, Olivia, Viola, and Maria choose their own mates and negotiate their own marriages. In the anthropological paradigm, as Gayle Rubin points out, since 'it is women who are being transacted, then it is the men who give and take them who are linked.'[16] In *Twelfth Night* the multiple marriages do not function to create alliances between men. Both Olivia and Orsino remark that Olivia becomes Orsino's sister through their marriages (V.i.317, 384), but Sebastian and Orsino do not address each other. Perhaps Sir Toby represents a debased version of the usual system. He relies on his blood ties to Olivia: 'Am I not consanguineous? Am I not of her blood?' (II.iii.77–8). And he tries to use Olivia as a means of exchange to cement his alliance with Sir Andrew. But Toby's plan is not merely thwarted; it is never a serious threat.

Another way in which the play's representation of social organization and process differs from anthropological accounts is its general untidiness. *Twelfth Night* notoriously leaves loose ends dangling: Malvolio's threat of revenge, Antonio's legal status in Illyria, the sea captain's imprisonment, Sir Andrew's broken head. Lévi-Strauss interprets the significance of reciprocity as the substitution of organization by rule for organization by kinship. In *Twelfth Night* social life proceeds not so much by rule as by a continuing process of negotiation. This open-endedness has caused many critics in recent years to see the play as more pessimistic than happy. Admittedly neither Shakespeare nor the anthropologists claim that awareness of the principle of reciprocity solves all problems. But *Twelfth Night*,

I think, suggests that by understanding our mutual needs, we can choose love, generosity, and alliance rather than isolation, stagnation, and division in the give-and-take of experience in the societies we construct.

CHAPTER TWELVE

Conclusion

Until recently Shakespeare's comedies usually have been valued for providing a holiday release from the problems of the real world, soaring above questions of politics or ethics into a world of imagination. While I agree that they grind no polemical axes, I have tried to demonstrate that the ten plays discussed in this book offer acute commentary on social situations and behavior. None of the plays presents itself as an accurate representation of a segment of contemporary culture much less as a comprehensive portrayal of sixteenth-century English society. Nevertheless these golden worlds of Italy, Arden, and Illyria scrutinize and seek to shape the society that shaped them. In the process of dramatizing the integration of marginal figures into an Italian city state, *The Taming of the Shrew* portrays contemporary English marriage customs, while *Love's Labor's Lost* examines the dynamics of courtly factionalism and the political implications of changing educational patterns. Geographical and chronological distance allow *The Merchant of Venice*, *Much Ado About Nothing*, and *As You Like It* to explore such indigenous institutions as nascent capitalism, colonialism, and primogeniture. For all their exotic settings and conspicuous artificiality, then, the comedies speak the language of the culture that produced them, representing social experience in familiar sixteenth-century terms. John Donne's analysis of human social structures in terms of the power of husbands over wives, parents over children, and masters over servants applies easily to these civil comedies. The plays include horizontal relationships between friends, siblings, and rivals as well as the vertical hierarchies of Donne's paradigm, but they consistently explore amatory, familial, economic, and political struggles within hierarchically structured societies and represent recognizable social institutions and practices.

Since attitudes and objects of attention vary in each play, the comedies provide nothing like a Shakespearean theory of society, but they all imply that human experience is unavoidably social and that fulfillment through social relations is desirable and possible. Comic confusion and complication result from tensions between characters' pursuits of their own interests and the expectations and demands of others and lead usually to comic denouements that reassure us that mutually satisfying balance is possible. Typically, happy endings result in the protagonists' integration into society, rather than, say, the hero's and heroine's escape to a better place. Even when romantic union is a deferred possibility rather than a dramatized achievement as in *Love's Labor's Lost* or when the happy ending is qualified by metatheatrical distancing as in *The Taming of the Shrew* and *As You Like It*, the image of human good suggested is individual fulfillment through communal participation. In the later tragedies this harmony of individual and group is not possible nor always even desirable: a Hamlet who accommodates to Denmark or an Antony who learns to balance successfully Egypt and Rome is inconceivable. But the comedies show people as social beings who reveal their worth and achieve some measure of satisfaction through relations with their kind.

Separation between citizens who can claim protection from the group and strangers who enter the community at risk is evident as early as *The Comedy of Errors* and as late as *Twelfth Night*, but the boundaries of the comic commonwealth and the criteria for belonging become increasingly relaxed. In *The Comedy of Errors* the standards are geographical and legal, and the penalty for violating boundaries is high. In *The Taming of the Shrew*, *The Two Gentlemen of Verona*, and *Love's Labor's Lost*, geographical and political barriers are less formidable, but exacting codes of language and behavior oppress as well as empower. In later comedies, cultural diversity balances social coercion, and exclusion is by and large voluntary. In *The Merry Wives of Windsor*, for example, Falstaff's assault on marital fidelity is intolerable, but the French doctor and the Welsh parson are citizens in good standing in the Windsor community. In *Much Ado About Nothing*, Dogberry and his colleagues function responsibly and significantly in Messina, however much they are objects of amused derision in the theater. The impulse towards inclusion in the comic denouements extends to violators of social norms like Falstaff and Oliver de Boys and attempts to co-opt even such antagonists to community solidarity as Shylock and Malvolio. Only the intractably anti-social Don John is still in jeopardy at the play's conclusion.

Since these comic worlds turn upside down only temporarily and since the inclusive and forgiving scenes of comic closure present social harmony in the framework of hierarchical social order, many critics conclude that the comedies implicitly endorse and support the institutions and policies of late Tudor and early Stuart England. Even though C.L. Barber presents *Love's Labor's Lost, A Midsummer Night's Dream, The Merchant of Venice, As You Like It*, and *Twelfth Night* as saturnalian celebrations of potentially anarchic forces, he argues that these festive comedies function to contain social discontent rather than to subvert settled orthodoxies. More recently, post-structuralist historical and materialist critics have demonstrated the inevitable complicity of all texts in the ideology of the culture producing them. Of course, their conclusions have not gone unchallenged. Other critics have argued persuasively that Shakespeare's plays constitute a powerful critique of contemporary political and social thought. These critical oppositions in themselves demonstrate the plays' resistance to readings based on Apollonian/Dionysian or conservative/subversive dichotomies. The comedies portray sympathetically rebellious daughters, impertinent servants, and irreverent wit, but they also satirize offenders against traditional social forms and group morality. Typically they present not so much the co-optation and containment of subversion or the triumph of amorous youth over social restraint as a sort of double helix in which society adjusts to meet challenge and change and individuals adjust – consciously or unconsciously, willingly or unwillingly – in order to take their places within society.

The representation of social harmony in the final scenes leaves the structures of Shakespeare's various comic commonwealths intact. Egeus' attempt to block the course of true love in *A Midsummer Night's Dream* is dismissed in Act IV, but his authority can be overruled only by the superior power of Duke Theseus. The last words of *The Comedy of Errors* gesture towards a more benign social order: 'We came into the world like brother and brother; / And now let's go hand in hand, not one before another' (*CE*, v.i.425–6), but the brotherhood and equality of Ephesian Dromio's invitation to his brother derive social rank from birth, the very principle that authorizes the violence that both twins, born of a 'mean woman' (I.i.54), are subjected to. Kate has more control of herself and others at the end than at the start of *The Taming of the Shrew*, but her empowerment is measured in terms of her deference to her husband. Yet while basic political structures never change, the actual disposition and exercise of power often shift significantly. Duke Frederick loses and Duke Senior regains a dukedom. Although the King of Navarre will return Aquitaine to France without compromising his political sovereignty, he binds himself to the Princess of France, becoming personally dependent on her favor instead of pursuing his own goals in splendid isolation. Count Orsino exercises power more forcefully in the last than in any earlier scene of *Twelfth Night*, threatening to execute Cesario and unhesitatingly issuing orders in Olivia's household, but he too voluntarily subjects himself to a woman, proclaiming Viola her 'master's mistress.' From one angle, of course, a position dependent on Orsino's capricious will could hardly be less secure, but in a play that repeatedly dramatizes how the constructions of the mind determine behavior, becoming the queen of Orsino's fancy has real significance.

Such changes of heart and voluntary relinquishments of power endorse hierarchical structures by representing them as capable of benign adjustment and reinterpretation. Still, even when fictional characters unquestioningly defer to authority, theatrical images of social harmony can function to invite critical examination of actual social structures. And the plays also present unflattering versions of social power. While the alien Shylock and the anti-social Don John are the most purely malicious villains and remain unforgiven, conflict and confusion result more often from oppressive conventionality – from maladroit young men pursuing courtly fashion and from fathers and rulers exercising legitimate power. Baptista auctioning his daughter to the highest bidder, the two gentlemen from Verona educating themselves in rivalry and duplicity, the King of Navarre irresponsibly indulging his whims, and Orlando suffering from primogeniture expose absurdities, cruelties, and injustices in contemporary institutions.

In addition to such direct satire, the comedies expose inconsistencies and contradictions within prevailing ideologies. In spite of their usually happy conclusions, they frequently highlight the tensions inherent in viewing marriage as at once economic, dynastic arrangement and personal emotional commitment. In the sermon I discussed briefly in chapter 1, John Donne divides human relationships into three homologous kinds, which he lists first as *'Prince and Subject,'* *'husband* and *wife,'* and *'parents* and *children'* and then as *'Master* and *Servant, Man* and *Wife, Father* and *Children.'* Shakespeare's comedies, like Donne's sermon and many Renaissance texts, often reduce parents to fathers, but *The Merry Wives of Windsor* explores conflict between father and mother. While Donne conflates the relation of prince to subject with that of master to man, the trial scene in *The Merchant of Venice* exposes opposing interests in the entanglements of political and economic power.

Perhaps even more disturbing to established ways of thinking is the drama's power to question the adequacy of conventional concepts and categories. Although the comedies do not condemn any specific political structure, they expose abuses of power and ideological inconsistencies, and they point to the gap between theory and practice. The representation of gender is a case in point. Female and male characters alike agree on the desirable subordination of women to men. Adriana's complaints are refuted, and Kate's rebellion suppressed. Clear-sighted women like Beatrice and Portia cheerfully choose their own subordination. But this gender hierarchy is by no means an expression of unconscious cultural assumptions. In their various ways, Adriana's complaints, Luciana's response, Kate's final paean to wifely submission, Beatrice's ironic rejection of marriage, and Portia's inventory of the wealth and independence she sacrifices by marrying all emphasize the social inequality of the sexes. And at the same time that female as well as male characters endorse this inequality, the plays deny rigid gender differences. The boy actors of the Elizabethan and Jacobean theater and the disguise conventions that allow Shakespearean heroines to impersonate men successfully blur gender distinctions. Characterization further undercuts traditional stereotypes. Women are represented not as reified objects of adoration nor as embodiments of male sexual fantasies and fears. As critics have always acknowledged, the comedies are dominated by women who are intelligent, courageous, and resourceful as well as loyal, generous, and loving. They display as much interiority as male characters, and the representation of subjectivity is surprisingly ungendered. When Rosalind witnesses a scene between Silvius and Phebe, for example, she identifies spontaneously with Silvius rather than with Phebe. And if Rosalind and Viola both attribute their abhorrence of physical violence to their womanly natures, their plays also make clear that masculine physical courage is a cultural expectation rather than a biological

Conclusion

reality: 'many ... mannish cowards ... outface it with their semblances' (*AYL*, I.iii.121–2). The fictional commonwealths of these plays are not partitioned into public masculine areas of war, business, and politics and private feminine areas of domesticity and human relations. Theseus and Hippolyta hunt together, the Princess of France and the King of Navarre conduct diplomacy, and Portia resolves the legal conundrum perplexing the Duke of Venice, while all the major characters devote most of their time to human relationships that are not divided into public and private categories. It is true that Portia can function successfully in the public law court only in masculine disguise, but it is equally true that despite her formal relinquishing of power and independence in order to marry Bassanio, she continues to exercise power independently. She uses her personal and financial resources for the benefit of her husband and his friend, but she refuses to be used as a commodity of exchange in the relationship between the two men, insisting that Antonio stand surety to her marriage instead of allowing herself to become a symbol of Antonio's generosity.

Thus Portia and the other heroines who do not challenge male authority nevertheless demonstrate that it is an arbitrary human arrangement unjustified by natural superiority. Hermia, who wonders 'what power' (*MND*, I.i.59) has emboldened her to speak in Theseus' august presence but acts on the promptings of her fancy, Portia, who claims that telling enough 'puny lies' (*MV*, III.iv.74) will make her male disguise convincing, Mistress Page and Mistress Ford, who pursue their own designs without their husbands' knowledge and against their wishes, and Rosalind, who deceives her father and lover with her doublet and hose, are similarly unawed and undeterred by masculine power. This gap between theoretical male dominance and actual female self-sufficiency does not imply that the theory is irrelevant to experience. The social mythology of gender affects action and shapes lives in all the plays. Indeed, awareness of its power correlates highly with the ability to act effectively. Katherine the shrew is not part of the tradition that represents female protest as failure rather than as rebellion.[1] Untamed Kate does not attack the patriarchal system: she ineffectually resents her own failure and her sister's success within it. In contrast, Portia, Beatrice, and Rosalind, who are aware of its artificiality, function effectively.

Shakespearean comedy, then, does not provide an image of gender equality. Although it presupposes that women can perform effectively in the public sphere, it does not condemn the social conventions that allow them to do so only in male disguise. It implicitly approves women who choose their own husbands when conventional procedures fail to provide them with satisfactory mates, but it does not strongly challenge the social arrangements that force them to deception in order to do so. Although the sexes are not polarized in individual characterizations, heterosexual union is consistently presented as the basis of society. Marriage in these plays is hierarchical, and women invariably prefer submission within marriage to isolation outside it. Nevertheless, there is a good deal of room to maneuver within and around the gender hierarchies of these comic commonwealths. These structures, moreover, are not inevitably or unalterably ordained by God or nature; they are flawed and mutable human social arrangements.

A similar gap opens between theoretical uniformity and constraint and actual variety and flexibility in the representation of political power. The comedies portray hierarchically structured commonwealths in which power resides in a ruler not accountable to those he governs. In most of the plays, the ruler figures prominently in the action. The two exceptions incorporate images of uncontested power: the figure of the Lord in *The Taming of the Shrew* and the image of the royal court in *The Merry Wives of Windsor*. Nevertheless, by their varied political settings the comedies as a group announce the variety and contingency of possible social orders. In addition, without explicitly condemning any particular political system, each play exposes the potential for violent cruelty and injustice. Even when individual dukes and kings are characterized as generally benevolent, harsh and unjust laws and irresponsible, unwise, and tyrannical uses of power demystify political hierarchy. The comedies support Donne's contention that 'the principall foundation ... of all States ... is *power,*' but they emphasize the multiple centers of power within societies: the power that enables Hermia to question authority as well as the power that threatens her, the power that allows the citizens of Windsor to resolve their conflicts without recourse to royal authority, the power of Dogberry and the nameless sexton to resolve the problems created by and for their political and social superiors. In these plays, as Dogberry says, when 'two men ride of a horse, one must ride behind,' but, in spite of the pervasive networks of privilege and deference, control slips away from titular authority. Duke Solinus interprets Ephesian law in response to Egeon's family fortunes, Duke Theseus ratifies the

Conclusion

betrothals arranged by his subjects, Don Pedro accedes to Leonato's wishes, Duke Senior plays the part Rosalind assigns him, and Duke Orsino's future happiness is subject to Viola and to contingencies involving Malvolio and an unnamed sea captain. Political control depends finally on willingness to be controlled. Power takes many forms, including prerogatives of rank and office, attractions of fashion and change, constraints of tradition, Malvolio's vengefulness, Rosalind's grace and resourcefulness, Petruchio's exuberant impatience, Silvia's loyalty, Dogberry's devotion to duty, and the wit and gaiety that allow Portia to see male presumption as funny rather than frightening.

Shakespeare's comedies acknowledge that arbitrary social structures, the duplicity of language, and the incompatibility and inconstancy of human purposes and desires make the project of living together complex and difficult. Open-ended plays like *Love's Labor's Lost* and *Twelfth Night* argue that such incalculable contingencies preclude certainty. Hero's vulnerability and the suffering of Shylock and his daughter deny the possibility of creating utopia. Like Schopenhauer's porcupines, the characters in these plays huddle together to protect themselves from the cold only to hurt each other with their quills.[2] But they don't draw Schopenhauer's moral and decide to keep their distance. If they are sometimes inconstant, they are also capable of making and keeping promises. If they fall short of perfection, they have the capacity to forgive. These plays remind us that both promising and forgiving depend on the presence of others.[3] Within the constrictive, sometimes oppressive structures of money, class, and gender hierarchies, characters in Shakespeare's comic commonwealths are able, with a bit of luck, to create social selves and to establish bonds with others. The comedies suggest that, in spite of causing unavoidable pain and irremediable loss, society is the happiness of life.

Notes

Chapter One: Introduction

1 Quotations throughout are from *The Riverside Shakespeare*, ed. G. Blakemore Evans et al. (Boston: Houghton Mifflin, 1974).
2 Of the first sort are such books as Larry Champion, *The Evolution of Shakespeare's Comedy: A Study in Dramatic Perspective* (Cambridge, Mass.: Harvard University Press, 1970); J. Dennis Huston, *Shakespeare's Comedies of Play* (New York: Columbia University Press, 1981); Karen Newman, *Shakespeare's Rhetoric of Comic Character: Dramatic Convention in Classical and Renaissance Comedy* (New York: Methuen, 1985); A.P. Riemer, *Antic Fables: Patterns of Evasion in Shakespeare's Comedies* (New York: St. Martin's Press, 1980); and Leo Salingar, *Shakespeare and the Traditions of Comedy* (Cambridge: Cambridge University Press, 1974). Examples of the second group are Arthur C. Kirsch, *Shakespeare and the Experience of Love* (Cambridge: Cambridge University Press, 1981); Alexander Leggatt, *Shakespeare's Comedy of Love* (London: Methuen, 1974); W. Thomas MacCary, *Friends and Lovers: The Phenomenology of Desire in Shakespearean Comedy* (New York: Columbia University Press, 1985); and Richard P. Wheeler, *Shakespeare's Development and the Problem Comedies* (Berkeley: University of California Press, 1981). Most criticism, of course, includes discussions of both thematic and formal matters; these groupings are meant only to indicate some primary emphases in work on the comedies.
3 Two exceptions to this generalization are Edward Berry, *Shakespeare's Comic Rites* (Cambridge: Cambridge University Press, 1984) and Richard A. Levin, *Love and Society in Shakespearean Comedy: A*

Study of Dramatic Form and Content (Newark: University of Delaware Press, 1985). Their approaches differ significantly from mine. Berry draws on anthropological studies to examine the pattern of separation, transition, and incorporation in the progress towards marriage of Shakespeare's young lovers. Levin sees in the plays 'conventional melodramatic structures' that celebrate the emergence of ideal societies, but prefers to present 'antiromantic' readings that stress the moral compromises characters make in their struggles for social advantage.

4 C.L. Barber, *Shakespeare's Festive Comedies: A Study of Dramatic Form and Its Relation to Social Custom* (Princeton: Princeton University Press, 1959); Northrop Frye, 'The Argument of Comedy,' *English Institute Essays*, ed. D.A. Robertson, Jr. (New York: Columbia University Press, 1949), 58–73; Northrop Frye, *A Natural Perspective: The Development of Shakespearian Comedy and Romance* (New York: Harcourt, Brace and World, 1965).

5 Thomas Greene, 'The Flexibility of the Self in Renaissance Literature' in *The Disciplines of Criticism*, ed. Peter Demetz, Thomas Greene, and Lowry Nelson, Jr. (New Haven: Yale University Press, 1968), 249.

6 Robert R. Hellenga, 'Elizabethan Dramatic Conventions and Elizabethan Reality,' *Renaissance Drama*, 12 (1981), 41.

7 See, for example, Stephen Greenblatt, *Renaissance Self-Fashioning: From More to Shakespeare* (Chicago: University of Chicago Press, 1980) and *Shakespearean Negotiations* (Berkeley: University of California Press, 1988); Louis Montrose, '"Shaping Fantasies": Figurations of Gender and Power in Elizabethan Culture,' *Representations*, 1:2 (1983), 61–94; Jonathan Dollimore and Alan Sinfield, eds., *Political Shakespeare* (Ithaca: Cornell University Press, 1985); Leonard Tennenhouse, *Power on Display: The Politics of Shakespeare's Genres* (New York: Methuen, 1986).

8 Wallace Stevens, *The Necessary Angel: Essays on Reality and the Imagination* (New York: Vintage, 1941), 36.

9 Anthony Giddens, *The Constitution of Society: Outline of the Theory of Structuration* (Berkeley: University of California Press, 1979), 163–4.

10 Thomas Smith, *The Common-Wealth of England, and Maner of Government Thereof* (London: John Windet for Gregorie Seton, 1589), 11. Smith's category of 'free men' apparently includes women, since he argues that two is the smallest possible social unit and that the 'naturalest, and first continuation of two, toward the making of a further societie of continuance, is of the husband & of the wife' (12).

Chapter Two

1 R.A. Foakes, 'Introduction' to the Arden edition of *The Comedy of Errors* (London: Methuen, 1962), xxix.
2 *The Sermons of John Donne*, ed. George R. Potter and Evelyn M. Simpson, 10 vols. (Berkeley: University of California Press, 1953-62), 5:114.
3 *Shakespeare's Romantic Comedies* (Chapel Hill: University of North Carolina Press, 1966), 25, 11. H.B. Charlton takes a similar view of Adriana as shrew and Luciana as romantic in *Shakespearean Comedy*, first published 1938 (London: Methuen, 1966), 68, 71.
4 Unhistoricized interpretations of this speech as evidence of Adriana's parasitic dependency ignore the force of the elm and vine as a traditional emblem of marriage, joining masculine strength with feminine fruitfulness. Adriana explicitly associates barren parasites with influences separating Antipholus from her. As Paul Stevens points out, Adriana's image of marriage contrasts with Titania's distorted version that replaces the vine with barren ivy to describe her embrace of Bottom (*MND*, IV.i.43-4). Paul Stevens, *Imagination and the Presence of Shakespeare in 'Paradise Lost'* (Madison: University of Wisconsin Press, 1985), 207.
5 I disagree with the critics who see this speech as evidence of Adriana's over-possessiveness. See Arden edition, note to II.ii.123-9; Phialas, 14; Ruth Nevo, *Comic Transformations in Shakespeare* (London: Methuen, 1980), 26.
6 For a perceptive discussion of time, money, and law in *The Comedy of Errors* see J. Dennis Huston, *Shakespeare's Comedies Of Play* (New York: Columbia University Press, 1981), 33-4.
7 Richard Henze discusses the chain as a symbol of social cohesion and of the play's recommended norm, 'the bridling of headstrong freedom and wandering individuality' (35). '*The Comedy of Errors*: A Freely Binding Chain,' *Shakespeare Quarterly*, 22 (1971), 35-41.
8 *Writings and Translations of Myles Coverdale* (Cambridge: The Parker Society, 1844), 175; quoted in John F. Danby, *Poets on Fortune's Hill* (London: Faber and Faber, 1952), 109. I am indebted throughout this paragraph to Danby's discussion of the distinction between classical and Christian patience (108-27).
9 James L. Sanderson has observed the importance of the theme of patience in *The Comedy of Errors* and discussed many of these passages in the context of Elizabethan iconographical and intellectual traditions but has reached different conclusions. He argues that errors

are caused and compounded by impatience and curable by patience and sees Egeon as an exemplar of patience. 'Patience in *The Comedy of Errors*,' *Texas Studies in Literature and Language*, 16 (1975), 603–18.
10 Arden edition, 'Introduction,' xlix.

Chapter Three

1 As is usual in the comedies, the absence of a wife and mother is not commented on.
2 Umberto Eco, *The Name of the Rose*, trans. William Weaver (San Diego: Harcourt, Brace, Jovanovich, 1983), 73. Puttenham calls hypotyposis '*the counterfait, otherwise called the figure of representation.*' George Puttenham, *The Arte of English Poesie*, intro. Baxter Hathaway (Kent, Ohio: Kent State University Press, 1970), 320.
3 See Alexander Leggatt, *Shakespeare's Comedy of Love* (London: Methuen, 1974), 46–9, and Peter G. Phialas, *Shakespeare's Romantic Comedies* (Chapel Hill: University of North Carolina Press, 1966), 28–30. Bertrand Evans and George R. Hibbard emphasize the contrast between the deception and disguise of the subplot and Petruchio's lack of subterfuge in the main plot. Evans, *Shakespeare's Comedies* (Oxford: Oxford University Press, 1967), 26; Hibbard, '*The Taming of the Shrew*: A Social Comedy' in *Shakespearean Essays*, ed. Alwin Thaler and Norman Sanders (Knoxville: University of Tennessee Press, 1964), 22.
4 Images of Bianca as confined or imprisoned and of her accessibility to suitors as freedom are recurrent; see I.i.87, 138; I.ii.118–19; I.i.138; I.ii.262.
5 Shakespeare has emphasized the rebelliousness of Bianca's and Lucentio's courtship by adding the clandestine marriage that does not appear in Gascoigne's *Supposes*, his source for the subplot.
6 According to Lawrence Stone, because the system of primogeniture fostered a growing reluctance to provide marriage portions, the proportion of the daughters of landed families who never married increased dramatically during the seventeenth century, rising to nearly 25 per cent in 1700. In the sixteenth century, however, more than 95 per cent of the daughters of the upper class married, a nuptial rate slightly higher than among the rest of the population. *The Family, Sex and Marriage in England, 1500–1800* (London: Weidenfeld & Nicolson, 1977), 43–5, graph 3 and 380. See also Miriam Slater, *Family Life in*

the Seventeenth Century (London: Routledge & Kegan Paul, 1985), 84–90.
7 Claude Lévi-Strauss, *The Raw and the Cooked*, trans. John Weightman and Doreen Weightman (New York: Harper & Row, 1969), 334–6.
8 Ibid., 338.
9 Kate's coming to terms with her society can be seen as an exploration of the self-conscious forging of human identity in the context of Renaissance culture described by Stephen Greenblatt in *Renaissance Self-Fashioning: From More to Shakespeare* (Chicago: University of Chicago Press, 1980). We should notice, however, that whereas Greenblatt describes Renaissance culture wholly in terms of its official cultural institutions, *The Taming of the Shrew* presents three distinct cultures – the plebeian world of the Hostess and Christopher Sly, the aristocratic world of the Lord and his retinue, and the middle-class world of Baptista's daughters and their suitors. In *The Taming of the Shrew*, emphasis on how a particular culture shapes individual identities is balanced by acknowledgment of the variety of cultures existing simultaneously and of the possibility of controlling cultural conventions whatever they are. Greenblatt's assumption of a monolithic Renaissance culture is criticized and supplemented by Michael Bristol in *Carnival and Theater: Plebeian Culture and the Structure of Authority in Renaissance England* (New York: Methuen, 1985).
10 Gervase Markham, *Country Contentments* (1615), 4th ed. (London, 1631), 36–7, as quoted in *The Taming of the Shrew*, ed. G.R. Hibbard (Harmondsworth: Penguin Books, 1968), n. to IV.i.176–82.
11 Marianne L. Novy, *Love's Argument: Gender Relations in Shakespeare*, (Chapel Hill: University of North Carolina Press, 1984), 61; J. Dennis Huston, *Shakespeare's Comedies of Play* (New York: Columbia University Press, 1981), 64.
12 In early modern England the family was usually thought of as the fundamental social unit rather than as a refuge from society. See Susan Amussen, 'Gender, Family and the Social Order, 1560–1725,' 196–217, in *Order and Disorder in Early Modern England*, ed. Anthony Fletcher and John Stevenson (Cambridge: Cambridge University Press, 1985), and Amussen, *An Ordered Society: Gender and Class in Early Modern England* (Oxford: Basil Blackwell, 1988).
13 In *The Taming of a Shrew*, which most scholars now see as a bad quarto or memorial reconstruction of *The Taming of the Shrew*, Sly falls asleep after commenting on the play several times and in an epilogue awakes in his own clothes and interprets his experience as a

dream. Some scholars have argued that Shakespeare intended *The Taming of the Shrew* to include similar scenes and have proposed various explanations for their loss. Other hypotheses are that Shakespeare deliberately dropped Sly from later scenes for artistic reasons or that Sly's expanded role is an unauthorized addition by those responsible for *The Taming of a Shrew*. For a discussion of the relationship of the texts see Brian Morris' 'Introduction' to the Arden edition (London: Methuen, 1981), 12–50.

14 Norbert Elias, *The Civilizing Process*, trans. Edmund Jephcott, 2 vols. (Oxford: Basil Blackwell, 1978 and 1982).

15 David Underdown, 'The Taming of the Scold: the Enforcement of Patriarchal Authority in Early Modern England,' in Fletcher and Stevenson, 116–36, and Underdown, *Revel, Riot, and Rebellion: Popular Politics and Culture in England, 1603–1660* (Oxford: Clarendon Press, 1985), 38–40.

16 On the development of the ironic reading of Kate's speech see Robert Heilman, 'The *Taming* Untamed, or the Return of the Shrew,' *Modern Language Quarterly*, 27 (1966), 147–61. Linda Woodbridge presents a sensible critique of ahistorical attempts to exonerate Shakespeare from the charge of sexism in *The Taming of the Shrew* in *Women and the English Renaissance: Literature and the Nature of Womankind, 1540–1620* (Urbana: University of Illinois Press, 1984), 221–2.

17 Lynda E. Boose, 'Scolding Brides and Bridling Scolds: Taming the Woman's Unruly Member,' *Shakespeare Quarterly*, 42 (1991), 181–2.

18 For the literary tradition, see Woodbridge, 201–7; for historical practices of controlling women, see Underdown, 'The Taming of the Scold,' and Boose, 179–213.

19 On the analogy between familial and political power and on Locke's undermining of the organic theory of patriarchal power, see Amussen, *An Ordered Society*, 37–66.

20 See John C. Bean, 'Comic Structure and the Humanizing of Kate in *The Taming of the Shrew*' in *The Woman's Part: Feminist Criticism of Shakespeare*, ed. Carolyn Ruth Swift Lenz, Gayle Green, and Carol Thomas Neely (Urbana: University of Illinois Press, 1980), 65–78, especially 68–71; Juliet Dusinberre, *Shakespeare and the Nature of Women* (London: Macmillan, 1975), 78–9; Morris, 148–9; Novy, 58–60.

21 Some historians attribute a growing emphasis on marriage as an affective rather than an economic relationship to the influence of Puritan ideas of spiritual equality. See Stone, *The Family, Sex and Marriage, 1500–1800*. Others stress that the ideal of marriage based on love appears throughout the period. See, for example, Ralph A.

Houlbrooke, *The English Family, 1450–1700* (London: Longman, 1984). Ann Jennalie Cook, whose useful study of marriage in Shakespeare's society appeared after I had completed this book, provides references on this controversy. *Making a Match: Courtship in Shakespeare and His Society* (Princeton: Princeton University Press, 1991), 13.

Chapter Four

1 M.C. Bradbrook, *Shakespeare and Elizabethan Poetry* (London: Chatto & Windus, 1951), 151.
2 Thomas Elyot, *The Book Named the Governor*, ed. S.E. Lehmberg (London: Dent, 1962), 136–51.
3 Ralph M. Sargent makes this point in 'Sir Thomas Elyot and the Integrity of *The Two Gentlemen of Verona*,' PMLA, 65 (1950), 1166–80.
4 'Introduction,' *The Two Gentlemen of Verona* (Cambridge: Cambridge University Press, 1921), xiv.
5 Bradbrook, 151.
6 A.C. Hamilton suggests a parallel with *The Franklin's Tale* in *The Early Shakespeare* (San Marino, Calif.: Huntington Library Press, 1967), 126.
7 See J.H. Hexter, 'The Education of the Aristocracy in the Renaissance' in his *Reappraisals in History* (London: Longmans, 1961), 45–70; Ruth Kelso, *The Doctrine of the English Gentleman in the Sixteenth Century* (Urbana: University of Illinois Press, 1929); Lawrence Stone, *The Crisis of the Aristocracy, 1558–1641* (Oxford: Clarendon Press, 1965).
8 Baldassare Castiglione, *The Book of the Courtier*, trans. Sir Thomas Hoby, in *Three Renaissance Classics*, ed. Burton A. Milligan (New York: Charles Scribner's Sons, 1953), 388, 408, 413.
9 Proteus' subsequent behavior suggests that the particular lie he fabricates may well express a subconscious desire for just what happens – avoidance of the emotional responsibility of his new relationship with Julia and a chance to join in his friend's adventures. If so, it does not mean that his feelings for Julia are feigned but that he finds the confusing intensity of a new kind of emotional experience difficult to deal with and intuitively recognizes that he is not ready to make that relationship public.
10 For example, Peter Lindenbaum points out that in Act I 'the perfect man' envisioned by Proteus' guardians, and presumably by those of Valentine as well, is merely a gentleman adept in the social arts'

(232). The significant dramatic action, he argues, is the education of the characters to redefine the 'perfect man' in religious rather than social terms. 'Education in *The Two Gentlemen of Verona*,' *Studies in English Literature*, 15 (1975), 229–44.

11 'Castiglione's *Courtier*: The Self as a Work of Art' in *Renaissance and Revolution* (New York: Pantheon, 1965), 147.

12 See Castiglione, *The Courtier*, 542; Elyot, *The Governor*, passim.

13 Like Frank Whigham's examination of conventions of courtly behavior in *Ambition and Privilege: The Social Tropes of Elizabethan Courtesy Theory* (Berkeley: University of California Press, 1984), *The Two Gentlemen of Verona* reveals how courtly discourse excludes the powerless while unifying the elite. But while Whigham stresses how the articulation of codes of courtly behavior ironically provides access to power for the socially mobile, *The Two Gentlemen* examines the social consequences of an ethic of self-fulfillment among the elite.

14 I quote from *The Poetical Works of Edmund Spenser*, ed. J.C. Smith and E. De Selincourt (London: Oxford University Press, 1912). In quoting from old spelling texts I have silently modernized i/j, u/v, and long s.

15 *The Courtier* explains the courtly lover's duty to serve his mistress. English courtesy books place less emphasis on love, but they insist 'that all gentlemen worthy of the name must be clerks' (Hexter, 49). On the distrust of love in English courtesy books, see Kelso, 85.

16 See Kelso, 78; Elyot, 172. According to Daniel Javitch, *Poetry and Courtliness in Renaissance England* (Princeton: Princeton University Press, 1978), 'Courtly grace, to the extent that it can be prescribed, is shown to rely on tactics of dissimulation ... For instance, *sprezzatura*, one of the chief sources of such grace, always entails deliberate subterfuge' (36).

17 He equivocates, for example, to protect Priscilla's reputation (*FQ*, VI.iii.16,18). On this and other instances of innocent duplicity in *FQ*, VI, see William Nelson, *The Poetry of Edmund Spenser* (New York: Columbia University Press, 1963), 283.

18 'The root of the word is from the verb *sprezzare*, "to disdain" or "to hold in contempt," and this sense is vaguely present in Castiglione's concept, although without pejorative connotations' (Mazzeo, 145).

19 In Spenser's 'Legend of Courtesy,' Despotto, Decetto, and Defetto (disdain, deceit, and detraction) appear as villains both because they are negators of courtesy and because they are the dangers courtesy or civility is most susceptible to.

20 Again, Shakespeare is dramatizing problems of behavior strikingly

similar to those Spenser treats in the nearly contemporary Book VI of *The Faerie Queene*: Proteus' willingness to slander Valentine demonstrates the absoluteness of his betrayal of his friend and the completeness of his degradation; the quest of Sir Calidore, the knight of courtesy, is to subdue the Blatant Beast, a monster embodying slander and calumny.

21 'Myth and Ritual in Shakespeare: *A Midsummer Night's Dream*,' in *Textual Strategies: Perspectives in Post-Structuralist Criticism*, ed. Josué V. Harari (Ithaca: Cornell University Press, 1979), 191.

22 On the gradual disappearance of the aristocratic warrior, see Stone, *Crisis*, especially 199–270.

23 A.C. Hamilton argues that until this point Proteus is the only gentleman of Verona, Valentine being lowly born and becoming a gentleman by merit (120–1). The Duke's reasoning – Valentine has merit and is therefore well-derived – may well parody the Elizabethans' penchant for constructing genealogies appropriate to their sense of their own dignity. Hexter, for example, mentions William Cecil's attempt 'to provide his grandfather ... with a fancier set of ancestors' ('The Myth of the Middle Class in Tudor England' in *Reappraisals*, 102), and Stone comments on the virtuosity of those 'imaginative creative writers, the Tudor heralds' who could provide family trees beginning with the Trojans or Old Testament figures such as Noah (*Crisis*, 23–4). I think, however, that Valentine's lineage is not as significant a factor as, say, Helena's in *All's Well That Ends Well*. Although the play is vague about Valentine's antecedents, it does not make a point of any social disparity between Valentine and Proteus. In *The Two Gentlemen of Verona*, Shakespeare is not interested in how the governing class is recruited but in the qualities desirable in its members.

24 For the importance of these ideas in Renaissance culture, see Thomas Greene, 'The Flexibility of the Self in Renaissance Literature,' 241–64; A. Bartlett Giametti, 'Proteus Unbound: Some Versions of the Sea God in the Renaissance,' 437–75, in *The Disciplines of Criticism: Essays in Literary Theory, Interpretation, and History*, ed. Peter Demetz, Thomas Greene, and Lowry Nelson, Jr. (New Haven: Yale University Press, 1968); Stephen J. Greenblatt, *Sir Walter Raleigh: The Renaissance Man and His Roles* (New Haven: Yale University Press, 1973), especially 31–41, and *Renaissance Self-Fashioning* (Chicago: The University of Chicago Press, 1980). Greene and Giametti stress the socially benign effects of flexibility, while Greenblatt is more interested in its darker aspects.

Chapter Five

1 In the 'Introduction' to the Arden edition, Richard David summarizes the scholarship on the play's topicality. Also helpful is Nancy Lenz Harvey and Anna Kirwan Carey, *'Love's Labor's Lost': An Annotated Bibliography* (New York: Garland Publishing, 1984). A useful study of allusions to figures prominent in contemporary French politics is Hugh M. Richmond, 'Shakespeare's Navarre,' *Huntington Library Quarterly*, 42 (1979), 193–216. The most detailed study of the play's connections with English literary figures is Frances Yates, *A Study of 'Love's Labour's Lost'* (Cambridge: Cambridge University Press, 1936).
2 Yates, 9.
3 *Riverside*, 174.
4 *Love's Labour's Lost*, ed. Richard David, The Arden Shakespeare (London: Methuen, 1951), xliii.
5 In the folio text the King is designated as Ferdinand in the stage directions and the speech headings in the first few pages, but he is never referred to by name in the text.
6 *The Complete Works of Shakespeare*, 3rd ed., David Bevington ed., (Glenview, Ill.: Scott, Foresman, 1980), 123.
7 A.C. Hamilton makes this point in *The Early Shakespeare* (San Marino, Calif.: Huntington Library Press, 1967), 139.
8 Francis Bacon, 'Of Discourse,' in *Francis Bacon: A Selection of His Works*, ed. Sidney Warhaft (Toronto: Macmillan, 1965), 132.
9 The fact that several lines are assigned to Katharine in the quarto and to Rosaline in the folio points to the characters' similarity. The confusion in speech headings may result from printers' errors or from revision. For a convincing argument that the 'Rosaline-Katherine tangle' and several other textual problems result from authorial reshaping of Berowne's character, see Grace Ioppolo, *Revising Shakespeare* (Cambridge, Mass.: Harvard University Press, 1991), 94–102.
10 See above, p. 66.
11 John Donne, *Selected Prose*, chosen by Evelyn Simpson, ed. Helen Gardner and Timothy Healy (Oxford: Clarendon Press, 1967), 111.
12 Jane Donawerth, *Shakespeare and the Sixteenth-Century Study of Language* (Urbana: University of Illinois Press, 1984), 153.
13 See, for example, Ralph Berry, *Shakespeare's Comedies: Explorations in Form* (Princeton: Princeton University Press, 1972), Chapter 4, 'The Words of Mercury,' and William Carroll, *The Great Feast of Language in 'Love's Labour's Lost'* (Princeton: Princeton University Press, 1976).

14 Lawrence Stone, 'The Educational Revolution in England, 1560–1640,' *Past and Present*, 28 (1964), 68.
15 Keith Wrightson, *English Society, 1580–1680* (New Brunswick, NJ: Rutgers University Press, 1982), 191.
16 See also David Cressy, 'Educational Opportunity in Tudor and Stuart England,' *History of Education Quarterly*, 16 (1976), 301–20, and *Literacy and the Social Order: Reading and Writing in Tudor and Stuart England* (Cambridge: Cambridge University Press, 1980).
17 Joan Simon, *Education and Society in Tudor England* (Cambridge: Cambridge University Press, 1967), 297.
18 Malcolm Evans and Terence Hawkes discuss the socially divisive effect of learning as part of a thematic opposition between speech and writing rather than between the educated and the uneducated. Malcolm Evans, 'Mercury Versus Apollo: A Reading of *Love's Labor's Lost*,' *Shakespeare Quarterly*, 26 (1975), 113–27; Terence Hawkes, *Shakespeare's Talking Animals: Language and Drama in Society* (Totowa, NJ: Rowan & Littlefield, 1974).
19 Noel Annan,'*Et Tu*, Anthony,' *New York Review of Books*, 34 (22 October 1987), 6.
20 Edward Said, 'Opponents, Audiences, Constituencies, and Community' in *The Politics of Interpretation*, ed. W.J.T. Mitchell (Chicago: University of Chicago Press, 1983), 12.
21 See Edgar Wind, *Pagan Mysteries in the Renaissance* (New Haven: Yale University Press, 1958), 79.
22 Theodore Spencer, *Shakespeare and the Nature of Man*, 2nd ed. (New York: Macmillan, 1949), 87 and Marlene Shindler, 'The Vogue and Impact of Pierre de La Primaudaye's "The French Academie" on Elizabethan and Jacobean Literature,' Dissertation, University of Texas, 1960.
23 Pierre de La Primaudaye, *The French Academie*, trans. T[homas] B[owes] (London, 1586), 39.
24 *The Essayes or Morall, Politike and Millitarie Discourses of Lo: Michaell de Montaigne ... now done into English by ... John Florio* (London, 1603), 125.
25 Hugh Richmond suggests that Berowne's line refers to the fact that the ladies-in-waiting who accompanied Catherine and Marguerite to Henry's court in 1578 were generally not of noble birth. Famous for beauty and charm, they allegedly used their sexual charm to spy for Catherine. While it seems possible that Berowne's remark might allude to the social rank of the famous *l'escadron volant*, I disagree with Richmond's judgment that the Princess, Rosaline, Maria, and

Katherine demonstrate a 'ruthlessly destructive attitude' and a 'startlingly manipulative view of sexual psychology' based on rumors about Catherine de Medici's attendants as 'sexual Machiavels.' Richmond, 200–1, 209–12.

26 Cf. La Primaudaye, 'If it were lawfull for every one to alleadge necessitie or constraint, thereby to cloake the breach of faith, to whome might a man trust in any matter?' 415.

27 Several critics have noted connections between Mercade and Mercury as the messenger of the gods and the god of oratory, but they have not commented on Mercury as the divine messenger recalling people to their social responsibilities. See, for example, Malcolm Evans, 'Mercury Versus Apollo'; Louis Montrose, 'Curious-Knotted Garden': The Form, Themes, and Contexts of Shakespeare's 'Love's Labour's Lost' (Salzburg: Universität Salzburg, 1977), 172; J.M. Nosworthy, 'The Importance of Being Mercade,' Shakespeare Survey, 32 (1979), 105–14.

28 Richard David, xliii.

Chapter Six

1 See Mark A. Kishlansky, *Parliamentary Selection: Social and Political Choice in Early Modern England* (Cambridge: Cambridge University Press, 1986), 1–9.

2 Harold F. Brooks discusses this hypothesis in his introduction to the Arden edition of *A Midsummer Night's Dream* (London: Methuen, 1979), liii–lvii.

3 Paul A. Olson, '*A Midsummer Night's Dream* and the Meaning of Court Marriage,' ELH 24 (1957), 95–119.

4 Frye, 'The Argument of Comedy' in *English Institute Essays* (New York: Columbia University Press, 1949), 58–73 and *A Natural Perspective* (New York: Columbia University Press, 1965); C.L. Barber, *Shakespeare's Festive Comedies* (Princeton: Princeton University Press, 1959), 119–62; Jan Kott, *Shakespeare Our Contemporary*, trans. Boleslaw Taborski (London: Methuen, 1967), 171–90; Girard, 'Myth and Ritual in Shakespeare' in *Textual Strategies: Perspectives in Post-Structuralist Criticism*, ed. Josué V. Harari (Ithaca: Cornell University Press, 1979), 189–212; Louis Adrian Montrose, ' "Shaping Fantasies": Figurations of Gender and Power in Elizabethan Culture,' *Representations* 1:2 (1983), 61–94; Leonard Tennenhouse, *Power on Display: The Politics of Shakespeare's Genres* (New York: Methuen, 1986), 73–6.

5 John Donne, 'The Good-morrow' and 'Loves Infiniteness' in *The*

Elegies and The Songs and Sonnets, ed. Helen Gardner (Oxford: Clarendon Press, 1965).

6 The Riverside edition glosses 'Therefore' in line 103 as 'in consequence of the breach between us.' Certainly Titania's point is that the quarrel is the ultimate cause of all the disasters ('We are their parents and original' [II.i.117]), but she also traces particular causal relations in the sequence. The moon misses human hymns and carols and therefore 'Pale in her anger, washes all the air,' just as the winds, missing the fairy dances, 'as in revenge' produce storms.

7 Barber, 133.

8 In general, critics regard change more sanguinely than do the characters involved. The changeling's transfer from Titania to Oberon, for example, has been seen as an appropriate step in his movement from the female-dominated world of the child to the adult masculine world, and Helena's betrayal of Hermia's secret has been interpreted as a healthy sign of a girl's transformation into a heterosexual woman. We never learn how the boy feels about the change, but Hermia and Helena mourn the loss of friendship and trust rather than enjoy maturation. See Barber, 130, 137, and J.L. Calderwood, '*A Midsummer Night's Dream*: The Illusion of Drama,' *Modern Language Quarterly,* 26 (1965), 511.

9 Edmund Spenser, 'Mutabilitie Cantos,' VII, 58; VIII, 2.

10 Pierre de La Primaudaye, *The French Academie,* trans. T[homas] B[owes] (London, 1586), 743.

11 Simultaneous belief in the need for social hierarchy and in government by consent, or at least government with due respect for community values and customs, was common in early modern England. See J.P. Sommerville, *Politics and Ideology in England, 1603–1640* (London: Longman, 1986), Chapter 2, 'Government by consent'; David Underdown, *Revel, Riot, and Rebellion: Popular Politics and Culture in England, 1603–1660* (Oxford: Clarendon Press, 1985), Chapter 5, 'Popular Politics before the Civil War.'

12 La Primaudaye, *French Academie,* 744.

13 David Young's discussion of the exchange between Theseus and Hippolyta about the lovers' account of their night in the woods argues that the play undercuts the traditional dichotomy between reason and imagination. Young points out the humor of Theseus' dismissing the means by which he himself exists but does not mention the comedy inherent in Hippolyta's argument for the lovers' credibility. Concurring testimony was a criterion associated with the new empirical and probabilistic approach to knowledge, which was often hostile to the

fictitious and imaginary. See David Young, *Something of Great Constancy: The Art of 'A Midsummer Night's Dream'* (New Haven: Yale University Press, 1966), 126–41, and Barbara J. Shapiro, *Probability and Certainty in Seventeenth-Century England* (Princeton: Princeton University Press, 1983), passim.
14 Stephen Orgel, *The Illusion of Power: Political Theater in the English Renaissance* (Berkeley: University of California Press, 1975).

Chapter Seven

1 *The Essayes or Morall, Politike and Millitarie Discourses of Lo: Michaell de Montaigne ... now done into English by ... John Florio* (London, 1603), 17.
2 Ralph Berry, *Shakespeare's Comedies: Explorations in Form* (Princeton: Princeton University Press, 1972), 121.
3 Sir Arthur Quiller-Couch, 'Introduction,' *The Merchant of Venice*, Cambridge edition (Cambridge: Cambridge University Press, 1926), xx.
4 Sigurd Burckhardt, 'The Merchant of Venice: The Gentle Bond,' in his *Shakespearean Meanings* (Princeton: Princeton University Press, 1968), 224.
5 John Russell Brown, 'Introduction,' *The Merchant of Venice*, Arden edition (London: Methuen, 1955), xli.
6 Lawrence Danson, *The Harmonies of 'The Merchant of Venice'* (New Haven: Yale University Press, 1978), 175–81.
7 Berry, 122.
8 On the extension of credit as an aspect of the virtue of neighborliness, see Keith Wrightson, *English Society, 1580–1680* (New Brunswick, NJ: Rutgers University Press, 1982), 51–3.
9 In this discussion I have drawn on my fuller discussion of Jessica in 'In Defense of Jessica: The Problem of the Run-away Daughter in *The Merchant of Venice*,' *Shakespeare Quarterly*, 31 (1980), 357–68.
10 Walter Cohen suggests this contrast in 'The Merchant of Venice and the Possibilities of Historical Criticism,' *ELH*, 49 (1982), 772.
11 See Ruth Nevo, *Comic Transformations in Shakespeare* (London: Methuen, 1980), 126.
12 Jan Lawson Hinely cites this passage and observes that Antonio and Bassanio show few similarities. 'Bond Priorities in *The Merchant of Venice*,' *Studies in English Literature*, 20 (1980), 233.
13 Valuable scholarship has illuminated the usury issue. See especially Benjamin Nelson, *The Idea of Usury*, 2nd ed. (Chicago: University of Chicago Press, 1969). The most important points to emerge, I think,

are that lending money for profit was not regarded as morally neutral in sixteenth-century England. It was never defended as simply permissible without qualification, but it was by no means universally condemned.

Recent articles considering the question of usury in *The Merchant of Venice* are Cohen, 'The Merchant of Venice and the Possibilities of Historical Criticism'; Richard Arneson, 'Shakespeare and the Jewish Question,' *Political Theory*, 13 (1985), 85–111; and Lars Engle, ' "Thrift is Blessing": Exchange and Explanation in *The Merchant of Venice*,' *Shakespeare Quarterly*, 37 (1986), 20–37. I agree with Arneson that the trial in Act IV does not concern usury but whether the state can and should control the antagonisms created within a market society. But while he argues that the contrast between Antonio and Shylock is between profit-taking and exploitation, I believe that the conflict between Antonio and Shylock over their normal business practices represents the mutual incomprehension of two honestly and deeply held positions. Antonio's aversion to Shylock's usury reflects the traditional condemnation of any profit-taking, while Shylock's defense of the honesty of receiving compensation for the use of capital reflects the more recent adjustment of moral thinking to the need for credit in a mercantile economy.

14 See, for example, René Girard, ' "To Entrap the Wisest" – A Reading of *The Merchant of Venice*,' in *Literature and Society*, ed. Edward Said (Baltimore: The Johns Hopkins University Press, 1980), 100–19, and Jean E. Howard, 'The Difficulties of Closure: An Approach to the Problematic in Shakespearan Comedy' in *Comedy from Shakespeare to Sheridan: Change and Continuity in the English and European Dramatic Tradition*, ed. A.R. Braunmuller and J.C. Bulman (Newark: University of Delaware Press, 1986), 113–130, especially 123–5. Richard Arneson comments shrewdly on the critical blurring of distinctions in 'Shakespeare and the Jewish Question.'

15 The emphasis on justice and the independence of the courts echoes contemporary accounts of Venice. For example, Lewis Lewkenor's translation of Gaspero Contarini's *The Common-wealth and Government of Venice* (London, 1599) notes that for all the '*royall dignitie*' of the Venetian doge, '*neverthelesse both he and his authority* [are] *wholy subjected to the lawes*' (A2 r–v). Contarini also comments on the provision of special judges who with 'speedier dispatch' deal with cases that 'do any way concerne Merchantes' (107). Fynes Moryson, in praising Venetian justice, also mentions these special courts. *Shakespeare's Europe: Unpublished Chapters of Fynes Moryson's*

Itinerary ..., ed. Charles Hughes (London: Sherratt & Hughes, 1903), 165.

16 I describe the principles and procedures of casuistry in *The Casuistical Tradition in Shakespeare, Donne, Herbert, and Milton* (Princeton: Princeton University Press, 1981). Closely related to casuistry is the concept of equity institutionalized in the Court of Chancery, the court of conscience. The relevance of the law of equity to *The Merchant of Venice* has been investigated by Mark Edwin Andrews, *Law versus Equity in 'The Merchant of Venice'* (Boulder: University of Colorado Press, 1965); George W. Keeton, *Shakespeare's Legal and Political Background* (London: Sir Isaac Pitman & Sons, 1967), 132–50; E.F.J. Tucker, 'The Letter of the Law in *The Merchant of Venice*,' *Shakespeare Survey*, 29 (1976), 93–101; W. Gordon Zeeveld, *The Temper of Shakespeare's Thought* (New Haven: Yale University Press, 1974), Chapter 3.

17 H.D. Kittsteiner, 'Kant and Casuistry,' in *Conscience and Casuistry in Early Modern Europe*, ed. Edmund Leites (Cambridge: Cambridge University Press, 1988), pp. 185–213. For the quotations following, Kittsteiner cites Jean-Jacques Rousseau, *Émile*, trans. Barbara Foxley, with an introduction by André Boutet de Monvel (London: Dent, 1957), 254; Adam Smith, *The Theory of Moral Sentiments*, ed. D.D. Raphael and A.L. Macfie, The Glasgow Edition of *The Works and Correspondence of Adam Smith*, 2nd ed. vol. 1 (Oxford: Clarendon Press, 1979), 339. Also see Roberto Unger on the modern antinomy of fact and value and of reason and desire in *Knowledge and Politics* (New York: Free Press, 1975).

18 I take 'attended' to mean 'given careful attention' as well as 'accompanied.' Portia balances her perception that we cannot see a small beauty when it must compete with a greater ('So doth the greater glory dim the less' [v.i.93]) with her realization that we may undervalue the greater when we are distracted. She relates accurate evaluation to attendant circumstances and to discriminating attention.

19 Hannah Arendt as quoted by W.H. Auden, *The Dyer's Hand* (New York: Random House, 1948), 218.

20 Although nothing in English common law required fathers to leave their property to their children, there was wide moral consensus that a father's duty is to leave his fortune to his children. See Alan Macfarlane, *The Origins of English Individualism: The Family, Property, and Social Transition* (New York: Cambridge University Press,

1978), pp. 83, 205; Ralph A. Houlbrooke, *The English Family, 1450–1700* (London: Longman, 1984), 228–52.
21 'A Narrative of the Late Proceedings at Whitehall, concerning the Jews' (London, 1656), in *The Harleian Miscellany*, ed. J. Malham, 12 vols. (London, 1808–1811), 6:445–54.
22 Michael Shapiro, 'Shylock the Jew Onstage: Past and Present,' *Shofar*, 4 (Winter, 1986), 1–11.
23 Richard Marienstras, *New Perspectives on the Shakespearean World*, trans. Janet Lloyd (Cambridge: Cambridge University Press, 1985), 122. Originally published as *Le Proche et le lointain* (Paris: Les Editions de Minuit, 1981).
24 Marienstras, 114.
25 William Salkeld, *Report of Cases Adjuged in the Court of King's Bench*, 6th ed. (London, 1795), vol. 1, p.46, as quoted in Marienstras, 125.
26 An analogy between Shylock's position in his society and that of nonconforming religious minorities in Elizabethan England seems to me a more fruitful historicizing possibility than identifying Shylock with Puritans or with Roman Catholics on the basis of similarities in ideas and attitudes. For discussion of the latter approach see Danson, 78–80.

Chapter Eight

1 Sherman Hawkins, 'The Two Worlds of Shakespearean Comedy,' *Shakespeare Studies*, 3 (1967), 62–80.
2 See, for example, Anne Barton's introduction to *The Merry Wives* in *The Riverside Shakespeare*, ed. G. Blakemore Evans (Boston: Houghton Mifflin, 1974); her 'Falstaff and the Comic Community' in *Shakespeare's 'Rough Magic': Renaissance Essays in Honor of C.L. Barber*, ed. Peter Erickson and Coppélia Kahn (Newark: University of Delaware Press, 1985), 131–48; and H.J. Oliver's introduction to the Arden edition (London: Methuen, 1971).
3 Ronald Huebert, 'Levels of Parody in *The Merry Wives of Windsor*,' *English Studies in Canada*, 3 (1977), 136–52. For useful discussions of the evidence for dating the play 1597, see Oliver's Arden introduction, lii–lvi, and Jeanne Addison Roberts, *Shakespeare's English Comedy: 'The Merry Wives of Windsor' in Context* (Lincoln: University of Nebraska Press, 1979), 41–50.
4 Thomas Sternhold and John Hopkins, *The Whole Book of Davids Psalmes* (London: John Daye, 1582), 343–44.

5 Huebert argues that since Psalm 137 concludes by calling for God's vengeance on the enemies of Israel, Evans implicitly is invoking divine wrath on Doctor Caius, and 'the threatening rumble of the Babylon Psalm is the bugle-call of the knight-at-arms.' Because Evans as knight is more notable for discretion than valor, the effect is mock heroic (Huebert, 141). I think that the original audience, like the modern, would have associated Psalm 137 with waters, willows, harps, and tears more readily than with bugles, that is, with elegiac pastoral rather than with heroic poetry or epic.

6 Calvin commented on Psalm 137: 'The writer of this Psalm ... drew up a form of lamentation, that by giving expression to their [the Jews'] sufferings in sighs and prayers, they might keep alive the hope of that deliverance which they despaired of. Another end he has in view, is to warn them against the decline of godliness in an irreligious land, and against defilement with the contamination of the heathen.' John Calvin, *Commentary on the Book of Psalms*, trans. James Anderson (Edinburgh: Calvin Translation Society, 1849), 5.189.

7 Cf. David Underdown: 'Villagers knew well enough that they differed in wealth and status, but in theory at least these inequalities were transcended by the reciprocal ties that bound them: the enduring ties of kinship, neighbourhood, the common experience of the stable certainties of the church calendar and the agricultural year. Like all such ideals, the harmony may have been more honoured in the breach than in the observance, but if it was a myth, it was a powerful one.' *Revel, Riot, and Rebellion: Popular Politics and Culture in England, 1603–1660* (Oxford: Clarendon Press, 1985), 11. Part of the cultural work performed by *The Merry Wives* is the nurturing of this myth.

8 Barbara Freedman, 'Falstaff's Punishment: Buffoonery as Defensive Posture in *The Merry Wives of Windsor*,' *Shakespeare Studies*, 14 (1981), 167.

9 Peter Erickson, 'The Order of the Garter, the Cult of Elizabeth, and Class-Gender Tension in *The Merry Wives of Windsor*' in *Shakespeare Reproduced: The Text in History and Ideology*, ed. Jean E. Howard and Marion F. O'Connor (New York: Methuen, 1987), 116–40.

10 See, for example, Georg Simmel, *Conflict*, trans. Kurt H. Wolff (Glencoe, Ill.: Free Press, 1955), Lewis A. Coser, *The Functions of Social Conflict* (Glencoe, Ill.: Free Press, 1956), and David D. Gilmore *Aggression and Community: Paradoxes of Andalusian Culture* (New Haven: Yale University Press, 1987).

11 Penry Williams, *The Tudor Regime* (Oxford: Clarendon Press, 1979), 10.

Notes to pages 157-72 263

12 Penry Williams, 'Emergence of the State,' *Times Literary Supplement*, 2 June 1990, 616.
13 Keith Wrightson, *English Society, 1580-1680* (New Brunswick, NJ: Rutgers University Press, 1982), 13 and throughout.
14 Linda Anderson, *A Kind of Wild Justice: Revenge in Shakespeare's Comedies* (Newark: University of Delaware Press, 1987).
15 Anderson, 19. Fredson Bowers, *Elizabethan Revenge Tragedy, 1587-1642* (Princeton: Princeton University Press, 1940), 5, and Francis Bacon, 'Of Revenge' in *The Essays of Lord Bacon* (London: Frederick Warne, 1889), 7-8, as quoted in Anderson, 14, 16.
16 According to Underdown, breaches of social norms in villages in early modern England normally were controlled by unofficial social pressure and reported to authorities only as a last resort; see *Revel, Riot, and Rebellion*, 15.
17 For the argument that hostility to courtly values is even more explicit in the 1602 Quarto text, which omits specific references to a Windsor setting, see Leah Marcus, 'Levelling Shakespeare: Local Customs and Local Texts,' *Shakespeare Quarterly*, 42 (1991), 168-78.
18 See Eve Kosofsky Sedgwick, *Between Men: English Literature and Male Homosocial Desire*, (New York: Columbia University Press, 1985), 48.
19 David Underdown, 'The Taming of the Scold: the Enforcement of Patriarchal Authority in Early Modern England' in *Order and Disorder in Early Modern England*, ed. Anthony Fletcher and John Stevenson (Cambridge: Cambridge University Press, 1985), 116-36, and *Revel, Riot, and Rebellion*, 99-102.
20 Walter R. Davis and R.A. Lanham, *Sidney's 'Arcadia'* (New Haven: Yale University Press, 1965), 35.
21 Davis, 38-9.
22 Davis, 175.
23 Erickson, 134.
24 William Empson, *Some Versions of Pastoral* (London, 1935); Louis Adrian Montrose, 'Of Gentlemen and Shepherds: The Politics of Elizabethan Pastoral Form,' *English Literary Renaissance*, 50 (1983), 415-59.

Chapter Nine

1 *Timber, or Discoveries* in *Ben Jonson*, ed. C.H. Herford, Percy Simpson, and Evelyn Simpson, 11 vols. (Oxford: Clarendon Press, 1925-52), 8:620-1.

2 Brian Vickers points out that Leonato creates his effect by using an image, a polyptoton, and an antimetabole; *The Artistry of Shakespeare's Prose* (London: Methuen, 1968), 174.
3 'Language used to comment directly on language itself is generally know[n] as *metalanguage* ... And by analogy, a use of language which in turn frames, or "goes beyond", language *in use* can be termed *metadiscourse*.' Kier Elam, *Shakespeare's Universe of Discourse: Language-Games in the Comedies* (Cambridge: Cambridge University Press, 1984), 19.
4 Louis LeRoy, *Aristotles Politiques or Discourses of Government* (London, 1598), 12.
5 See Arnold Williams, *The Common Expositor: An Account of the Commentaries on Genesis 1527–1633* (Chapel Hill: University of North Carolina Press, 1948), 81. Williams quotes Francis Bacon's prediction that when man 'shall be able to call the creatures by their true names he shall again command them.' *Of the Interpretation of Nature* in *The Works of Francis Bacon*, ed. James Spedding, Robert Ellis, Douglas Heath (London, 1857), 3:222. Alastair Fowler's notes to the naming of the creatures in *Paradise Lost*, VIII, 343–56, cite Andrew Willet's opinion that one of the purposes for the naming of the creatures in Genesis 2 is 'that mans authoritie and dominion over the creatures might appeare: *for howsoever man named every living creature, so was the name thereof*.' Andrew Willet, *Hexapla ... Sixfold Commentary upon Genesis* (London, 1608), 36. *The Poems of John Milton*, ed. John Carey and Alastair Fowler (London: Longmans, 1968).
6 See Jane Donawerth, *Shakespeare and the Sixteenth-Century Study of Language* (Urbana: University of Illinois Press, 1984), 32.
7 Ralph Lever, *Arte of Reason* (London, 1573), vi, as cited in Donawerth, 32.
8 A sizable body of recent scholarship describes sixteenth-century ideas about women. On the association of deceit and sexuality, see, for example, Lisa Jardine, *Still Harping on Daughters: Women and Drama in the Age of Shakespeare* (Sussex: Harvester Press, 1983), Chapter 4, and Linda Woodbridge, *Women and the English Renaissance: Literature and the Nature of Womankind, 1540–1620* (Urbana: University of Illinois Press, 1984).
9 'Messina. A city in N.E. Sicily ... Pedro of Arragon took it from the French, and it remained a possession of the Spanish royal house from 1282 to 1713.' Edward H. Sudgen, *A Topographical Dictionary to the Works of Shakespeare and His Fellow Dramatists* (Manchester: Manchester University Press, 1925), 343. A sixteenth-century account is

included in *The Historie of Philip de Commines* ..., trans. Thomas Danett (London, 1596), 24–5.
10 *La Prima Parte De Le Novella Del Bandello* (Lucca, 1554), trans. Geoffrey Bullough, *Narrative and Dramatic Sources of Shakespeare*, 8 vols. (London: Routledge & Kegan Paul, 1958), 2:112.
11 The French translation of Bandello's story in Francois de Belleforest's *Le Troisiesme Tome des Histories Tragiques Extraictes des oeuvres Italiennes de Bandel', Histoire XVIII* (1569) emphasizes this tension, describing the prince as 'ce roy inhumaine Pierre d'Aragon.' See A.R. Humphreys' 'Introduction' to the Arden *Much Ado*, 14.
12 The infamous Sicilian Vespers seems to be the most common association with Sicily for sixteenth-century Englishmen. Although Englishmen visited Venice, Milan, Padua, Florence, Rome, and Naples as centers of culture, few ventured to Sicily. See E.S. Bates, *Touring in 1600: A Study in the Development of Travel as a Means of Education* (New York: Burt Franklin, 1911), 113; John Walter Stoye, *English Travellers Abroad, 1604–1667: Their Influence in English Society and Politics* (London: Jonathan Cape, 1952), 124.

Although such notable Elizabethan tourists as Thomas Coryat and Fynes Moryson did not go to Sicily, George Sandys stopped there on his return from the Levant in 1611. His account emphasizes the violent history of foreign control and contemporary colonial status: ' ... at length *Clement* the fourth did give it from *Conradine*, unto *Charles* of *Aniou* the *French* Kings brother; betraying him [Conrad] to the slaughter, who was overcome neare *Naples* in a mortall battell, and his head stricken off by *Clements* appointment. So fell the *Germans*, and so rise the *French* men to the Kingdome of *Naples* and both the *Sicilias*. But here some seventeene yeares after they were bid to a bitter banquet: al slaine at the tole of a bell throughout the whole Iland, which is called to this day the *Sicilian* Even-song. A just reward (if justice will countenance so bloudy a designe) for their intollerable insolencies ... *Don Pedro* King of Aragon, had married *Constantia* the onely daughter of *Manfroy*. In whose right (although *Manfroy* was a bastard, a parricide, and usuper) he entred *Sicilia* in this tumult whereunto he was privy, and was crowned King with the general consent of the *Sicilians*: it continuing in the house of *Aragon*, untill united to *Castile*. So it remaineth subject unto *Spaine* ... They [the Sicilians] have their commodities fetch from them by forrainers, and withall the profit ... The chiefe of the ancient *Sicilain* Nobility attend in the Court of *Spaine*: a course of life, rather politickly commanded, then elected' (237–8).

In Messina, Sandys was most struck by the Spanish influence and by the violence of the society: 'The better sort are *Spanish* in attire ... The Gentlemen put their monies into the common table, "for which the Citie stands bound" and receive it againe upon their bils, according to their uses. For they dare not venture to keepe it in their houses, so ordinarily broken open by theeves (as are the shops and ware-houses) for all their crosse-bard windowes, iron doores, locks, bolts, and barres on the inside: wherein, and in their private revenges, no night doth passe without murder ... The Duke of Osuna their new Vice-roy, was here daily expected; for whom a sumptuous landing place was made ...' (245–6). George Sandys, *A Relation of a Journey begun An: Dom: 1610* (London, 1615).

13 In all other versions of the story, a rival lover is responsible for the slander. See Charles T. Prouty, *The Sources of 'Much Ado About Nothing'* (New Haven: Yale University Press, 1950), 34.

14 Of course, anxiety about foreign domination, specifically fear of Spanish power, was intense in England. The possible application of Sicilian history to English politics is illustrated by John Hoskyns' speech in Parliament in 1614 which compared England dominated by James I's Scottish favorites to Sicily under the French at the time of the Sicilian Vespers. Hoskyns was committed to the Tower the following day. Louise Brown Osborn, *The Life, Letters, and Writings of John Hoskyns, 1566–1638* (New Haven: Yale University Press, 1937), 38. I am indebted for this reference to Annabel Patterson, 'All Donne,' in *Soliciting Interpretation: Literary Theory and Seventeenth-Century English Poetry*, ed. Elizabeth Harvey and Katharine Maus (Chicago: University of Chicago Press, 1990), 57.

15 Mikhail Bakhtin, *The Dialogic Imagination*, ed. Michael Holquist, trans. Caryl Emerson and Michael Holquist (Austin: University of Texas Press, 1981), 263.

16 Carl Dennis points out that the deception successfully appeals to Benedick and Beatrice's social natures: 'They want to fulfill the values of their community' (228). See 'Wit and Wisdom in *Much Ado About Nothing*,' *Studies in English Literature*, 13 (1973), 223–37.

17 Joyce Hengerer Sexton observes that the emphasis on publicizing the truth about Hero in the denouement represents a significant divergence from the sources and analogues; see 'The Theme of Slander in *Much Ado About Nothing*,' *Philological Quarterly*, 54 (1975), 423, 428.

18 Anthony Dawson points out that Dogberry's desire to be 'writ down

an ass' (IV.ii.87) alludes to writing as a mark of cultural validity. 'Much Ado About Signifying,' *Studies in English Literature*, 22 (1982), 218-19. On sixteenth-century respect for the stability of the written word in contrast with ephemeral speech, see Terence Hawkes, *Shakespeare's Talking Animals: Language and Drama in Society* (Totowa, NJ: Rowman & Littlefield, 1974), 38.

Chapter Ten

1 See Louis Montrose, ' "The Place of a Brother" in *As You Like It*: Social Process and Comic Form,' *Shakespeare Quarterly*, 32 (1981), 28-54.
2 According to Ralph Houlbrooke, 'For a growing proportion of the population ... individual resilience, strength and skill were assets more significant than inherited possessions.' *The English Family, 1450-1700* (New York: Longman, 1984), 228. My discussion of inheritance practices in this and the following paragraphs is indebted to Houlbrooke, 228-52. See also Susan Amussen, *An Ordered Society: Gender and Class in Early Modern England* (Oxford: Basil Blackwell, 1988), 86-91; Keith Wrightson, *English Society, 1580-1680* (New Brunswick, NJ: Rutgers University Press, 1984), 111-12.
3 Houlbrooke, 233.
4 Houlbrooke, 230.
5 'The Place of a Brother,' especially 31.
6 Among the influential essays emphasizing growth and self-discovery are Harold Jenkins, 'As You Like It,' *Shakespeare Survey*, 8 (1955), 40-51; Helen Gardner, 'As You Like It' in *More Talking of Shakespeare*, ed. John Garrett (New York: Theatre Arts Books, 1959), reprinted in *Modern Shakespearean Criticism*, ed. Alvin B. Kernan (New York: Harcourt, Brace & World, 1970), 190-203; and Albert R. Cirillo, '*As You Like It*: Pastoralism Gone Awry,' *ELH*, 38 (1971), 19-39.
7 Many critics have discussed *As You Like It* as pastoral. The best of them, such as David Young, recognize that 'there was something fundamentally equivocal in pastoral which ... tended to undermine and invert its familiar antitheses.' David Young, *The Heart's Forest* (New Haven: Yale University Press, 1972), 34.
8 'Venatical attitudes,' Renato Poggioli observes, 'consistently oppose the pastoral: on the one side they resemble too closely martial exploits; on the other, they are connected with Diana, the goddess of

chastity, whom shepherds ... neglect in favor of Venus.' *The Oaten Flute: Essays on Pastoral Poetry and the Pastoral Ideal* (Cambridge, Mass.: Harvard University Press, 1975), 7.
9 *New Perspectives on the Shakespearean World*, trans. Janet Lloyd (Cambridge: Cambridge University Press, 1985), 11–39.
10 *A Treatise and Discourse of the Lawes of the Forrest* (1592) as quoted in Marienstras, 30.
11 Orlando's rhetorical question resembles that of George Herbert's vocationless gallant who asks 'whether he shall mend shoes, or what he shall do.' Orlando's predicament illustrates Herbert's judgment that the failure to prepare younger brothers for some profession is 'a shamefull wrong both to the Common-wealth, and their own House.' *A Priest to the Temple or, The Country Parson* in *The Works of George Herbert*, ed. F.E. Hutchinson (Oxford: Clarendon Press, 1941), 275, 277.
12 In an important essay, Madeleine Doran traces Orlando's claim of being 'inland bred' (II.vii.96) to the opposition between the civil and the rude or uncivil in Shakespeare's plays and in Elizabethan thought. ' "Yet am I inland bred," ' *Shakespeare Quarterly*, 15 (1964), 99–114.
13 The figure of Phebe makes *As You Like It* more disturbing from a feminist perspective than *The Taming of the Shrew* because, while Kate and Bianca are empowered in the course of the dramatic action, Phebe is denied the right to reject a suitor appropriate in terms of class.
14 Pierre de La Primaudaye, *The French Academie*, trans. T[homas] B[owes] (London, 1586), 743. See above, p. 121–2.
15 *Patriarchal Structures in Shakespeare's Drama* (Berkeley: University of California Press, 1985), 33.
16 Judy Z. Kronenfeld argues that, rather than mystifying social relations in the interests of a dominant social class, *As You Like It* uses pastoralism to reaffirm the virtues of charity, humility, and nobility that should control relations between social ranks. 'Social Rank and the Pastoral Ideals of *As You Like It*,' *Shakespeare Quarterly*, 29 (1978), 333–48. According to Louis Montrose in ' "The Place of a Brother",' *As You Like It* reconciles social inequality with spiritual brotherhood through 'acts of theatrical prestidigitation' (31). Peter Erickson concludes in *Patriarchal Structures* that the play achieves and endorses patriarchal power by containing and subordinating female power. In 'Conservative Fools in James's Court and Shakespeare's Plays,' *Shakespeare Studies*, 19 (1987), 219–37, Theodore B. Leinwand argues that *As You Like It* 'resists Elizabethan

pastoral's typical social mystification' (227) in order to insist on hierarchical distinctions.
17 Lawrence Danson, 'Jonsonian Comedy and the Discovery of the Social Self,' *PMLA*, 99 (1984), 185.
18 Natalie Zemon Davis, 'Boundaries and the Sense of Self in Sixteenth-Century France' in *Reconstructing Individualism: Autonomy, Individuality, and the Self in Western Thought*, ed. Thomas C. Heller, Morton Sosna, and David E. Wellbery (Stanford: Stanford University Press, 1986), 63.
19 Davis, 61.
20 *Areopagitica* in *John Milton: Complete Poems and Major Prose*, ed. Merritt Y. Hughes (New York: Odyssey Press, 1957), 744.

Chapter Eleven

1 *The Elementary Structures of Kinship*, trans. James Harle Bell, John Richard von Sturmer, and Rodney Needham, rev. ed. (Boston: Beacon Press, 1969), 496–7. Originally published as *Les Structures élémentaires de la Parenté* (Paris, 1949).
2 'Mistakes in *Twelfth Night* and Their Resolution,' *PMLA*, 76 (1961), 194.
3 Williams, 194.
4 Marcel Mauss, *The Gift: Forms and Functions of Exchange in Archaic Societies*, trans. Ian Cunnison, intro. E.E. Evans-Pritchard (Glencoe, Ill.: Free Press, 1954). Originally published as *Essai sur le don, forms archaique de l'échange* (Paris, 1925). Claude Lévi-Strauss, *Elementary Structures*, especially Chapter. 5, 'The Principle of Reciprocity.'
5 Lévi-Strauss, 84. The social function of exchanging gifts had not, of course, escaped earlier observation. Seneca's *De Beneficiis* seeks to explain the rules of giving, receiving, and repaying, 'a practice that constitutes the chief bond of human society.' *Moral Essays*, trans. John W. Basore, Loeb Classical Library (London: William Heinemann, 1935), 3:19.
6 Bradley, 'Feste the Jester' in *A Miscellany* (London: Macmillan, 1929), 212.
7 Cf. Seneca, *De Beneficiis*: 'A gift is not a benefit if the best part of it is lacking – the fact that it was given as a mark of esteem' (49).
8 III.iv.354–7. Cf. Seneca: 'Homicides, tyrants, thieves, adulterers, robbers, sacrilegious men, and traitors there always will be; but worse than all these is the crime of ingratitude ... ' (33).

9 Mauss, *The Gift*, intro., v.
10 See above, p. 177.
11 Andrew Marvell, 'The Definition of Love' in *Poems and Letters*, 2nd ed., ed. H.M. Margoliouth (Oxford: Oxford University Press, 1952).
12 Ralph Lever, *Arte of Reason* (London, 1573), vi ; Ben Jonson, *Timber* in *Ben Jonson*, ed. C.H. Herford, Percy Simpson, and Evelyn Simpson (Oxford: Clarendon Press, 1925–52), 8:622. Jane Donawerth quotes these passages in *Shakespeare and the Sixteenth-Century Study of Language* (Urbana: University of Illinois Press, 1984), 32.
13 Cf. Pierre Bourdieu: 'if it is not to constitute an insult, the counter-gift must be *deferred* and *different*, because the immediate return of an exactly identical object clearly amounts to a refusal ... ' *Outline of a Theory of Practice*, trans. Richard Nice (Cambridge: Cambridge University Press, 1977), 5.
14 William Slights analyzes the transformation of Cesario into two marital unions in the context of Renaissance mythography, tracing Cesario's dual sexuality to myths of the monstrous androgyne and the united lovers to myths of ideal androgynous union. ' "Maid and Man" in Twelfth Night,' *Journal of English and Germanic Philology*, 80 (1981), 327–48. Marianne Novy presents the meeting of Sebastian and Viola as emblematic of mutual love between man and woman. Marianne L. Novy, *Love's Argument: Gender Relations in Shakespeare* (Chapel Hill: University of North Carolina Press, 1984), 37. Without denying that the loving reunion is crucial to the mutual happiness of the ending, I want to argue that its primary function is to divide Cesario, the brother-sister amalgam, into two people, a division which allows new love relationships to succeed long-established biological ones.
15 On the implications for gender construction of Lévi-Strauss' work on kinship systems, see Gayle Rubin, 'The Traffic in Women: Notes on the "Political Economy" of Sex' in *Toward an Anthropology of Women*, ed. Rayna R. Reiter (New York: Monthly Review Press, 1975), 157–210.
16 Rubin, 174.

Chapter Twelve

1 Dale Spender identifies the tradition of describing recalcitrant women not as disobedient but as neurotic failures. *Man Made Language*, 2nd ed. (London: Routledge & Kegan Paul, 1985), 2.

2 Arthur Schopenhauer, *Studies in Pessimism: A Series of Essays*, trans. T. Bailey Saunders, 2nd ed. (London: Swan Sonnenchein, 1891), 142. I owe this reference to Roberto Unger, who cites it in a similar context. *Knowledge and Politics* (New York: Free Press, 1975), 156.
3 See above, p. 145.

Bibliography

Amussen, Susan. 'Gender, Family and the Social Order, 1560–1725.' *Order and Disorder in Early Modern England*. Ed. Anthony Fletcher and John Stevenson. Cambridge: Cambridge University Press, 1985. 196–217.
– *An Ordered Society: Gender and Class in Early Modern England*. Oxford: Basil Blackwell, 1988.
Anderson, Linda. *A Kind of Wild Justice: Revenge in Shakespeare's Comedies*. Newark: University of Delaware Press, 1987.
Andrews, Mark Edwin. *Law versus Equity in 'The Merchant of Venice'*. Boulder: University of Colorado Press, 1965.
Annan, Noel. 'Et Tu, Anthony.' *New York Review of Books*, 34 (22 October, 1987): 3–8.
Anon. 'A Narrative of the Late Proceedings at Whitehall, concerning the Jews.' London, 1656. Rpt. *The Harleian Miscellany*. Ed. J. Malham. Vol. 6. London, 1808–11. 12 vols.
Arneson, Richard. 'Shakespeare and the Jewish Question.' *Political Theory*, 13 (1985): 85–111.
Auden, W.H. *The Dyer's Hand*. New York: Random House, 1948.
Bacon, Francis. 'Of Discourse.' *Francis Bacon: A Selection of His Works*. Ed. Sidney Warhaft. Toronto: Macmillan, 1965. 132–6.
Bakhtin, Mikhail. *The Dialogic Imagination*. Ed. Michael Holquist. Trans. Caryl Emerson and Michael Holquist. Austin: University of Texas Press, 1981.
Barber, C.L. *Shakespeare's Festive Comedies: A Study of Dramatic Form and Its Relation to Social Custom*. Princeton: Princeton University Press, 1959.
Barton, Anne. 'Falstaff and the Comic Community.' *Shakespeare's*

'Rough Magic': Renaissance Essays in Honor of C.L. Barber. Ed. Peter Erickson and Coppélia Kahn. Newark: University of Delaware Press, 1985. 131–48.

Bates, E.S. *Touring in 1600: A Study in the Development of Travel as a Means of Education*. New York: Burt Franklin, 1911.

Bean, John. 'Comic Structure and the Humanizing of Kate in *The Taming of the Shrew*.' *The Woman's Part: Feminist Criticism of Shakespeare*. Ed. Carolyn Ruth Swift Lenz, Gayle Green, and Carol Thomas Neely. Urbana: University of Illinois Press, 1980. 65–71.

Berry, Edward. *Shakespeare's Comic Rites*. Cambridge: Cambridge University Press, 1984.

Berry, Ralph. *Shakespeare's Comedies: Explorations in Form*. Princeton: Princeton University Press, 1972.

Boose, Lynda E. 'Scolding Brides and Bridling Scolds: Taming the Woman's Unruly Member.' *Shakespeare Quarterly*, 42 (1991): 179–213.

Bourdieu, Pierre. *Outline of a Theory of Practice*. Trans. Richard Nice. Cambridge: Cambridge University Press, 1977.

Bowers, Fredson. *Elizabethan Revenge Tragedy, 1587–1642*. Princeton: Princeton University Press, 1940.

Bradbrook, M.C. *Shakespeare and Elizabethan Poetry*. London: Chatto & Windus, 1951.

Bradley, Andrew C. *A Miscellany*. London: Macmillan, 1929.

Bristol, Michael. *Carnival and Theater: Plebeian Culture and the Structure of Authority in Renaissance England*. New York: Methuen, 1985.

Bullough, Geoffrey, ed. *Narrative and Dramatic Sources of Shakespeare*. London: Routledge & Kegan Paul, 1957–75. 8 vols.

Burckhardt, Sigurd. '*The Merchant of Venice*: The Gentle Bond.' *Shakespearean Meanings*. Princeton: Princeton University Press, 1968.

Calderwood, James L. '*A Midsummer Night's Dream*: The Illusion of Drama.' *Modern Language Quarterly*, 26 (1965): 506–22.

Calvin, John. *Commentary on the Book of Psalms*. Trans. James Anderson. Edinburgh: Calvin Translation Society, 1849.

Carroll, William. *The Great Feast of Language in 'Love's Labour's Lost'*. Princeton: Princeton University Press, 1976.

Castiglione, Baldassare. *The Courtier*. Trans. Sir Thomas Hoby. *Three Renaissance Classics*. Ed. Burton A. Milligan. New York: Charles Scribner's Sons, 1953. 241–624.

Champion, Larry. *The Evolution of Shakespeare's Comedy: A Study in Dramatic Perspective*. Cambridge, Mass.: Harvard University Press, 1970.

Charlton, H.B. *Shakespearean Comedy*. 1938. London: Methuen, 1966.
Cirillo, Albert. '*As You Like It*: Pastoralism Gone Awry.' *ELH*, 38 (1971): 19–39.
Cohen, Walter. 'The *Merchant of Venice* and the Possibilities of Historical Criticism.' *ELH*, 49 (1982): 765–89.
Commines, Philip de. *The Historie of Philip de Commines* ... Trans. Thomas Danett. London, 1596.
Contarini, Cardinal Gasper. *The Commonwealth and Government of Venice*. Trans. Lewis Lewkenor. London, 1599.
Cook, Ann Jennalie. *Making a Match: Courtship in Shakespeare and His Society*. Princeton: Princeton University Press, 1991.
Coser, Lewis A. *The Functions of Social Conflict*. Glencoe, Ill.: Free Press, 1956.
Cressy, David. 'Educational Opportunity in Tudor and Stuart England.' *History of Education Quarterly*, 16 (1976): 301–20.
– *Literacy and the Social Order: Reading and Writing in Tudor and Stuart England*. Cambridge: Cambridge University Press, 1980.
Danby, John F. *Poets on Fortune's Hill*. London: Faber and Faber, 1952.
Danson, Lawrence. *The Harmonies of 'The Merchant of Venice'*. New Haven: Yale University Press, 1978.
– 'Jonsonian Comedy and the Discovery of the Social Self.' *PMLA*, 99 (1984): 179–93.
Davis, Natalie Zemon. 'Boundaries and the Sense of Self in Sixteenth-Century France.' *Reconstructing Individualism: Autonomy, Individuality, and the Self in Western Thought*. Ed. Thomas C. Heller, Morton Sosna, and David E. Wellbery. Stanford: Stanford University Press, 1986. 53–63.
Davis, Walter R., and R.A. Lanham. *Sidney's 'Arcadia'*. New Haven: Yale University Press, 1965.
Dawson, Anthony. 'Much Ado About Signifying.' *Studies in English Literature*, 22 (1982): 211–21.
Dennis, Carl. 'Wit and Wisdom in *Much Ado About Nothing*.' *Studies in English Literature*, 13 (1973): 223–37.
Dollimore, Jonathan, and Alan Sinfield, eds. *Political Shakespeare*. Ithaca: Cornell University Press, 1985.
Donawerth, Jane. *Shakespeare and the Sixteenth-Century Study of Language*. Urbana: University of Illinois Press, 1984.
Donne, John. *The Elegies and The Songs and Sonnets*. Ed. Helen Gardner. Oxford: Clarendon Press, 1965.
– *Selected Prose*. Chosen by Evelyn Simpson. Ed. Helen Gardner and Timothy Healy. Oxford: Clarendon Press, 1967.

- *The Sermons of John Donne.* Ed. George R. Potter and Evelyn M. Simpson. Berkeley: University of California Press, 1953–62. 10 vols.
Doran, Madeleine. ' "Yet am I inland bred." ' *Shakespeare Quarterly*, 15 (1964): 99–114.
Dusinberre, Juliet. *Shakespeare and the Nature of Women.* London: Macmillan, 1975.
Eco, Umberto. *The Name of the Rose.* Trans. William Weaver. San Diego: Harcourt, Brace, Jovanovich, 1983.
Elam, Kier. *Shakespeare's Universe of Discourse: Language-Games in the Comedies.* Cambridge: Cambridge University Press, 1984.
Elias, Norbert. *The Civilizing Process.* Trans. Edmund Jephcott. Oxford: Basil Blackwell, 1978 and 1982. 2 vols.
Elyot, Thomas. *The Book Named the Governor.* Ed. S.E. Lehmberg. London: Dent, 1962.
Empson, William. *Some Versions of Pastoral.* 1935. Norfolk, Conn.: New Directions, 1960.
Engle, Lars. ' "Thrift is Blessing": Exchange and Explanation in *The Merchant of Venice*.' *Shakespeare Quarterly*, 37 (1986): 20–37.
Erickson, Peter. 'The Order of the Garter, the Cult of Elizabeth, and Class-Gender Tension in *The Merry Wives of Windsor*.' *Shakespeare Reproduced: The Text in History and Ideology.* Ed. Jean E. Howard and Marion F. O'Connor. New York: Methuen, 1987. 116–40.
- *Patriarchal Structures in Shakespeare's Drama.* Berkeley: University of California Press, 1985.
Evans, Bertrand. *Shakespeare's Comedies.* Oxford: Oxford University Press, 1967.
Evans, Malcolm. 'Mercury Versus Apollo: A Reading of *Love's Labor's Lost*.' *Shakespeare Quarterly*, 26 (1975): 113–27.
Freedman, Barbara. 'Falstaff's Punishment: Buffoonery as Defensive Posture in *The Merry Wives of Windsor*.' *Shakespeare Studies*, 14 (1981): 163–74.
Frye, Northrop. 'The Argument of Comedy.' *English Institute Essays.* Ed. D. A. Robertson, Jr. New York: Columbia University Press, 1949. 58–73.
- *A Natural Perspective: The Development of Shakespearean Comedy and Romance.* New York: Columbia University Press, 1965.
Gardner, Helen. 'As You Like It.' *More Talking of Shakespeare.* Ed. John Garrett. New York: Theatre Art Books, 1959. 17–32.
Giametti, A. Bartlett. 'Proteus Unbound: Some Versions of the Sea God in the Renaissance.' *The Disciplines of Criticism: Essays in Literary Theory, Interpretation, and History.* Ed. Peter Demetz, Thomas

Greene, and Lowry Nelson, Jr. New Haven: Yale University Press, 1968. 437–75.
Giddens, Anthony. *The Constitution of Society: Outline of the Theory of Structuration*. Berkeley: University of California Press, 1979.
Gilmore, David D. *Aggression and Community: Paradoxes of Andalusian Culture*. New Haven: Yale University Press, 1987.
Girard, René. 'Myth and Ritual in Shakespeare: *A Midsummer Night's Dream*.' *Textual Strategies: Perspectives in Post-Structuralist Criticism*. Ed. Josué V. Harari. Ithaca: Cornell University Press, 1979. 187–212.
– ' "To Entrap the Wisest" – A Reading of *The Merchant of Venice*.' *Literature and Society*. Ed. Edward Said. Baltimore: The Johns Hopkins University Press, 1980. 100–19.
Greenblatt, Stephen J. *Renaissance Self-Fashioning: From More to Shakespeare*. Chicago: University of Chicago Press, 1980.
– *Shakespearean Negotiations*. Berkeley: University of California Press, 1988.
– *Sir Walter Ralegh: The Renaissance Man and His Roles*. New Haven: Yale University Press, 1973.
Greene, Thomas. 'The Flexibility of the Self in Renaissance Literature.' *The Disciplines of Criticism*. Ed. Peter Demetz, Thomas Greene, and Lowry Nelson, Jr. New Haven: Yale University Press, 1968. 241–64.
Hamilton, A.C. *The Early Shakespeare*. San Marino, Calif.: Huntington Library Press, 1967.
Harvey, Nancy Lenz, and Anna Kirwan Carey. *'Love's Labor's Lost': An Annotated Bibliography*. New York: Garland, 1984.
Hawkes, Terence. *Shakespeare's Talking Animals: Language and Drama in Society*. Totowa, NJ: Rowan & Littlefield, 1974.
Hawkins, Sherman. 'The Two Worlds of Shakespearean Comedy.' *Shakespeare Studies*, 3 (1967): 62–80.
Heilman, Robert. 'The *Taming* Untamed, or the Return of the Shrew.' *Modern Language Quarterly*, 27 (1966): 147–61.
Hellenga, Robert R. 'Elizabethan Dramatic Conventions and Elizabethan Reality.' *Renaissance Drama*, 12 (1981): 27–50.
Henze, Richard. '*The Comedy of Errors*: A Freely Binding Chain.' *Shakespeare Quarterly*, 22 (1971): 35–41.
Herbert, George. *A Priest to the Temple or, The Country Parson*. *The Works of George Herbert*. Ed. F.E. Hutchinson. Oxford: Clarendon Press, 1941. 223–290.
Hexter, J.H. *Reappraisals in History*. London: Longmans, 1961.
Hibbard, George R. '*The Taming of the Shrew*: A Social Comedy.'

Shakespearean Essays. Ed. Alwin Thaler and Norman Sanders. Knoxville: University of Tennessee Press, 1964. 15–28.
Hinely, Jan Lawson. 'Bond Priorities in *The Merchant of Venice.*' *Studies in English Literature,* 20 (1980): 217–39.
Houlbrooke, Ralph A. *The English Family, 1450–1700.* London: Longman, 1984.
Howard, Jean. 'The Difficulties of Closure: An Approach to the Problematic in Shakespearian Comedy.' *Comedy from Shakespeare to Sheridan: Change and Continuity in the English and European Dramatic Tradition.* Ed. A.R. Braunmuller and J.C. Bulman. Newark: University of Delaware Press, 1986. 113–28.
Huebert, Ronald. 'Levels of Parody in *The Merry Wives of Windsor.*' *English Studies in Canada,* 3 (1977): 136–52.
Huston, J. Dennis. *Shakespeare's Comedies of Play.* New York: Columbia University Press, 1981.
Ioppolo, Grace. *Revising Shakespeare.* Cambridge, Mass.: Harvard University Press, 1991.
Jardine, Lisa. *Still Harping on Daughters: Women and Drama in the Age of Shakespeare.* Sussex: Harvester Press, 1983.
Javitch, Daniel. *Poetry and Courtliness in Renaissance England.* Princeton: Princeton University Press, 1978.
Jenkins, Harold. 'As You Like It.' *Shakespeare Survey,* 8 (1955): 40–51.
Jonson, Ben. *Timber, or Discoveries. Ben Jonson.* Ed. C.H. Herford, Percy Simpson, and Evelyn Simpson. Vol. 8. Oxford: Clarendon Press, 1947. 1925–52. 11 vols.
Keeton, George W. *Shakespeare's Legal and Political Background.* London: Sir Isaac Pitman & Sons, 1967.
Kelso, Ruth. *The Doctrine of the English Gentleman in the Sixteenth Century.* Urbana: University of Illinois Press, 1929.
Kirsch, Arthur C. *Shakespeare and the Experience of Love.* Cambridge: Cambridge University Press, 1981.
Kishlansky, Mark A. *Parliamentary Selection: Social and Political Choice in Early Modern England.* Cambridge: Cambridge University Press, 1986.
Kittsteiner, H.D. 'Kant and Casuistry.' *Conscience and Casuistry in Early Modern Europe.* Ed. Edmund Leites. Cambridge: Cambridge University Press, 1988. 185–213.
Kott, Jan. *Shakespeare Our Contemporary.* Trans. Boleslaw Taborski. London: Methuen, 1967.
Kronenfeld, Judy Z. 'Social Rank and the Pastoral Ideals of *As You Like It.*' *Shakespeare Quarterly,* 29 (1978): 333–48.

La Primaudaye, Pierre de. *The French Academie*. Trans. T[homas] B[owes]. London, 1586.
Leggatt, Alexander. *Shakespeare's Comedy of Love*. London: Methuen, 1974.
Leinwand, Theodore B. 'Conservative Fools in James's Court and Shakespeare's Plays.' *Shakespeare Studies*, 19 (1987): 219–37.
LeRoy, Louis. *Aristotles Politiques or Discourses of Government*. London, 1598.
Lever, Ralph. *Arte of Reason*. London, 1573.
Levin, Richard A. *Love and Society in Shakespearean Comedy: A Study of Dramatic Form and Content*. Newark: University of Delaware Press, 1985.
Lévi-Strauss, Claude. *The Elementary Structures of Kinship*. Trans. James Harle Bell, John Richard von Sturmer, and Rodney Needham. Rev. ed. Boston: Beacon Press, 1969.
– *The Raw and the Cooked*. Trans. John Weightman and Doreen Weightman. New York: Harper & Row, 1969.
Lindenbaum, Peter. 'Education in *The Two Gentlemen of Verona*.' *Studies in English Literature*, 15 (1975): 229–44.
MacCary, W. Thomas. *Friends and Lovers: The Phenomenology of Desire in Shakespearean Comedy*. New York: Columbia University Press, 1985.
Macfarlane, Alan. *The Origins of English Individualism: The Family, Property, and Social Transition*. New York: Cambridge University Press, 1978.
Marcus, Leah. 'Levelling Shakespeare: Local Customs and Local Texts.' *Shakespeare Quarterly*, 42 (1991): 168–78.
Marienstras, Richard. *New Perspectives on the Shakespearean World*. Trans. Janet Lloyd. Cambridge: Cambridge University Press, 1985.
Markham, Gervase. *Country Contentments*. 1615. 4th ed. London, 1631.
Marvell, Andrew. *Poems and Letters*. 2nd ed. Ed. H.M. Margoliouth. Oxford: Oxford University Press, 1952.
Mauss, Marcel. *The Gift: Forms and Functions of Exchange in Archaic Societies*. Trans. Ian Cunnison. Intro. E.E. Evans-Pritchard. Glencoe, Ill.: Free Press, 1954.
Mazzeo, J.A. 'Castiglione's *Courtier*: The Self as a Work of Art.' *Renaissance and Revolution*. New York: Pantheon, 1965. 138–60.
Milton, John. *Areopagitica. John Milton: Complete Poems and Major Prose*. Ed. Merritt Y. Hughes. New York: Odyssey Press, 1957.
– *The Poems of John Milton*. Ed. John Carey and Alastair Fowler. London: Longmans, 1968.

Montaigne, Michel de. *The Essayes or Morall, Politike and Millitarie Discourses of Lo: Michaell de Montaigne.* Trans. John Florio. London, 1603.

Montrose, Louis Adrian. *'Curious-Knotted Garden': The Form, Themes, and Contexts of Shakespeare's 'Love's Labour's Lost'.* Salzburg: Universität Salzburg, 1977.

– 'Of Gentlemen and Shepherds: The Politics of Elizabethan Pastoral Form.' *English Literary Renaissance,* 50 (1983): 415–59.

– ' "The Place of a Brother" in *As You Like It*: Social Process and Comic Form.' *Shakespeare Quarterly,* 32 (1981): 28–54.

– ' "Shaping Fantasies": Figurations of Gender and Power in Elizabethan Culture.' *Representations,* 1:2 (1983): 61–94.

Moryson, Fynes. *Shakespeare's Europe: Unpublished Chapters of Fynes Moryson's Itinerary...* Ed. Charles Hughes. London: Sherratt & Hughes, 1903.

Nelson, Benjamin. *The Idea of Usury.* 2nd ed. Chicago: University of Chicago Press, 1969.

Nelson, William. *The Poetry of Edmund Spenser.* New York: Columbia University Press, 1963.

Nevo, Ruth. *Comic Transformations in Shakespeare.* London: Methuen, 1980.

Newman, Karen. *Shakespeare's Rhetoric of Comic Character: Dramatic Conventions in Classical and Renaissance Comedy.* New York: Methuen, 1985.

Nosworthy, J.M. 'The Importance of Being Mercade.' *Shakespeare Survey,* 32 (1979): 105–14.

Novy, Marianne L. *Love's Argument: Gender Relations in Shakespeare.* Chapel Hill: University of North Carolina Press, 1984.

Olson, Paul A. '*A Midsummer Night's Dream* and the Meaning of Court Marriage.' *ELH,* 24 (1957): 95–119.

Orgel, Stephen. *The Illusion of Power: Political Theater in the English Renaissance.* Berkeley: University of California Press, 1975.

Osborn, Louise Brown. *The Life, Letters, and Writings of John Hoskyns, 1566–1638.* New Haven: Yale University Press, 1937.

Phialas, Peter. *Shakespeare's Romantic Comedies.* Chapel Hill: University of North Carolina Press, 1966.

Poggioli, Renato. *The Oaten Flute: Essays on Pastoral Poetry and the Pastoral Ideal.* Cambridge, Mass.: Harvard University Press, 1975.

Prouty, Charles T. *The Sources of 'Much Ado About Nothing'.* New Haven: Yale University Press, 1950.

Puttenham, George. *The Arte of English Poesie*. Intro. Baxter Hathaway. Kent, Ohio: Kent State University Press, 1970.
Richmond, Hugh M. 'Shakespeare's Navarre.' *Huntington Library Quarterly*, 42 (1979): 193–216.
Riemer, A.P. *Antic Fables: Patterns of Evasion in Shakespeare's Comedies*. New York: St. Martin's Press, 1980.
Roberts, Jeanne Addison. *Shakespeare's English Comedy: 'The Merry Wives of Windsor' in Context*. Lincoln: University of Nebraska Press, 1979.
Rubin, Gayle. 'The Traffic in Women: Notes on the "Political Economy" of Sex.' *Toward an Anthropology of Women*. Ed. Rayna R. Reiter. New York: Monthly Review Press, 1975. 157–210.
Said, Edward. 'Opponents, Audiences, Constituencies, and Community.' *The Politics of Interpretation*. Ed. W.J.T. Mitchell. Chicago: University of Chicago Press, 1983. 7–32.
Salingar, Leo. *Shakespeare and the Traditions of Comedy*. Cambridge: Cambridge University Press, 1974.
Sanderson, James L. 'Patience in *The Comedy of Errors*.' *Texas Studies in Literature and Language*, 16 (1975): 603–18.
Sandys, George. *A Relation of a Journey begun An: Dom: 1610*. London, 1615.
Sargent, Ralph M. 'Sir Thomas Elyot and the Integrity of *The Two Gentlemen of Verona*.' *PMLA*, 65 (1950): 1166–80.
Schopenhauer, Arthur. *Studies in Pessimism: A Series of Essays*. Trans. T. Bailey Saunders. 2nd ed. London: Swan Sonnenchein, 1891.
Sedgwick, Eve Kosofsky. *Between Men: English Literature and Male Homosocial Desire*. New York: Columbia University Press, 1985.
Seneca. *De Beneficiis*. *Moral Essays*. Trans. John W. Basore. Loeb Classical Library. London: William Heinemann, 1935. 3 vols.
Sexton, Joyce Hengerer. 'The Theme of Slander in *Much Ado About Nothing*.' *Philological Quarterly*, 54 (1975): 419–33.
Shakespeare, William. *The Comedy of Errors*. Ed. R.A. Foakes. Arden Edition. London: Methuen, 1962.
– *The Complete Works of Shakespeare*. Ed. David Bevington. 3rd ed. Glenview, Ill.: Scott, Foresman, 1980.
– *Love's Labour's Lost*. Ed. Richard David. Arden Edition. London: Methuen, 1951.
– *The Merchant of Venice*. Ed. John Russell Brown. Arden Edition. London: Methuen, 1955.
– *The Merchant of Venice*. Ed. Sir Arthur Quiller-Couch. Cambridge Edition. Cambridge: Cambridge University Press, 1926.

- *The Merry Wives of Windsor.* Ed. H.J. Oliver. Arden Edition. London: Methuen, 1971.
- *A Midsummer Night's Dream.* Ed. Harold F. Brooks. Arden Edition. London: Methuen, 1979.
- *Much Ado About Nothing.* Ed. A.R. Humphreys. Arden Edition. London: Methuen, 1981.
- *The Riverside Shakespeare.* Ed. G. Blakemore Evans et al. Boston: Houghton Mifflin, 1974.
- *The Taming of the Shrew.* Ed. G.R. Hibbard. New Penguin Shakespeare. Harmondsworth: Penguin Books, 1968.
- *The Taming of the Shrew.* Ed. Brian Morris. Arden Edition. London: Methuen, 1981.
- *The Two Gentlemen of Verona.* Ed. Sir Arthur Quiller-Couch. Cambridge: Cambridge University Press, 1921.

Shapiro, Barbara J. *Probability and Certainty in Seventeenth-Century England.* Princeton: Princeton University Press, 1983.

Shapiro, Michael. 'Shylock the Jew Onstage: Past and Present.' *Shofar,* 4 (1986): 1–11.

Shindler, Marlene. 'The Vogue and Impact of Pierre de La Primaudaye's "The French Academie" on Elizabethan and Jacobean Literature.' Diss. University of Texas, 1960.

Simmel, Georg. *Conflict.* Trans. Kurt H. Wolff. Glencoe, Ill.: Free Press, 1955.

Simon, Joan. *Education and Society in Tudor England.* Cambridge: Cambridge University Press, 1967.

Slater, Miriam. *Family Life in the Seventeenth Century.* London: Routledge & Kegan Paul, 1985.

Slights, Camille Wells. *The Casuistical Tradition in Shakespeare, Donne, Herbert, and Milton.* Princeton: Princeton University Press, 1981.

- 'In Defense of Jessica: The Problem of the Run-away Daughter in *The Merchant of Venice.*' *Shakespeare Quarterly,* 31 (1980): 357–68.

Slights, William W.E. ' "Maid and Man" in *Twelfth Night.*' *Journal of English and Germanic Philology,* 80 (1981): 327–48.

Smith, Thomas. *The Common-wealth of England, and Maner of Government Thereof.* London, 1589.

Sommerville, J.P. *Politics and Ideology in England, 1603–1640.* London: Longman, 1986.

Spencer, Theodore. *Shakespeare and the Nature of Man.* 2nd ed. New York: Macmillan, 1949.

Spender, Dale. *Man Made Language*. 2nd ed. London: Routledge & Kegan Paul, 1985.
Spenser, Edmund. *The Poetical Works of Edmund Spenser*. Ed. J.C. Smith and E. De Selincourt. London: Oxford University Press, 1912.
Sternhold, Thomas, and John Hopkins. *The Whole Book of Davids Psalmes*. London, 1582.
Stevens, Paul. *Imagination and the Presence of Shakespeare in 'Paradise Lost'*. Madison: University of Wisconsin Press, 1985.
Stevens, Wallace. *The Necessary Angel: Essays on Reality and the Imagination*. New York: Vintage, 1941.
Stone, Lawrence. *The Crisis of the Aristocracy, 1558–1641*. Oxford: Clarendon Press, 1965.
- 'The Educational Revolution in England, 1560–1640.' *Past and Present*, 28 (1964): 41–80.
- *The Family, Sex and Marriage in England, 1500–1800*. London: Weidenfeld & Nicolson, 1977.
Stoye, John Walter. *English Travellers Abroad, 1604–1667: Their Influence in English Society and Politics*. London: Jonathan Cape, 1952.
Sudgen, Edward H. *A Topographical Dictionary to the Works of Shakespeare and His Fellow Dramatists*. Manchester: Manchester University Press, 1925.
Tennenhouse, Leonard. *Power on Display: The Politics of Shakespeare's Genres*. New York: Methuen, 1986.
Tucker, E.F.J. 'The Letter of the Law in *The Merchant of Venice*.' *Shakespeare Survey*, 29 (1976): 93–101.
Underdown, David. *Revel, Riot, and Rebellion: Popular Politics and Culture in England, 1603–1660*. Oxford: Clarendon Press, 1985.
- 'The Taming of the Scold: The Enforcement of Patriarchal Authority in Early Modern England.' *Order and Disorder in Early Modern England*. Ed. Anthony Fletcher and John Stevenson. Cambridge: Cambridge University Press, 1985. 116–36.
Unger, Roberto. *Knowledge and Politics*. New York: Free Press, 1975.
Vickers, Brian. *The Artistry of Shakespeare's Prose*. London: Methuen, 1968.
Wheeler, Richard P. *Shakespeare's Development and the Problem Comedies*. Berkeley: University of California Press, 1981.
Whigham, Frank. *Ambition and Privilege: The Social Tropes of Elizabethan Courtesy Theory*. Berkeley: University of California Press, 1984.

Willet, Andrew. *Hexapla ... Sixfold Commentary upon Genesis*. London, 1608.

Williams, Arnold. *The Common Expositor: An Account of the Commentaries on Genesis 1527–1633*. Chapel Hill: University of North Carolina Press, 1948.

Williams, Penry. 'The Emergence of the State.' *Times Literary Supplement* (2 June, 1990): 616.

– *The Tudor Regime*. Oxford: Clarendon Press, 1979.

Williams, Porter, Jr. 'Mistakes in *Twelfth Night* and Their Resolution.' *PMLA*, 76 (1961): 193–99.

Wind, Edgar. *Pagan Mysteries in the Renaissance*. New Haven: Yale University Press, 1958.

Woodbridge, Linda. *Women and the English Renaissance: Literature and the Nature of Womankind, 1540–1620*. Urbana: University of Illinois Press, 1984.

Wrightson, Keith. *English Society, 1580–1680*. New Brunswick, NJ: Rutgers University Press, 1982.

Yates, Frances. *A Study of 'Love's Labour's Lost'*. Cambridge: Cambridge University Press, 1936.

Young, David. *The Heart's Forest*. New Haven: Yale University Press, 1972.

– *Something of Great Constancy: The Art of 'A Midsummer Night's Dream'*. New Haven: Yale University Press, 1966.

Zeeveld, W. Gordon. *The Temper of Shakespeare's Thought*. New Haven: Yale University Press, 1974.

Index

All's Well That Ends Well 253 n23
Amussen, Susan 249 n12, 250 n19, 267 n2
Anderson, Linda 158, 263 nn14, 15
Andrews, Mark Edwin 260 n16
Annan, Noel 88, 255 n19
Antony and Cleopatra 237
Arendt, Hannah 144–5, 260 n19
Aristotle 89, 174
Arneson, Richard 258–9 n13, 259 n14
As You Like It 9, 22, 36, 162, 193–215, 216–17, 236–40, 243
Auden, W.H. 144–5, 260 n19

Bacon, Sir Francis 5, 77, 158, 183, 197, 254 n8, 263 n15, 264 n5
Bakhtin, Mikhail 183, 266 n15
Barber, C.L. 4, 104–5, 116, 238, 246 n4, 256 n4, 257 nn7, 8
Barton, Anne 75, 261 n2
Bates, E.S. 265–6 n12
Bean, John C. 250 n20
Berry, Edward 245–6 n3
Berry, Ralph 131, 133, 254 n13, 258 nn2, 7

Bevington, David 76, 254 n6
Bible 85; Ephesians 13, 15, 18, 24–6, 28; Genesis 264 n2; Psalms 154, 261 n4, 262 n5
Blunt, Anthony 88
Boose, Lynda 52, 250 nn 17, 18
Bourdieu, Pierre 270 n13
Bowers, Fredson 158, 263 n15
Bradbrook, M.C. 59, 251 nn1, 5
Bradley, A.C. 223, 269 n6
Bristol, Michael 249 n9
Brooks, Harold F. 256 n2
Brown, John Russell 258 n5
Bullough, Geoffrey 265 n10
Burckhardt, Jacob 213–14
Burckhardt, Sigurd 131, 258 n4
Burgess, Guy 88

Calderwood, James L. 257 n8
Calvin, John 262 n6
Carey, Anna Kirwan 254 n1
Carroll, William 254 n13
Castiglione, Baldassare 5, 59–60, 63–5, 251 n8, 252 nn11, 12
Champion, Larry 245 n2
Chapman, George 75–7
Charlton, H.B. 247 n3

Chaucer, Geoffrey 59, 104
Cirillo, Albert R. 267 n6
civility and incivility 21, 28, 31, 44, 64, 73, 90, 106, 118, 174–5, 204–6
civilization 32, 49–50, 70–2, 116, 172
Cohen, Walter 258 n10, 258–9 n13
Coke, Edward 146
colonialism 178–83
Comedy of Errors, A 8, 9, 13–31, 37, 46, 50, 52, 57, 106, 120, 127, 151, 152, 216, 233, 237, 238, 240, 242
comedy: generic conventions of 4, 66, 98–9, 103–4, 132, 147, 152
Commines, Philip de 264–5 n9
conscience 130–2, 142–4
Contarini, Gaspero 259 n15
Cook, Ann Jennalie 251 n21
Coriolanus 103
Coser, Lewis A. 262 n10
courtesy 73, 118, 120, 252 n19, 252–3 n20
courtesy books 63–4, 252 n15
Cressy, David 255 n16

Danby, John F. 247 n8
Danson, Lawrence 213, 258 n6, 261 n26, 269 n17
David, Richard 75–6, 254 nn1, 4, 256 n28
Davis, Natalie Zemon 214, 269 nn18, 19
Davis, Walter R. 164–5, 263 nn20–2
Dawson, Anthony 266–7 n18
Dekker, Thomas 152
Dennis, Carl 266 n16
dissimulation: courtly and social 62–7, 252 n16
Dollimore, Jonathan 246 n7

Donawerth, Jane 82, 254 n12, 264 nn6, 7, 270 n12
Donne, John 13–14, 18, 19, 30, 57, 81, 110, 128, 236, 239–40, 242, 247 n2, 254 n11, 256–7 n5
Doran, Madeleine 268 n12
Dusinberre, Juliet 250 n20

Eco, Umberto 37, 248 n2
education 36, 51, 59–64, 80–8, 194–5, 205, 251–2 n10
Elam, Kier 173, 264 n3
Elias, Norbert 51, 250 n14
Elizabeth I of England 85, 104, 147
Elyot, Thomas 5, 58, 59, 251 n3, 252 nn12, 16
Empson, William 169, 263 n24
Engle, Lars 258–9 n13
Erasmus, Desiderius 5
Erickson, Peter 157, 168, 211, 262 n9, 268 nn15, 16
Essex, Earl of 75–8
Evans, Bertrand 248 n3
Evans, Malcolm 255 n18, 256 n27

Florio, John 75–6, 255 n24, 258 n1
Foakes, R.A. 30, 247 n1
Fowler, Alastair 264 n5
Freedman, Barbara 156, 262 n8
Frye, Northrop 4, 104–5, 151, 246 n4, 256 n4

Gardner, Helen 267 n6
Giametti, A. Bartlett 253 n24
Giddens, Anthony 6–7, 246 n9
Gilmore, David D. 262 n10
Girard, René 68–9, 104–5, 253 n21, 256 n4, 259 n14
government 7, 122, 157–8, 188, 193–4, 257 n11

Index 287

Greenblatt, Stephen J. 5, 246 n7, 249 n9, 253 n24
Greene, Thomas 5, 246 n5, 253 n24

Hamilton, A.C. 251 n7, 253 n23, 254 n24
Hamlet 237
Harriot, Thomas 75–6
Harvey, Gabriel 75
Hawkes, Terence 255 n18, 266–7 n18
Hawkins, Sherman 151, 261 n1
Heilman, Robert 250 n16
Hellenga, Robert R. 5, 246 n6
Henry III of France 90
Henry IV of France 74–5
Henze, Richard 247 n7
Herbert, George 268 n11
heteroglossia 183
Hexter, J.H. 251 n7, 252 n15, 253 n23
Hibbard, George R. 50, 248 n3, 249 n10
Hinely, Jan Lawson 258 n12
Hoskyns, John 266 n14
Houlbrooke, Ralph A. 197, 250–1 n21, 260–1 n20, 267 nn2–4
Howard, Jean E. 259 n14
Huebert, Ronald 153, 261 n3, 262 n5
Humphreys, A.R. 265 n11
Huston, J. Dennis 51, 245 n2, 247 n6, 249 n11

identity 213–14; individual 5, 19–20, 31, 45, 69, 73, 107–8, 117–18, 199, 205; social 7, 23, 29, 32–5, 37, 79–80, 129, 161, 171, 214, 249 n9
Ioppolo, Grace 254 n9

James I of England 74, 266 n14
Jardine, Lisa 264 n8
Jenkins, Harold 267 n6
Jonson, Ben 152, 172, 186, 230, 263 n1, 270 n12

Keeton, George W. 260 n16
Kelso, Ruth 251 n7, 252 nn15, 16
Kirsch, Arthur 245 n2
Kishlansky, Mark A. 256 n1
Kittsteiner, H.D. 143, 260 n17
Kott, Jan 104–5, 256 n4
Kronenfeld, Judy Z. 268 n16

language: cohesive power of 60–4, 80–3, 91, 129, 172–4, 183, 187, 227–8; divisive power of 65–8, 85–8, 91, 137–8, 174–8, 187; courtly discourse 65–6, 173, 208, 252 n13
Lanham, R.A. 263 n20
La Primaudaye, Pierre de 89, 90–1, 98, 121–2, 255 n23, 256 n26, 257 nn10, 12, 268 n14
Leggatt, Alexander 245 n2, 248 n3
Leinwand, Theodore B. 268–9 n16
LeRoy, Louis 174, 264 n4
Lever, Ralph 175, 230, 264 n7, 270 n12
Levin, Richard A. 245–6 n3
Lévi-Strauss, Claude 49, 219, 222, 233–4, 249 n7, 269 nn1, 4, 5, 270 n15
Lindenbaum, Peter 251–2 n10
Locke, John 53, 250 n19
Love's Labor's Lost 3, 7, 9, 57, 74–100, 103, 106–7, 121, 123, 126, 127, 147, 151, 236–8, 243, 254 nn1, 4, 13, 255 n18, 256 n27

Macbeth 21, 103

MacCary, Thomas 245 n2
Macfarlane, Alan 260-1 n20
Manwood, John 203, 268 n10
Marcus, Leah 263 n17
Marienstras, Richard 146, 202-3, 261 nn23-25, 268 nn9, 10
Markham, Gervase 50, 249 n10
Marlowe, Christopher 153-4
marriage 9, 38, 98, 129, 144, 161, 204, 233-4, 239; companionate 54; patriarchal 17-18, 38, 40, 47-8, 52-4, 107, 109, 168, 175-8, 181-3, 211, 214, 234, 241
Marvell, Andrew 229, 270 n11
Mauss, Marcel 222, 228, 269 n4, 270 n9
Mazzeo, Joseph A. 63-5, 252 n18
Medici, Catherine de 75, 255-6 n25
Merchant of Venice, The 8, 125-48, 152, 196, 216, 220, 236, 238, 239, 240, 243
Merry Wives of Windsor, The 3, 7, 103, 151-70, 193, 201, 214, 215, 237, 240, 242
Midsummer Night's Dream, A 3, 41, 68-9, 91, 103-24, 125-6, 127, 136-7, 141, 142, 201, 202, 216, 238, 241, 242-3
Milton, John 215, 269 n20
Montaigne, Michel de 89-90, 129, 255 n24, 258 n1
Montrose, Louis Adrian 5, 104-5, 169, 197, 246 n7, 256 nn27, 4, 263 n24, 267 nn1, 5, 268 n16
Morris, Brian 250 nn13, 20
Moryson, Fynes 259-60 n15, 265 n12
Much Ado About Nothing 8, 61, 79, 151-2, 171-89, 193, 206, 211, 215, 228, 236, 237, 238, 240, 242, 243

Nashe, Thomas 75
nature 14-17, 25, 46, 114-16, 201-4, 212, 216-17
neighbor 3, 80, 159, 167, 258 n8, 262 n7
Nelson, William 252 n17
Nevo, Ruth 247 n5, 258 n11
Newman, Karen 245 n2
Nosworthy, J.M. 256 n27
Novy, Marianne L. 51, 249 n11, 250 n20, 270 n14

oaths. *See* vows and oaths
Oliver, H.J. 261 nn2, 3
Olson, Paul A. 256 n3
Orgel, Stephen 123, 258 n14
Osborn, Louise Brown 266 n14
outsider 19, 30, 88, 90, 100, 151. *See also* stranger

Paston, William 197
pastoralism 70, 153-5, 160, 161-70, 201-2, 212, 267-8 n8, 268-9 n16
patience 26-7, 247 nn8, 9
Patterson, Annabel 266 n14
Petrarchism 39, 43, 202, 207-8, 228-31
Phialas, Peter G. 17, 247 n5, 248 n3
Plutarch 103-4
Poggioli, Renato 267-8 n8
Prouty, Charles T. 266 n13
Puttenham, George 248 n2

Quiller-Couch, Arthur 59, 131, 258 n3

Ralegh, Sir Walter 75-8
reciprocity 220-34
revenge 26, 142, 144, 158, 161-7, 225-7
Richard III 97

Index

Richmond, Hugh M. 254 n1, 255–6 n25
Riemer, A.P. 245 n2
Roberts, Jeanne Addison 261 n3
Romeo and Juliet 61
Rousseau, Jean-Jacques 143, 260 n17
Rubin, Gayle 234, 270 nn15, 16

Said, Edward 88, 255 n20
Salingar, Leo 245 n2
Salkeld, William 147, 261 n25
Sanderson, James L. 247–8 n9
Sandys, George 265–6 n12
Sargent, Ralph M. 251 n3
Schopenhauer, Arthur 243, 271 n2
Sedgwick, Eve Kosofsky 263 n18
Seneca 269 nn5, 7, 8
Sexton, Joyce Hengerer 266 n17
Shapiro, Barbara J. 257–8 n13
Shapiro, Michael 261 n22
Shindler, Marlene 255 n22
Sicilian Vespers 179, 265–6 n12
Sidney, Sir Philip 162, 165
Simmel, Georg 262 n10
Sinfield, Alan 246 n7
Slater, Miriam 248–9 n6
Slights, Camille Wells 258 n9, 260 n16
Slights, William W.E. 270 n14
Smith, Adam 143, 260 n17
Smith, Thomas 7, 246 n10
social convention 29–30, 38, 44, 48, 106, 111, 202; clothing and costume as 37, 44–9; courtship 9, 34, 41–2, 97, 204, 248 n5; law as 15–16, 23, 25, 29–30, 33, 57, 71, 104–9, 114, 122, 125, 139, 142–7, 158, 194, 202; money as 23–4, 40, 133, 140, 155–6, 220–6, 243; time as 23–4, 29, 46–7, 208, 234
social hierarchy 7–8, 13, 30–1, 70, 74, 78–9, 124, 146, 188, 238–9; and gender 17–18, 38–42, 52–4, 91–5, 112, 168, 175–6, 229, 240–2; and rank 33, 73, 84–6, 90, 106–9, 121–2, 151, 155–6, 158–9, 194–5, 203–4, 210–11, 242–3
social role and relations 4–5, 9, 13, 17–24, 28–31, 35, 48, 144, 172, 199–200, 203, 206, 208–9, 211, 213–14, 217, 222, 231–2, 236–7, 239–40
society: definition of 6–7; as human construction 8, 50, 128, 198; heterogeneity in 121–3, 127–9, 136, 142, 159–60, 209–10
Sommerville, J.P. 257 n11
Sonnets 39, 43
Southampton, Earl of 74–7, 99–100
Spencer, Theodore 255 n22
Spender, Dale 270 n1
Spenser, Edmund 59, 64, 65, 73, 120, 164–5, 169, 252 nn17, 19, 252–3 n20, 257 n9
Stevens, Paul 247 n4
Stevens, Wallace 6, 246 n8
Stone, Lawrence 83–5, 88, 248 n6, 250–1 n21, 251 n7, 253 nn22, 23, 255 n14
Stoye, John Walter 265 n12
stranger 20, 217, 222, 237. See also outsider
Sudgen, Edward H. 264 n9

Taming of the Shrew, The 8, 32–54, 57, 79, 106, 120, 127, 147, 151–2, 208, 215, 236, 237, 240, 242, 243
Tempest, The 103–4, 212, 220, 227

Tennenhouse, Leonard 104–5, 246 n7, 256 n4
Tucker, E.F.J. 260 n16
Twelfth Night 4, 151, 193, 216–35, 237–9, 240, 243
Two Gentlemen of Verona, The 57–73, 74, 78, 79, 99, 107, 121, 126, 205, 207, 237, 239

Underdown, David 52, 250 nn15, 18, 257 n11, 262 n7, 263 nn16, 19
Unger, Roberto 260 n17, 271 n2

Valois, Margurite de 75, 76, 90, 255–6 n25
Vickers, Brian 264 n2
vows and oaths 74, 94–9, 109, 144–5

Wheeler, Richard P. 245 n2

Whigham, Frank 252 n13
Willet, Andrew 264 n5
Williams, Arnold 264 n5
Williams, Penry 157, 262 n11, 263 n12
Williams, Porter, Jr. 220, 269 nn2, 3
Wind, Edgar 255 n21
Woodbridge, Linda 250 nn16, 18, 264 n8
wooing 34, 163, 207–8, 213
Wrightson, Keith 83–8, 157–8, 159, 255 n15, 258 n8, 263 n13, 267 n2

Yates, Frances 75, 100, 254 nn1, 2
Young, David 257–8 n13, 267 n7

Zeeveld, W. Gordon 260 n16

www.ingramcontent.com/pod-product-compliance
Lightning Source LLC
Chambersburg PA
CBHW020357080526
44584CB00014B/1058